Scan... Eu... phrasebook

Ingibjörg Árnadóttir
Peter A Crozier
Markus Lehtipuu
Doekes Lulofs
Pär Sörme

Scandinavian Europe Phrasebook
  1st edition

Published by
  Lonely Planet Publications
  Head Office: PO Box 617, Hawthorn, Vic, 3122, Australia
  Branches: PO Box 2001A, Berkeley, CA 94702, USA and London, UK

Printed by
  Singapore National Printers Ltd, Singapore

Published
  December 1992

National Library of Australia Cataloguing in Publication Data

Scandinavian Europe Phrasebook

  Includes Index.
  ISBN 0 86442 154 0.

  1. Danish language – Conversation and phrase books – English 2. Finnish
  language – Conversation and phrase books – English. 3. Icelandic language
  - Conversation and phrase books - English. 4. Norwegian language -
  Conversation and phrase books - English. 5. Swedish language - Conversation and phrase books - English. I. Crozier, Peter. (Series: Language
  survival kit).

439.5

Contents

Acknowledgements

The Danish section was written by Peter A Crozier. Markus Lehtipuu wrote the Finnish chapter and the Icelandic was written by Ingibjörg Árnadóttir. Doekes Lulofs wrote the Norwegian chapter. Swedish was written by Pär Sörme.

The editor of this book is Sally Steward, and Tamsin Wilson was responsible for design and illustrations. Thanks to Dan Levin for computer assistance.

From the Publisher

In this book Lonely Planet uses a simplified phonetic translation, based on the International Phonetic Alphabet. While this can only approximate the exact sounds of each language, it serves as the most useful guide for readers attempting to speak the various words and phrases. As you spend time in a country, listening to native speakers and following the rules offered here in the pronunciation sections, you should be able to read directly from the language itself.

All the languages in this book have masculine, feminine and sometimes neuter, forms of words. The different forms are separated in the text by slashes and/or the bracketed letters (m), (f) and (neut), when appropriate. Many words share the same form, so no indication of gender is required.

Several of the languages in this book have both formal and informal ways of speech, which means that for one word in English you may find two in the other language, one being the polite, formal, word and the other being more casual, informal. For the purposes of this book the formal way of speech has been adopted throughout, as this will ensure that at least you will not offend anyone by using the more intimate speech. In instances where the informal is commonly used, we have included it in brackets after the formal, or indicated with the letters (inf).

Danish

Danish

Introduction

The Danish language belongs to the North Germanic language group, together with Swedish, Norwegian, Icelandic and Faroese. Consequently written Danish bears a strong resemblance to these languages. Spoken Danish, on the other hand, has evolved in a different direction, introducing sounds and pronunciation not found elsewhere. Grammatically it has the same general rules and syntax as the other Germanic languages of Scandinavia. Nouns have two genders: masculine *(en)* and neuter *(et)*. Definite articles ('the' in English) are added to the noun: *-en* and *-et* for singular nouns, and *-ne* (indefinite) and *-ene* (definite) for plural nouns regardless of gender.

Danish has a polite form of address, using the personal pronouns *De* and *Dem*. The words and phrases in this chapter are mostly in the familar form using *du* and *deg*, except where it is more appropriate to use the formal form. In general, use the formal form when speaking to senior citizens and officials, and the familiar form the rest of the time.

As Danish is a minor language and few visitors take the time or effort to learn it, most Danes speak English. However, an effort to at least learn the basics is well received. It's a good idea to memorise the words for 'thank you', 'goodbye', 'hello' and 'I'm sorry'. This minimum effort will be appreciated, and with an increased command of the language you'll be rewarded by gaining a greater insight into Denmark and the Danes. The pronunciation of each phrase and word in this chapter is transcribed using a simplified phonetic system, so with not too much effort it should be possible to grasp the basic sentence structure and begin creating your own sentences.

Pronunciation

Danish varies from island to island as well as from north to south, with each region having its distinct dialect. The translation and pronunciation presented here follows the form of Danish known as *Nudansk*, (literally 'Now Danish'). This is the form of Danish spoken in Copenhagen, and understood throughout the country.

In Danish the stress is usually placed on the first syllable, or on the first letter of the word. Stressed syllables in polysyllabic words are printed here in bold type, and some longer syllables have been split into more manageable lengths.

Danes do not necessarily pronounce what they write. The pronunciation of vowels in particular varies depending on the word, and unfortunately there are no hard and fast rules as to how a given letter is to be pronounced. Following is a list of Danish letters, how they sound using English words, and their equivalent in our pronunciation guide. Letters in parenthesis determine when the letter in bold type is to be pronounced as described. This should make it easier for the reader to pronounce words encountered which are not included in the text. In general though, the best advice for good pronunciation is to listen and learn. Good luck.

10 Danish

Danish	Pronunciation Guide	Sounds
a	*aa*	a long flat 'a' as in 'father'
a, æ	*a*	a long sharp 'a' as in 'act'
u(n), å, o	*ā*	a long rounded 'a' as in 'walk'
e(g)	*ai*	as in 'eye'
e, i	*e*	a short flat 'e', as in the Italian *che*
i	*i*	a long sharp 'e' as in 'see'
æ	*eh*	a long flat 'e' as in 'bet'
ø	*er*	as in 'fern' and 'earn'
i	*i*	a short flat 'i' as in 'pit' and 'in'
o, u	*oo*	a long 'o' as in 'zoo'
o	*o*	a short 'o' as in 'pot'
o(v)	*ow*	somewhat shorter sound than 'out' or 'vow'
o(v)	*or*	with less emphasis on the 'r', as in 'more'
u	*u*	as in 'pull'
y	*ü*	a long sharp 'u' as in the German *über*

Semiconsonants

w	*w*	similar to the 'wh' in 'what'
j	*y*	as in 'yet'
	'	the glottal stop, similar to the swallowed sound in 'bottle' as pronounced by a cockney: 'bo'l'. Usually occurs with words ending in 'er'.

Consonants

sj	*sh*	as in 'ship'
ch	*tj*	as the 'ch' in 'cheque'

Danish 11

DANISH

j(o)	j	a short sharp 'j' as in 'jaw' or 'age'
(o)d	ð	a flat 'dth' sound as in 'these'
ng	ng	as in 'sing'
g	gh	when followed by a vowel, a hard 'g' as in 'get'
h	h	as the 'h' in 'horse', but silent before j and v
k	k	as the 'c' in 'cat'
b	b	as in 'box'
r	R	a rolling r abruptly cut short – there's no English equivalent
v	v	as in 'very'
c	c	as in 'cell'

All other consonants are pronounced as in English.

Greetings & Civilities
Top Useful Phrases

Hello./Goodbye.
　haa-lo/faar-vel　　　　　Hallo./Farvel.
Yes./No.
　ya/naay　　　　　　　　Ja./Nej.
Excuse me.
　ān-sghül　　　　　　　　Undskyld.
May I? Do you mind?
　mā yai? te-laðˈ dee?　　Må jeg? Tillader De?
Sorry. (excuse me, forgive me)
　ān-sghül. be-klaa　　　　Undskyld. Beklager.
Please.
　mā yai beðe. vehrs-gho　Må jeg bede. Værsgo.
Thank you.
　taagh　　　　　　　　　Tak.

Many thanks.
   maang-e taagh   Mange tak.
That's fine. You're welcome.
   de ehR ee oh-den   Det er i orden.
   sehl taagh   Selv tak.

Greetings

Good morning.
   *gho **mor**-on*   God morgen.
Good afternoon.
   *gho **efd'**-meda*   God eftermiddag.
Good evening/night.
   *gho-**aafden**/gho-**nad*** Godaften/Godnat.
How are you?
   *vo-**dan** haa dee de?*   Hvordan har De det?
Well, thanks.
   gaad, taagh   Godt, tak.

Forms of Address

Madam/Mrs	*froo*	fru
Sir/Mr	*hehr*	herr
Miss	*frer-ghen*	frøken
companion, friend	*kaame-rad, ven*	kammerat, ven

Small Talk
Meeting People

What is your name?
   *vað **he**-ð' du?*   Hvad hedder du?
My name is ...
   mid naown ehR ...   Mit navn er ...

I'd like to introduce you to ...
yai vel ad du sgha merðe ...　　Jeg vil at du skal møde ...
I'm pleased to meet you.
det ehR hüge-lid ad　　　　　Det er hyggeligt at træffe
tref-feh dem　　　　　　　　Dem.

Nationalities

Where are you from?
vor-fraa k'm-m' du?　　　　　Hvorfra kommer du?

I am from ...
jai ehR fra ...　　　　　　　　Jeg er fra ...

Australia	*aaow-sdraa-lien*	Australien
Canada	*kan-ada*	Canada
Denmark	*dan-maagh*	Danmark
England	*ehng-lan*	England
Ireland	*iR-lan*	Irland
New Zealand	*nü-se-lan*	New Zealand
Scotland	*sgh'd-lan*	Skotland
the USA	*dee f'-eneðe*	De Forenede
	sdaa-d'	Stater
Wales	*wa-ehls*	Wales

Age

How old are you?
vor gaa-mel ehR du?　　　　Hvor gammel er du?
I am ... years old.
yai ehR ... ā gaa-mel　　　　Jeg er ... år gammel.

Occupations

What do you do?
vað f' ed aa-baay-de　　　　Hvad for et arbejde
lav' du?　　　　　　　　　　laver du?

I am (a/an) .../I work as ...

yai ehR ...		Jeg er ...
yai aa-baay-d' sām ...		Jeg arbejder som ...
artist	*kāns-d'*	kunster
business person	*f'-radnengs-dree-vene*	forretningsdrivende
doctor	*leh-e*	læge
engineer	*enshe-nyerR*	ingeniør
farmer	*bāne*	bonde
journalist	*shuRna-lisd*	journalist
lawyer	*aðvo-kaa-d*	advokat
manual worker	*kr'bs-aa-baay-d'*	krobsarbeider
mechanic	*me-kaa-nigh'*	mekaniker
nurse	*sile-plaay*	sygeplejer
office worker	*k'nto-risd'*	kontorist
scientist	*for-sgh'*	forsker
student	*sdu-dehd*	student
teacher	*leh'*	lærer
waiter	*kehl-n'*	kelner
writer	*sghree-behnd*	skribent

Religion

What is your religion?

vað f' en reli-ghyoon haa du? — Hvad for en religion har du?

I am not religious.

yai ehR eghe relee-ghyers — Jeg er ikke religiøs.

I am ...
yai ehR ...   Jeg er ...

Buddhist	*bu-**deesd***	buddist
Catholic	*kato-**leegh***	katolik
Christian	***krehs**-den*	kristen
Hindu	***hen**-du*	hindu
Jewish	*yer-ðe*	jøde
Muslim	*mus-**leem***	muslim

Family

Are you married?
   *ehR du **gheefd**?*   Er du gift?

I am single.
   *yai ehR u-**gheefd***   Jeg er ugift.

I am married.
   *yai ehR **gheefd***   Jeg er gift.

How many children do you
have?
   *vor **maang**-e berRn haa du?*   Hvor mange børn har du?

I don't have any children.
   yai haa eng-en berRn   Jeg har ingen børn.

I have a daughter/a son.
   *yai haa en **da**-d'/en sern*   Jeg har en datter/en søn.

How many brothers/sisters do
you have?
   *vor **maang**-e **brer**-ðr'/
ser-ðr' haa du?*   Hvor mange brødre/søstre
har du?

Is your husband/wife here?
   ehR deen man/koone hehR?   Er din mand/kone her?

Do you have a boyfriend/
girlfriend?
*haa du en **kehR's**-de?*   Har du en kæreste?

brother	*broR*	bror
children	*bern*	børn
daughter	***da**-d'*	datter
family	*fa-**milye***	familie
father	*faa*	far
grandfather	***behsde**-fað'*	bestefader
grandmother	***behsde**-mooð'*	bestemoder
husband	*man*	mand
mother	*mooð'*	moder
sister	*ser-ð'*	søster
son	*sern*	søn
wife	*koone*	kone

Feelings

I like ...
yai kan g'd leeðe ...   Jeg kan godt lide ...
I don't like ...
yai kan eghe leeðe ...   Jeg kan ikke lide ...
(I am) in a hurry.
*(yai haa) **hasd**-vaRgh*   (Jeg har) astværk.
(I am) well.
(yai haa de) g'd   (Jeg har det) godt.
I am sorry. (condolence)
de gherR mai ānd ad her'   Det gør mig ondt at høre.
I am grateful.
*yai ehR taag-**nehm**-li*   Jeg er taknemlig.

I am ...
  yai ehR ...   Jeg er ...

angry	*vrehð*	vred
cold/hot	*k'l/vaam*	kold/varm
happy/sad	*glaŏ/trisd*	glad/trist
hungry/thirsty	*sul-den/terRs-di*	sulten/tørstig
right (correct)	*rehd*	ret
sleepy	*serv-ni*	søvnig
tired (fatigued)	*trehd*	træt
worried	*be-kerm-r'ð*	bekymret

Language Difficulties

Do you speak English?
  tal' dee ehng-elsgh?   Taler De engelsk?
Does anyone speak English?
  ehR de nooen s'm tal'   Er det nogen som taler
  ehng-elsgh?   engelsk?
I speak a little ...
  yai tal' en smoole ...   Jeg taler en smule ...
I don't speak ...
  yai tal' eghe ...   Jeg taler ikke ...
I (don't) understand.
  yai f'-sdor (eghe)   Jeg forstår (ikke).
Could you repeat that?
  kune dee ghehn-ta de?   Kunne De gentage det?
Could you speak more slowly
please?
  kune dee tale me' laand-   Kunne De tale mere
  s'md, mā yai beðe?   langsomt, må jeg bede?
How do you say ...?
  vo-dan see' man ð?   Hvordan siger man ...?

What does ... mean?
*vað be-**tilð**ð?*　　　　　　Hva betyder ...?

I speak ...
yai tal' ...　　　　　　Jeg taler ...
English　　*ehng-elsgh*　　engelsk
French　　*fraansgh*　　fransk
German　　*tüsgh*　　tysk
Italian　　*itali-ensgh*　　italiensk

Some Useful Phrases
Sure.
sel-sagd　　　　　　Selvsagt.
Just a minute.
ehd 'je-blegh　　　　Et øjeblikk.
It's (not) important.
de ehr eghe så vegh-did　　Det er (ikke) så vigtigt.
It's (not) possible.
de ehR eghe mu-lid　　Det er (ikke) muligt.
Wait!
ven-d!　　　　　　Vent!
Good luck!
ler-ghe tel!　　　　Lykke til!

Signs

BAGGAGE COUNTER	BAGAGE SKRANKE
CHECK-IN COUNTER	INDCHECKINGS SKRANKE
CUSTOMS	TOLD
EMERGENCY EXIT	NØDUDGANG
ENTRANCE	INDGANG

EXIT	UDGANG
FREE ADMISSION	GRATIS ADGANG
HOT/COLD	VARM/KOLD
INFORMATION	INFORMATION
NO ENTRY	INGEN ADGANG
NO SMOKING	IKKE-RYGERE
OPEN/CLOSED	ÅBEN/LUKKET
PROHIBITED	FORBUDT
RESERVED	RESERVERET
TELEPHONE	TELEFON
TOILETS	TOILETTER

Emergencies

| POLICE | POLITI |
| POLICE STATION | POLITISTATION |

Help!
yehlb!
Hjælp!

It's an emergency!
dehde ehR en nerŏs-situa-shoon!
Dette er en nødssituation!

There's been an accident!
de haa veh'ŏ en uler-ghe!
Det har været en ulykke!

Call a doctor!
reng efd' en leh-e!
Ring efter en læge!

Call an ambulance!
reng efd' en süle-v'v!
Ring efter en sygevogn!

I've been raped.
yai haa bleveŏ v'-taed
Jeg har blevet voldtaget.

I've been robbed.
yai haa bleveŏ raneŏ
Jeg har blevet ranet.

Call the police!
  *reng efd' poli-**tee**-eð!*   Ring efter politiet!
Where is the police station?
  *vor ehR poli-tee-sda-**shoo**-*   Hvor er politistationen?
  nen?
Go away!
  *f'-**sven**!*   Forsvind!
I'll call the police!
  *yai kal' pā poli-**tee**-eð!*   Jeg kalder på politiet!
Thief!
  tüv!   Tyv!
I am/My friend is ill.
  yai ehR/meen ven ehR sü   Jeg er/Min ven er syg.
I am lost.
  yai haa gāeð vil   Jeg har gået vild.
Where are the toilets?
  *vor ehR toa-**ledene**?*   Hvor er toilettene?
Could you help me please?
  kune dee yelbe mai?   Kunne De hjælpe mig?
Could I please use the telephone?
  mā yai fā broo-e   Må jeg få bruge telefonen?
  *tele-**foo**-nen?*
I'm sorry. I apologise.
  *be-**klaa** an-sgül*   Beklager. Undskyld.
I didn't realise I was doing
anything wrong.
  yai vesde eghe ad yai gyoo'   Jeg vidste ikke at jeg gjorde
  nāeð ghald   noget galt.
I didn't do it.
  de vaa eghe mai dehR   Det var ikke mig der gjorde
  gyoo' de   det.

I wish to contact my embassy/
consulate.

*yai **ern**-sgh' ad k'n-**taaghde**
meen aamba-saðe/mid
k'nsu-lad*

Jeg ønsker at kontakte min
ambassade/mit konsulat.

I speak English.

*yai tal' **ehng**-elsgh*

Jeg taler engelsk.

I have medical insurance.

*yai haa süe-f'-**segh**-reng*

Jeg har sygeforsikring.

My possessions are insured.

*meene **aayen**-dele ehR
f'-**segh**-red*

Mine ejendele er forsikret.

My ... was stolen.

*mid ... haa bleveð
sdyā-leð*

Mit ... har blevet stjålet.

I've lost ...

yai haa taabd ...

Jeg har tabt ...

my bags	*meen ba-**gashe***	min bagage
my handbag	*meen h'n-**tasghe***	min håndtaske
my money	*meene **pehng**-e*	mine penge
my passport	*mid pas*	mit pas
my travellers' cheques	*meene raayse-**sheghs***	mine rejsechecks

Paperwork

name	*naaown*	navn
address	*a-**dras**-se*	adresse
date of birth	*fersels-**dato***	fødselsdato
place of birth	*ferðe-**sdeð***	fødested
age	*al'*	alder
sex	*kern*	køn

nationality	*nasho-nali-ted*	nationalitet
religion	*reli-ghyoon*	religion
reason for travel	*for-māleð með raaysen*	formålet med rejsen
profession	*profe-shoon*	profession
marital status	*si-veel-sdan*	civilstand
passport	*pas*	pas
passport number	*pas-nām'*	pasnummer
visa	*veesām*	visum
identification	*leghitima-shoon*	legitimation
birth certificate	*fersels-atesd/dābs-atesd*	fødslesattest/dåbsattest
driver's licence	*sehRtifi-kad*	certifikat
car owner's title	*v'own-kord*	vognkort
car registration	*v'own-kord*	vognkort
customs	*t'l*	told
immigration	*imighra-shoon*	immigration
border	*granse*	grænse

Getting Around

ARRIVALS	ANKOMSTER
BUS STOP	BUSHOLDEPLADS
DEPARTURES	AFGANGER
STATION	STATION
SUBWAY	UNDERGRUNDSBANEN
TICKET OFFICE	BILLETKONTOR
TIMETABLE	KØREPLAN
TRAIN STATION	JERNBANESTATION/ BANEGÅRD

What time does the ... leave/
arrive?

*vo-**nor** gor/**an**-k'm'* ...	Hvornår går/ankommer ...
(air)plane	*flü-eð*	flyet
boat	*bā-ðen*	båden
bus (city)	*busen*	bussen
bus (intercity)	*rude-beelen*	rutebilen
train	*tā-weð*	toget
tram	*sbooR-v'ow-nen*	sporvognen

Directions

Where is ...?
    vor ehR ...?   Hvor er ...?
How do I get to ...?
    *vo-**dan** k'm' yai tel ð?*   Hvordan kommer jeg til ...?
Is it far from here?
    ehR de langd hehR-fraa?   Er det langt herfra?
Is it near here?
    ehR de ee nehr-heðen?   Er det i nærheden?
Can I walk there?
    *kan yai gā dehR-**hen**?*   Kan jeg gå derhen?
Can you show me (on the
map)?
    kune dee veese mai (pā   Kunne De vise mig (på
    kord-eð)?   kortet)?
Are there other means of
getting there?
    ehR dehR aandr' māð' ad   Er der andre måder at
    *k'me dehR-**hen**?*   komme derhen?
ˈ want to go to ...
    vai ern-sgh' ad k'me tel ...   Jeg ønsker at komme til ...

Go straight ahead.
  gā lee-e-fram — Gå ligefrem.
It's two streets down.
  de ehR too gað' u-na — Det er to gader unna.
Turn left ...
  draay tel vehns-dr' ... — Drej tel venstre ...
Turn right ...
  draay tel h'yr' ... — Drej til højre ...
at the next corner
  ve nehsde yerR-ne — ved næste hjørne
at the traffic lights
  ve traa-figh-lü-seð — ved trafiklyset

behind	*ba*	bag
far	*fyehRn*	fjern
near	*nehR*	nær
in front of	*for-an*	foran
opposite	*pā moð-sad seeð a*	på modsat side af

Buying Tickets

Excuse me, where is the ticket office?
  ān-sghül, vor ehR bi-lehd-k'n-too-'ð? — Undskyld, hvor er billetkontoret?
Where can I buy a ticket?
  vor kaa yai ker-be en bi-lehd? — Hvor kan jeg købe en billet?

I want to go to ...
  yai ern-sgh' ad raay-se tel ... — Jeg ønsker at rejse til ...

Do I need to book?
*ehR de nerð-**vehn**-did ad be-**sdel**-le plas?*

Er det nødvendigt at bestille plads?

You need to book.
*de ehR nerð-**vehn**-did ad be-**sdel**-le plas*

Det er nødvendig at bestille plads.

I'd like to book a seat to ...
*yai **ern**-sgh' ad be-**sde**-le plas tel ...*

Jeg ønsker at bestille plads til ...

It is full.
*de ehR **ful**-d*

Det er fuldt.

Is it completely full?
*ehR de held **ful**-d?*

Er det helt fuldt?

Can I get a stand-by ticket?
*kan yai mä-**sghe** ker-be en stand-by be-**lehd**?*

Kan jeg måske købe en stand-by billet?

I would like ... *yai vel **gaR**-ne ha-ve ...*		Jeg vil gerne have ...
a one-way ticket	*en **eng**-gheld-bi-lehd*	en enkeltbillet
a return ticket	*en tooR-re-**tooR** bi-lehd*	en tur-retur billet
two tickets	*too bi-**lehd**'*	to billetter
tickets for all of us	*bi-**lehd**' f' a-le-saa-men*	billetter for allesammen
a student's fare	*sdu-**dehnd**-ra-bad*	studentrabat
a child's/pensioner's fare	*en berne/paangsho-nisd bi-**lehd***	en børne/pensionist billet
1st class	*fers-de **klas**-e*	første klasse
2nd class	*anen **klas**-e*	anden klasse

Air

CHECKING IN LUGGAGE PICKUP REGISTRATION	INDCHECKING BAGAGE AFHENTING REGISTRERING

Is there a flight to ...?
ehR dehR ed flü tel ...? Er der et fly til ...?

When is the next flight to ...?
*vo-nor gor nehs-de flü
tel ...?* Hvornår går næste fly til ...?

How long does the flight take?
vor lang tið ta' flüve-tu'n? Hvor lang tid tager
flyveturen?

What is the flight number?
vað ehR flaihd nā-m'-'ð? Hvad er flight nummeret?

You must check in at ... (time)
du mā tjeghe en kl'-ghen ... Du må checke ind klokken ...

airport tax	*lāfd-haawne-aow-ghifd*	lufthavneavgift
boarding pass	*boarding-kord*	boardingkort
customs	*t'l*	told

Bus

BUS/TRAM STOP	BUS/SPORVOGN HOLDEPLADS

Where is the bus/tram stop?
*vor ehR bus/sboR-v'own
h'le-plasen?* Hvor er bus/sporvogns
holdepladsen?

Which bus goes to ...?
   vel-ghen bus gor tel ...?

Hvilken bus går til ...?

Does this bus go to ...?
   gor dehne bus-sen tel ...?

Går denne bussen til ...?

How often do buses pass by?
   vor 'fde k'm-m' bus-sen
   f'-bee?

Hvor ofte kommer bussen
forbi?

Could you let me know when
we get to ...?
   ku-ne dee la mai veeð nor
   vi k'm-m' tel ...?

Kunne De lade mig vide når
vi kommer til ...?

I want to get off!
   yai vel a!

Jeg vil af!

What time is the ... bus?
   vo-nor gor ... bus?

Hvornår går ... bus?

next	*nehs-de*	næste
first	*fers-de*	første
last	*sis-de*	sidste

Metro

METRO/UNDERGROUND	UNDERGRUNDSBANEN
CHANGE (for coins)	VÆKSEL
THIS WAY TO	DENNE VEJ TIL
WAY OUT	UDGANG

Which line takes me to ...?
   vel-ghen bane gor tel ...?

Hvilken bane går til ...?

What is the next station?
   vað ehR nehs-de sda-
   shoon?

Hvad er næste station?

Train

DINING CAR	SPISEVOGN
EXPRESS	EKSPRES
PLATFORM NO	PLATFORM NUMMER
SLEEPING CAR	SOVEVOGN

Is this the right platform
for ...?
  ehR dehde rehgh-di pa-r'ng   Er dette rigtig perron for
  f' tā-oweð tel ...?   toget til ...?
The train leaves from
platform ...
  tā-oweð gor fraa   Toget går fra perron ...
  pa-r'ng ð

Passengers must change
trains/platforms.
  pasa-she-'ne mā bü-de   Passagerene må bytte
  tā-ow/pa-r'ng   tog/perron

dining car	*sbeese-v'own*	spisevogn
express	*ehghs-pras*	ekspres
local	*lo-kal*	lokal
sleeping car	*s'owe-v'own*	sovevogn

Taxi
Can you take me to ...?
  kan du ker' mai tel ...?   Kan du køre mig til ...?

Please take me to ...
    *va's' **vehn**-lid ad ker' mai tel ...*

Vær så venligt at køre mig til ...

How much does it cost to go to ...?
    *vor **maa**-yeð kāsd' de ad ker' tel ...?*

Hvor meget koster det at køere til ...?

Instructions

Here is fine, thank you.
    sd'b hehR, taagh

Stop her, tak.

The next corner, please.
    *veð **nehs**-de yerR-ne, taagh*

Ved næste hjørne, tak.

Continue!
    ford-sehd!

Fortsæt!

The next street to the left/right.
    nehs-de gað tel vens-dr'/h'yr'

Næste gade til venstre/højre.

Stop here!
    sd'b hehR!

Stop her!

Please slow down.
    *va's' **vehn**-li ad kerR **laang**-s'm-m"*

Vær så venlig at køre langsommere.

Please wait here.
    ***vehn**-lid **vehn**-d hehR*

Venligt vent her.

Some Useful Phrases

The train is delayed/cancelled.
    *tā-oweð ehR f'-**sen**-gheð/en-sdel-eð*

Toget er forsinket/indstilt.

How long will it be delayed?
vor lehnge blee-v' tä-oweð f'-sen-gheð?

Hvor lenge bliver toget forsinket?

There is a delay of ... hours.
de ehR en f'-seng-ghelse på ... teem'

Det er en forsinkelse på ... timer.

Can I reserve a place?
ehR de moo-lid ad reh-saR-ve' plas?

Er det muligt at reservere plads?

How long does the trip take?
vor laang tið taa' too-'n?

Hvor lang tid tager turen?

Is it a direct route?
ehr de en di-raghde f'-ben-else?

Er det en direkte forbindelse?

Is that seat taken?
ehr seed-ed 'b-taa-eð?

Er sædet optaget?

I want to get off at ...
yai ern-sgh' ad gä a ved ...

Jeg ønsker at gå af ved ...

Excuse me.
än-sghül

Undskyld.

Where can I hire a bicycle?
vor kan yai laa-ye en sül-ghel?

Hvor kan jeg leje en cykel?

Car

DETOUR	OMKØRSEL
FREEWAY	MOTORVEJ
GARAGE	GARAGE
GIVE WAY	VIGEPLIKT
MECHANIC	MEKANIKER
NO ENTRY	INDKØRSEL FORBUDT

NO PARKING	PARKERING FORBUDT
NORMAL	NORMAL
ONE WAY	ENRETTET FÆRDSEL
REPAIRS	REPARATIONER
SELF SERVICE	SELVBETJENING
STOP	STOP
SUPER	SUPER
UNLEADED	BLYFRIT

Where can I rent a car?
   *vor kan yai **laa**-ye en beel?*

How much is it daily/weekly?
   *vor **maa**-yeð k's-d' de par da/par ooe?*

Does that include insurance/ mileage?
   *en-klu-**de'** de f'-**segh**-reng/ **ube**-ghran-seð me kilo-**me**-d'?*

Where's the next petrol station?
   *vor ehR **nehs**-de behn-**seen**-sda-shoon?*

Please fill the tank.
   ful taanggh, taagh

I want ... litres of petrol (gas).
   *yai **ern**-sgh' ... lid' me behn-**seen***

Please check the oil and water.
   *va's' **vehn**-li ad tjehghe olyen ' **van**-eð*

Hvor kan jeg leje en bil?

Hvor meget koster det per dag/per uge?

Inkluderer det forsikring/ ubegrænset med kilometer?

Hvor er næste benzinstation?

Fuld tank, tak.

Jeg ønsker ... liter med benzin.

Vær så venlig at checke olien og vandet.

How long can I park here?
vor lehnge kan yai paa-ke'
hehR?
Does this road lead to ...?
fer' dehne vaay-en tel ...?

Hvor længe kan jeg parkere her?

Fører denne vejen til ...?

air (for tyres)	*lāfd*	luft
battery	*bade-ree*	batteri
brakes	***bram-s'***	bremser
clutch	*k'b-leng*	kobling
driver's licence	*saR-tifi-kaad*	certifikat
engine	***moo-to***	motor
lights	*lüs*	lys
oil	*olye*	olie
puncture	*pāng-te-Reng*	punktering
radiator	*raadi-aa-to*	radiator
road map	***vaay-kord***	vejkort
tyres	*dehgh*	dæk
windscreen	*f'-rooðe*	forrude

Car Problems

I need a mechanic.
yai haa broo f' en
me-ka-nigh'
What make is it?
vað f' ed maR-ghe ehR de?
The battery is flat.
bade-ree-eð ehR derð
The radiator is leaking.
raadi-ato-on leh-gh'

Jeg har brug for en mekaniker.

Hvad for et mærke er det?

Batteriet er dødt.

Radiatoren lækker.

I have a flat tyre.
*yai haa pāng-**te**-'ð*   Jeg har punkteret.

It's overheating. (engine)
moo-to-on kā-ow' ow'   Motoren koger over.

It's not working.
*dehn **viR**-gh' eghe*   Den virker ikke.

Accommodation

CAMPING GROUND	CAMPINGPLADS
GUESTHOUSE	GJÆSTGIVERI
INN	KRO
HOTEL	HOTEL
MOTEL	MOTEL
YOUTH HOSTEL	VANDREHJEM

I am looking for ...
*yai **le**-ð' efd' ...*   Jeg leder efter ...

Where is a ...?
vor ehR ed ...?   Hvor er et ...?

cheap hotel	*bi-lid ho-**tehl***	billigt hotel
good hotel	*g'd ho-**tehl***	godt hotel
nearby hotel	*ho-**tehl** ee nehR-heden*	hotel i nærheden

What is the address?
*vað ehR a-**dra**-sen?*   Hvad er adressen?

Could you write the address, please?
*ku-ne dee va' s' **vehn**-li ad **sghree**-ve neð a-**dra**-sen?*   Kunne De være så venlig at skrive ned adressen?

At the Hotel

Do you have any rooms
available?
  haa ee leðee e vaR'l-s'?   Har I ledige værelser?

I would like ...   Jeg ønsker ...
  yai ern-sgh' ...
a single room   *ed eng-gheld-vaR'l-se*   et enkeltværelse
a double room   *ed d'beld-vaR'l-se*   et dobbeltværelse
a room with a   *ed vaR'l-se meh bað*   et værelse med
  bathroom   bad
to share a dorm   *plas ee en s'owe-saal*   plads i en sovesal
a bed   *en sehng*   en seng

I want a room with a ...   Jeg ønsker et værelse
  yai ern-sgh' ed vaR'l-se   med ...
  meh ...
bathroom   *bað*   bad
shower   *broose-bað*   brusebad
TV   *tele-vi-shoon*   television
window   *ven-dooe*   vindue

I'm going to stay for ...
  yai blee-v' ...   Jeg bliver ...
one day   *en nad*   en nat
two days   *too nehð'*   to nætter
one week   *en ooe*   en uge

Do you have identification?
  haa du leghi-tima-shoon?   Har du legitimation?
Your membership card, please.
  yaR-'s mehð-lehms-kord,   Jeres medlemskort, tak.
  taagh

Sorry, we're full.
be-klaa', de ehR ful-d
How long will you be staying?
vor lehnge blee-v' du?
How many nights?
vor maang-e nehð'?
It's ... per day/per person.
de kāsd'... par da/par paR-soon

Beklager, det er fuldt.

Hvor længe bliver du?

Hvor mange nætter?

Det koster ... per dag/per person.

How much is it per night/per person?
vor maa-yeð kāsd' de par nad/par paR-soon?
Can I see it?
mā yai fāse vaR'l-seð?
Are there any others?
ehR dehR aandr' vaR'l-s'?
Are there any cheaper rooms?
fen-es dehr bilee-'e vaR'l-s'?
Can I see the bathroom?
mā yai fā se baaðe-vaR'l-seð?
Is there a reduction for students/children?
ehR dehR sdu-dehnd-raa-bad/berR-ne-raa-bad?
Does it include breakfast?
ehR moron-mað en-klu-de'-eð?

Hvor meget koster det per nat/per person?

Må jeg få se værelset?

Er der andre værelser?

Findes der billigere værelser?

Må jeg få se badeværelset?

Er det studentrabat/børnerabat?

Er morgenmad inkluderet?

DANISH

It's fine, I'll take it.
  de ehR fee-nd, yai taa' de   Det er fint, jeg tager det.
I'm not sure how long I'm
staying.
  yai veð eghe vor lehng-e   Jeg ved ikke hvor længe jeg
  yai blee-v'   bliver.
Where is the bathroom?
  vor ehR toa-leh-deð?   Hvor er toilettet?
Is there somewhere to wash
clothes?
  ehR dehR ed ehl' aneð   Er der et eller andet sted for
  sdehð f' ad vasghe kle-ð'?   at vaske klæder?
Is there hot water all day?
  ehR dehR vaamd-van hele   Er der varmtvand hele
  d'y-neð?   døgnet?
Is there a lift?
  ehR dehR ele-vaa-tor?   Er der elevator?
Can I use the kitchen?
  kan yai broo-e ker-ghe-neð?   Kan jeg bruge køkkenet?
Can I use the telephone?
  kan yai be-ner-de tele-foo-   Kan jeg benytte telefonen?
  nen?

Requests & Complaints
Please wake me up at ...
  ku-ne dee veh-ghe mai   Kunne De vække mig
  kl'-ghen ...   klokken ...
The room needs to be cleaned.
  vaR'l-seð mā rü-ðes   Værelset må ryddes.
Please change the sheets.
  va' s' vehn-li ad sghif-de   Vær så venligt at skifte
  laay-n'ne   lagnene.

I can't open/close the window.
  yai kan eghe **ābne/lā**-ghe
  ven-du-eð

Jeg kan ikke åbne/lukke vinduet.

I've locked myself out of my room.
  yai haa **lā**-sd mai ooðe a
  va**R'l**-seð

Jeg har låst mig ude af værelset.

The toilet won't flush.
  *toa-**leh**-deð* **sgher**-l' eghe

Toilettet skyller ikke.

I don't like this room.
  yai **sünes** eghe 'm dehde
  va**R'l**-seð

Jeg synes ikke om dette værelset.

It's (too) ...
  de ehR (f') ...

Det er (for) ...

small	*li-le*	lille
noisy	*sd'y-ene*	støjende
dark	*morR-ghd*	mørkt
expensive	*düR-d*	dyrt

Some Useful Phrases

I am/We are leaving ...
  yai/vi **raay**-s' ...

Jeg/Vi rejser ...

now/tomorrow
  nu/i **mor**-orn

nu/i morgen

I would like to pay the bill.
  yai **ern**-sgh' ad be-**taa**-le
  raay-neng-en

Jeg ønsker at betale regningen.

name	*naown*	navn
surname	*ehfd'-naown*	efternavn
room number	va**R'l**-se-näm'	værelsenummer

Some Useful Words

address	*a-dra-se*	adresse
air-conditioned	*lā-fd-k'ndi-sho-ne-'ð*	luftkonditionert
balcony	*bal-k'ng*	balkon
bathroom	*bað*	bad
bed	*sehng*	seng
bill	*raay-neng*	regning
blanket	*teh-be*	tæppe
candle	*lüs*	lys
chair	*sdool*	stol
clean	*rehn*	ren
dark	*morRgh*	mørk
dirty	*snaow-seð*	snavset
double bed	*d'beld-sehng*	dobbeltseng
electricity	*elehgh-trisi-teð*	elektricitet
excluded	*ehghsklu-de-eð*	ekskluderet
fan	*vef-de*	vifte
included	*enklu-de-'ð*	inkluderet
key	*n'y-le*	nøgle
lift (elevator)	*ele-vaato*	elevator
light bulb	*e-lehgh-trisgh peh'*	elektrisk pære
lock (n)	*lās*	lås
mattress	*ma-dras*	madras
mirror	*sbai-l*	spejl
padlock	*hehnge-lās*	hængelås
pillow	*hooeð-pooðe*	hovedpude
quiet	*sdele*	stille
room (in hotel)	*var'l-se*	værelse
sheet	*laay-en*	lagen
shower	*broose-bað*	brusebad

soap	*sehbe*	sæpe
suitcase	*kā-f'd*	kuffert
swimming pool	*sver-me-ba-seng*	svømmebassin
table	*booR*	bord
toilet	*toa-lehd*	toilet
toilet paper	*toa-lehd-pa-peeR*	toiletpapir
towel	*h'n-klehðe*	håndklæde
water	*van*	vand
cold water	*k'ld van*	koldt vand
hot water	*vaa-md van*	varmt vand
window	*ven-dooe*	vindue

Around Town

I'm looking for ...		Jeg søger efter ...
yai ser' ehfd' ...		
the art gallery	*kān-sd-mu-seheð*	kunstmuseet
a bank	*en bang-gh*	en bank
the church	*kiR-ghen*	kirken
the city centre	*sehn-trām*	centrum
the ... embassy	*dehn ... amba-saa-ðe*	den ... ambassade
my hotel	*mid ho-tehl*	mit hotel
the market	*maa-gheð-ed*	markedet
the museum	*mu-seh-eð*	museet
the police	*poli-tee-eð*	politiet
the post office	*p'sd-k'n-tooR-eð*	postkontoret
a public toilet	*ed 'fend-lid toa-lehd*	et offentligt toilet
the telephone centre	*tele-foon-sehn-traa-len*	telefoncentralen
the tourist information office	*tu-risd-enforma-shoo-nen*	turistinformationen

What time does it open?
*vo-**nor** ābn' de?*   Hvornår åbner det?
What time does it close?
*vo-**nor** lā-gh' de?*   Hvornår lukker det?

What ... is this?
vað f' en ... ehR dehde?   Hvad for en ... er dette?
street   ***gaa-**ðe*   gade
suburb   *f'-**sdað***   forstad

For directions, see the Getting Around section, page 23.

At the Bank
I want to exchange some
money/traveller's cheques.
*yai **ern**-sgh' ad **vehgh**-sle   Jeg ønsker at veksle nogle
noo-le **pehng**-e/**raayse**-   penger/reisechecks.
sheghs*
What is the exchange rate?
*vað ehR **kuR**-sen?*   Hvad er kursen?
How many kroner per dollar?
*vor **maang**-e **kroo**-n' par   Hvor mange kroner per
d'-la?*   dollar?
Can I have money transferred
here from my bank?
*kan yai fā **pehng**-e'   Kan jeg få penge overført
ow'-fer' hid fra meen   hit fra min bank?
baang-gh?*
How long will it take to
arrive?
*vor laang tið vel de ta ferR   Hvor lang tid vil det tage
de **an**-k'm'?*   før de ankommer?

Has my money arrived yet?
   *haa meene **pehng**-e
   an-k'm-eð e-nu?*

Har mine penge ankommet
endnu?

bank draft	***baang**-gh-an-vee-sneng*	bankanvisning
bank notes	***sehð**l'*	sedler
cashier	*ka-**seh**-'*	kasserer
coins	***mern**-d'*	mønter
credit card	***kreh**-did-kord*	kreditkort
exchange	***vehgh**-sle*	veklse
loose change	***smā**-pehng-e*	småpenge
signature	*sin-ya-**tooR***	signatur

At the Post Office

I would like to send ...
   *yai **ern**-sgh' ad seh-ne ...*

Jeg ønsker at sende ...

a letter	*ed brehv*	et brev
a postcard	*ed **p'sd**-kord*	et postkort
a parcel	*en **pa**-ghe*	en pakke
a telegram	*ed tele-**ghram***	et telegram

I would like some stamps.
   *yai vel **gaR**-ne **haa**-ve
   noo-le fri-**maRgh**'*

Jeg vil gerne have nogle
frimerker.

How much is the postage?
   *vor **maa**-yeð ehR **portoo**-en?*

Hvor meget er portoen?

How much does it cost to
send this to ...?
   *vor **maa**-yeð k's-d' de ad
   seh-ne dehne tel ...?*

Hvor meget koster det at
sende denne til ...?

an aerogram	*ed ahRo-**graam***	et aerogram
air mail	*lā-fd-p'sd*	luftpost
envelope	*k'nvo-**lud***	konvolut
mailbox	*p'sd-kase*	postkasse
parcel	*paa-ghe*	pakke
registered mail	*rehk'-man-de-'ð*	rekommanderet
surface mail	*ow'-flaað-p'sd*	overfladepost

Telephone

I want to ring ...
   yai ern-sgh' ad rehng-e tel ...
      Jeg ønsker at ringe til ...

The number is ...
   nām-r'ð ehR ...
      Nummeret er ...

I want to speak for three minutes.
   yai ern-sgh' ad taa-le treh mi-nud'
      Jeg ønsker at tale tre minutter.

How much does a three-minute call cost?
   vor maa-yeð k's-d' de f' treh mi-nud'?
      Hvor meget koster det for tre minutter?

How much does each extra minute cost?
   vor maa-yeð k's-d' vehRd mi-nud ehghs-dra?
      Hvor meget koster hvert minutt ekstra?

I would like to speak to Mr Pedersen.
   yai ern-sgh' ad taa-le meh haR peh-d'-sen
      Jeg ønsker at tale med Hr Pedersen.

It's engaged.
   de ehR 'b-taa-eð
      Det er optaget.

I want to make a reverse-
charges phone call.
  yai ern-sgh' ad mod-
  taa-'en sgha be-taa-le
I've been cut off.
  yai bleh-v aw-brud

Jeg ønsker at modtageren
skal betale.

Jeg blev afbrudt.

Sightseeing

Do you have a guidebook/
local map?
  haa ee en raay-se-h'n-
  bāow/lo-kaal-kord?
What are the main attractions?
  vað ehR hoo-veð-atraagh-
  shoo-nene?
What is that?
  vað ehR de?
How old is it?
  vor gaa-mel ehR dehn?
Can I take photographs?
  mā yai fā ta be-leð'?
What time does it open/close?
  vo-nor ābn'/lā-gh' de?

Har I en rejsehåndbog/
lokalkort?

Hvad er hovedattraktionene?

Hvad er det?

Hvor gammel er den?

Må jeg få tage billeder?

Hvornår åbner/lukker det?

ancient	*ehl-gaa-mel*	ældgammel
archaeological	*akeho-loo-isgh*	arkæologisk
beach	*sdran*	strand
building	*būgh-neng*	bygning
castle	*sl'd*	slot

cathedral	*kade-**draal***	katedral
church	*kiR-ghe*	kirke
concert hall	*k'n-saRd-saal*	koncertsal
library	*biblio-**tehgh***	bibliotek
main square	*hoo-veð-torv*	hovedtorv
market	*maa-gheð*	marked
monastery	*kl's-d'*	kloster
monument	*monu-**mehnd***	monument
mosque	*m'-sghe*	moské
old city	*gaam-le büen*	gamle byen
opera house	*oo-bera*	opera
palace	*pa-las*	palads
ruins	*ru-ee-n'*	ruiner
stadium	*sdaa-di'n*	stadion
statues	*sdaa-too'*	statuer
synagogue	*süna-**ghooe***	synagoge
temple	*tehm-bel*	tempel
university	*uni-vaRsi-**teh-deð***	universitet

Entertainment

What's there to do in the evenings?

  vað ehR dehR ad gher' 'm aaf-denen?

Hvad er der at gøre om aftenen?

Are there any discos?

  *ehR dehR disgh'-**tehgh'***?

Er der disoteker?

Are there places where you can hear local folk music?

  *fen-es dehR **sdeh**-ð' vor de ehR moo-lid ad her' f'lghe-mu-sigh?*

Findes der steder hvor det er muligt at høre folkemusik?

How much does it cost to get in?

*vor **maa**-yeð **k**'s-d' de ad **k**'m-me en?*		Hvor meget koster det at komme ind?

cinema	*bio-**ghraaf***	biograf
concert	*k'n-**saRd***	koncert
discotheque	*disgh'-**tehgh***	diskotek
theatre	*te-**aa**-d'*	teater

In the Country
Weather

What's the weather like?

*vor-**dan** ehR veh-'ð?* Hvordan er vejret?

The weather is ... today.

de ehR ... ee daa Det er ... i dag.

Will it be ... tomorrow?

*k'm-m' de ad **blee**-ve ... ee **mor**-orn?* Kommer det at blive ... i morgen?

cloudy	***ow**'-sghü-eð*	overskyet
cold	*k'ld*	koldt
foggy	***tä**-weð*	tågede
frosty	*fr'sd*	frost
hot	*hed*	hedt
raining	***raay**-n*	regn
snowing	*sne*	sne
sunny	*sool*	sol
windy	***bleh**-se-vehR*	blæsevejr

Camping

Am I allowed to camp here?
mā yai fā kaam-peh' hehR? Må jeg få campere her?

Is there a campsite nearby?
fen-es dehR en kaam-peng- Findes der en campingplads
plas ee nehR-heðen? i nærheden?

backpack	*rergh-sehgh*	rygsække
can opener	*dāse-ābn'*	dåseåbner
compass	*k'm-pas*	kompas
crampons	*kladr'-yaRn*	klatrejern
firewood	*brane*	brænde
gas cartridge	*gas-be-h'l'*	gasbeholder
hammock	*hehnge-k'ye*	hængekøje
ice axe	*ees-erghse*	isøkse
mattress	*ma-dras*	madras
penknife	*l'me-kneev*	lommekniv
rope	*t'w*	tov
sleeping bag	*s'owe-poose*	sovepose
stove	*kaam-peng-'own*	campingovn
tent	*tehld*	telt
tent pegs	*tehld-pehle*	teltpæle
torch (flashlight)	*l'me-lerghde*	lommelygte
water bottle	*fehld-flasghe*	feltflaske

Food

Traditional Danish cooking is dominated, although not to the same extent as the other Scandinavian countries, by smoked, cured, pickled or otherwise preserved food, due to the short growing season and long winters. Regional variations are not great, though proximity to the ocean flavours menus with seafood.

breakfast	**mor**-orn-mað	morgenmad
lunch	**frā**-k'sd	frokost
dinner	**meda**	middag

Table for ..., please.
  ed booR f' ..., taagh — Et bord for ..., tak.
Can I see the menu please?
  mā yai fā seh menüen? — Må jeg få se menuen?
I would like the set lunch, please.
  yai taa'**daaens** rad, taagh — Jeg tager dagens ret, tak.
What does it include?
  vað enklu-**deh'** dehn? — Hvad inkluderer den?
Is service included in the bill?
  ehR **ser**-vis enklu-**deh**-'ð ee **raay**-nengen? — Er service inkluderet i regningen?
Not too spicy please.
  eghe f'**krüð**-r'ð 'm yai mā behðe — Ikke for krydret, om jeg må bede.

Vegetarian Meals

I am a vegetarian.
  yai ehR veghe-taai-**aan'** — Jeg er vegetarianer.
I don't eat meat.
  yai sbees' eghe kerð — Jeg spiser ikke kød.
I don't eat chicken, or fish, or ham.
  yai sbees' eghe **kü**-leng ehl' fesgh ehl' **sgheng**-ghe — Jeg spiser ikke kylling eller fisk eller skinke.

ashtray	*asghe-beh'*	askebæger
the bill	*raay-nengen*	regningen
a cup	*en k'b*	en kop
dessert	*deh-sehR*	dessert
a drink	*ed dreh-ghe*	et drikke
a fork	*en ghaa-fel*	en gaffel
fresh	*faRsgh*	fersk
a glass	*ed glas*	et glas
a knife	*en kneev*	en kniv
a plate	*en ta-laR-ghen*	en tallerken
spicy	*krüð-r'ð*	krydret
a spoon	*en sgheh*	en ske
stale	*gaa-mel*	gammel
sweet	*serð*	sød
teaspoon	*teh-sgheh*	teske
toothpick	*tan-sdegh'*	tandstikker

Breakfast

	Morgenmad
fried egg (always sunny side up)	*spejlæg*
hardboiled egg	*hårdkogte æg*
oatmeal	*havregrød*
pancakes	*pandekager*
scrambled eggs	*røræg*
scrambled eggs with bacon	*flæskeæggekage*
scrambled eggs with onions, potatoes and bacon	*æggekage*
softboiled egg	*blødkogte æg*
toast	*ristet brød*

Sandwiches   Smørebrød

Danish sandwiches are ornate and tasty. A feast for the eye and a delight to the palate.

Bøftartar
  Beef tartar: raw ground beef topped with a raw egg yolk, onion and capers.

Hakkebøf med løg
  Hamburger covered with fried onions, served cold.

Leverpostej
  Liver paté.

Rejemad
  Small shrimp served with mayonnaise and lemon slices.

Røget ål
  Smoked eel, a delicacy.

Røget laks
  Smoked salmon, served with scrambled eggs.

Røget sild
  Smoked herring on bread with a raw egg yolk and chives

Ost
  Cheese. Denmark is famous for its cheeses, and produces an enormous variety.

bread	*brød*
crusty roll	*rundstykke*
Danish pastry	*wienerbrød*
French bread, baguette	*franskbrød*
rye bread	*rugbrød*
soft roll	*bolle*

Soup   Suppe

Fiskesuppe
Fish soup, usually creamy.
Grøntsagssuppe
Vegetable soup.
Hønsekødsuppe
Chicken soup.
Sødsuppe
A sweet barley or sago soup with raisins and prunes.
Ølebrød
A smooth beer and bread soup served with whipped cream.
Ærter gule
Split pea soup served with pork.

Meat   Kød

Denmark is a major meat exporter, and is best known for its pork, ham and bacon.

Benløse fugle
Meatloaf shaped to resemble small game birds.
Bankekød
Similar to Weinerschnitzel.
Forloren skilpadde
Imitation turtle stew made with tongue, veal, meatballs and fishballs.
Frikadeller med surt
Meat patties served with potatoes, brown sauce, and pickled cucumbers.
Fyldt hvidkålshoved
Cabbage leaves wrapped around ground beef.

Høns i karri
  Stewed chicken in a curry sauce.
Ruskomsnusk
  Hash made with bits of ham, carrots, potatoes and onions,
  fried in butter.

chicken	*kylling*
hamburger	*hakkebøf*
lamb chops	*lammekoteletter*
roast beef	*oksesteg*
roast lamb	*lammesteg*
roast pork	*flæskesteg*
sausage	*pølse*
steak	*engelsk bøf*

Seafood   Fisk

Ål stegt med stuvede kartofler
  Fried eel with either fried or boiled diced potatoes.
Kogt torsk
  Poached cod in a mustard sauce served with boiled potatoes.
Kryddersild
  Herring pickled in different marinades, onion, mustard,
  tomato, etc.

haddock	*kuller*
halibut	*helleflynde*
herring	*sild*
plaice	*rødspætte*
salmon	*laks*
shrimp	*rejer*
sole	*søtunge*
trout	*forel*

Vegetables	Grøndsager
beets (usually served pickled)	*rødbeder*
cabbage	*kål*
carrots	*gulerødder*
cauliflower	*blomkål*
celery	*bladselleri*
cucumber	*augurk*
lettuce	*grøn salat*
mashed potatoes	*kartoffelmos*
mushrooms	*champignons*
onions	*løg*
peas	*ærter*
pickled cucumbers	*surt*
potato (boiled/baked)	*kartoffel (kogt/bagt)*
rice	*ris*
string beans	*snittebønner*

Condiments	Surt og Sødt
butter	*smør*
garlic	*hvidløg*
mustard	*sennep*
oil	*olie*
pepper	*peber*
salt	*salt*
sugar	*sukker*
vinegar	*eddik*

Dessert   Dessert

Bindepige med slør

'Peasant girl with a veil'. Browned breadcrumbs mixed with chocolate and covered with whipped cream.

Chokoladeis/vanilleis
Chocolate ice cream/Vanilla ice cream.

Kage
Cake.

Konditorkager
French pastry.

Rødgrød med fløde
Red currant or raspberry pudding served with cream or custard.

Pandekager
Crepes rolled around a jam filling and sprinkled with powdered sugar.

Drinks – Nonalcoholic   **Drikke**
coffee (with cream)   *kaffe (med fløde)*
orange juice   *orangesaft*
skim milk   *skummet mælk*
soft drink, carbonated water   *sodavand*
tea   *te*
water, ice water.   *vand, isvand*
whole milk   *sødmælk*

Drinks – Alcoholic   **Drikke**
øl
beer, lager.

bajer
Beer. Specifically means a darker beer more like ale, but is used colloquially to mean any beer.

snapps
Various kinds of grain alcohol flavoured with different herbs. *Jægermeister, Gammel Dansk*, etc. Traditionally consumed with fatty foods to help digestion.

Shopping

How much is it?

*vor **maa**-yeð **k**'s-d' de?* Hvor meget koster det?

bookshop	*bāw-han-el*	boghandel
camera shop	*foto-han-el*	fotohandel
clothing store	*kleh-ð-magha-seen*	klædemagasin
delicatessen	*delika-tehse*	delikatesse
general store, shop	*lan-han-el, bu-tigh*	landhandel, butik
laundry	*vasghe-ree*	vaskeri
market	*maa-gheð*	marked
newsagency	*a-vees-ki-'sgh*	aviskiosk
pharmacy	*aapo-tegh*	apotek
shoeshop	*sgho-t'ys-f'rad-neng*	skotøjsforretning
souvenir shop	*suve-neer-bu-tigh*	souvenirbutik
stationers	*pa-peeR-han-el*	papirhandel
supermarket	*soo-b'-maa-gheð*	supermarked
vegetable shop	*grernd-han-el*	grønthandel

I would like to buy ...

*yai **ern**-sgh' ad kerbe ...* Jeg ønsker at købe ...

Do you have others?

*haa du **an**-eð?* Har du andet?

I don't like it.

dehn kan yai eghe leeðe Den kan jeg ikke lide.

Can I look at it?

*mā yai fā **ki**-ghe pā dehn?* Må jeg få kikke på den?

I'm just looking.

*yai **baa**-a **ki**-gh'* Jeg bare kikker.

Can you write down the price?
ku-ne du sghree-ve pree-sen?

Kunne du skrive prisen?

Do you accept credit cards?
aagh-sehb-teh'ee kreh-did-kord?

Accepterer I kreditkort?

Can I help you?
mā yai fā yehl-be dehm?

Må jeg få hjælpe Dem?

Will that be all?
ehr de de heh-le?

Er det det hele?

Would you like it wrapped?
ern-sgh' dee de paa-gheð en?

Ønsker De det pakket ind?

Sorry, this is the only one.
des-vaR', dehde ehR dehn enesde

Desværre, dette er den eneste.

How much/many do you want?
vor maa-yeð/maang-e ern-sgh' dee?

Hvor meget/mange ønsker De?

Souvenirs

earrings	*er'n-rehnge*	ørenringe
handicraft	*kā-nsd-h'n-vaRgh*	kunsthåndværk
necklace	*hals-b'n*	halsbånd
pottery	*keaa-migh*	keramik
ring	*rehng*	ring
rug	*teh-be*	tæppe

Clothing

clothing	*kleh'*	klæder
coat	*fraa-ghe*	frakke
dress	*kyoo-le*	kjole
jacket	*yaa-ghe*	jakke
jumper (sweater)	*sweh-d'*	sweater
shirt	*sghyoR-de*	skjorte
shoes	*sghoo*	sko
skirt	*neð'-dehl*	nederdel
trousers	*bā'-gh-s'*	bukser

It doesn't fit.
   dehn pa-s' eghe — Den passer ikke.

It is too ...
   dehn ehR f' ... — Den er for ...

big	*sdooR*	stor
small	*li-le*	lille
short	*kord*	kort
long	*laang*	lang
tight	*traang*	trang
loose	*lers*	løs

Materials

cotton	*bām-ul*	bomuld
handmade	*h'n-laa-veð*	håndlavet
leather	*lehð'*	læder
of brass	*a mehs-eng*	af messing
of gold	*a gul*	af guld
of silver	*a serl*	af sølv
pure alpaca	*rehn al-paaka*	ren alpaka
silk	*sel-ghe*	silke
wool	*ul*	uld

Toiletries

comb	*kaam*	kam
condoms	*k'n-doom-'*	kondomer
deodorant	*deo-do-raand*	deodorant
hairbrush	*hor-borRs-de*	hårbørste
moisturising cream	*fågh-di-heðs-krehm*	fugtighedscreme
razor	*baa-behR-kneev*	barberkniv
sanitary napkins	*ben*	bind
shampoo	*sham-pu*	shampoo
shaving cream	*baa-behR-krehm*	barbercreme
soap	*seh-be*	sæbe
sunblock cream	*sool-krehm*	solcreme
tampons	*taam-p'ng'*	tamponer
tissues	*ranse-sarvi-ehd*	rense-serviet
toilet paper	*toa-lehd-pa-peeR*	toiletpapir
toothbrush	*tan-berRs-de*	tandbørste
toothpaste	*tan-pasda*	tandpasta

Stationery & Publications

map	*kord*	kort
newspaper	*a-vees*	avis
newspaper in English	*en a-vees på eng-elsgh*	en avis på engelsk
novels in English	*ro-maa-n' på eng-elsgh*	romaner på engelsk
paper	*pa-peeR*	papir
pen (ballpoint)	*koo-le-pehn*	kuglepen
scissors	*saaghs*	saks

Photography

How much is it to process this film?

> *vor **maa**-yeð k's-d' de ad*   Hvor meget koster det at
> *fram-kale dehne fil-men?*   fremkalde denne filmen?

When will it be ready?

> *vor-**nor** blee-v' dehn*   Hvornår bliver den ferdig?
> *faR-di?*

I'd like a film for this camera.

> *yai **ern**-sgh' ad ker-be film*   Jeg ønsker at købe film til
> *tel dehde **kaa**-meraa-eð*   dette kameraet.

B&W (film)	**soRd**-við	sort-hvid
camera	**kaa**-meraa	kamera
colour (film)	**faa**-ve	farve
film	film	film
flash	blids	blitz
lens	'b-yehgh-**teev**	objektiv
light meter	**lüs**-mål'	lysmåler

Smoking

A packet of cigarettes, please.

> *en **paa**-ghe sighaa-**rad'**,*   En pakke cigaretter, tak.
> *taagh*

Are these cigarettes strong/ mild?

> *ehR dise sighaa-**rad'** sdaR-*   Er disse cigaretter
> *ghe/mile?*   stærke/milde?

Do you have a light?

> *kan yai få il hås dai?*   Kan jeg få ild hos deg?

cigarette papers	*sighaa-**rad**-pa-peeR*	cigaretpapir
cigarettes	*sigha-**rad**'*	cigaretter
filtered	*með fil-d'*	med filter
lighter	*füR-t'y*	fyrtøj
matches	*teh-sde-gh'*	tændstikker
menthol	*mehn-**tool***	mentol
pipe	***pee**-be*	pibe
tobacco (pipe)	***pee**-be-to-baagh*	pibetobak

Colours

black	*soRd*	sort
blue	*blā*	blå
brown	*broon*	brun
green	*grern*	grøn
orange	*o-**rang**-she*	orange
pink	*roosa*	rosa
purple	*li-la*	lilla
red	*rerð*	rød
white	*við*	hvid
yellow	*gool*	gul

Sizes & Comparisons

small	*li-le*	lille
big	*sdooR*	stor
heavy	*tāng*	tung
light	*lehd*	let
more	*mehR*	mer
less	***men**-dr'*	mindre
too much/many	*f'**maa**-yeð/**maang**-e*	for meget/mange
many	***maang**-e*	mange
enough	*n'gh*	nok
also	*'ows'*	også
a little bit	*en **li**-le smoole*	en lille smule

Health

Where is ...?
vor ehR ...?   Hvor er ...?

the doctor	**leh**-en	lægen
the hospital	hosbi-**taa**-leð	hospitalet
the chemist	aapo-**teh**-gh'	apoteker
the dentist	**tan**-leh-en	tandlægen

I am sick.
yai ehR sü   Jeg er syg.

My friend is sick.
meen vehn ehR sü   Min ven er syg.

Could I see a female doctor?
*mā yai fā seh en **kvene**-li*   Må jeg få se en kvindelig
leh-e?   læge?

What's the matter?
*vað ehR dehR ee **vaay**-en?*   Hvad er der i vejen?

Where does it hurt?
vor gerR de ānd?   Hvor gør det ondt?

It hurts here.
de gerR ānd hehR   Det gør ondt her.

My ... hurts.
meen/mid ... gerR ānd   Min/mitt ... gør ondt.

Parts of the Body

ankle	**aang**-ghel	ankel
arm	aam	arm
back	rergh	ryg
chest	brersd	bryst
ear	er'	øre
eye	'ye	øje

finger	*feng-'*	finger
foot	*fooð*	fod
hand	*h'n*	hånd
head	*hooðe*	hoved
heart	*yaR-de*	hjerte
leg	*behn*	ben
mouth	*mān*	mund
ribs	*riben*	ribben
skin	*huð*	hud
stomach	*maave*	mave
teeth	*tehn'*	tænder
throat	*hals*	hals

Ailments

I have ... *yai haa ...*		Jeg har ...
an allergy	*alaR-ghee*	allergi
anaemia	*aneh-mee*	anæmi
a blister	*en vaa-ble*	en vable
a burn	*ed braan-sor*	et brandsår
a cold	*en f'-kerl-else*	en forkølelse
constipation	*f'-sd'b-else*	forstoppelse
a cough	*en hoos-de*	en hoste
diarrhoea	*dia-reh*	diarré
fever	*fe-b'*	feber
a headache	*hoo-ðe-peene*	hovedpine
hepatitis	*hepa-titis*	hepatitis
indigestion	*maa-ve-be-svehR-li-heð'*	mavebesværli-gheder
an infection	*en en-fehgh-shoon*	en infektion
influenza	*en-flu-ehnsa*	influenza
lice	*loos*	lus

low/high blood pressure	*laa-vd/h'yd **bloð**-trergh*	lavt/højt blodtryk
a pain	*en **smaR**-de*	en smerte
sore throat	*ānd ee hal-sen*	ondt i halsen
sprain	*f'-sdoo-neng*	forstuvning
a stomachache	*ānd ee maaven*	ondt i maven
sunburn	*sool-f'-bran-eng*	solforbrænding
a temperature	*fe-b'*	feber
a venereal disease	*en **kerns**-sü-d'm*	kønssygdom
worms	*oRm*	orm

Some Useful Words & Phrases

I'm ...
  yai ehR ...   Jeg er ...

diabetic	*dia-**be**-tigh'*	diabetiker
epileptic	*epi-**lehb**-tisgh*	epileptisk
asthmatic	*asd-**maa**-tisgh*	astmatisk

I'm allergic to ...
  *yai ehR a-**laR**-ghisgh i-mooð...*   Jeg er allergisk imod ...

| antibiotics | *anti-bi-**oo**-tikām* | antibiotikum |
| penicillin | *penisi-**leen*** | penicillin |

I'm pregnant.
  *yai ehR graa-**við***   Jeg er gravid.

I'm on the pill.
  yai broo' pe-pelen   Jeg bruger p-pillen.

I haven't had my period for ... months.
  *yai haa eghe haafd mehns-drua-**shoon** pā ... māneð'*   Jeg har ikke haft menstruation på ... måneder.

I have been vaccinated.
 yai haa ble-veð vaaghsi-
 neh-'ð
         Jeg har blevet vaccineret.
I have my own syringe.
 yai haa meen aayen
 ka-nüle
         Jeg har min egen kanyle.
I feel better/worse.
 yai fer-l' mai behðr'/vaR' Jeg føler mig bedre/værre.

accident	*u-lerghe*	ulykke
addiction	*aaw-hengi-heð*	afhængighed
antibiotics	*anti-bi-oo-tikām*	antibiotikum
aspirin	*asbi-reen*	aspirin
a bandage	*en ban-daashe*	en bandage
blood test	*bloð-prer-ve*	blodprøve
contraceptive	*prehvehn-teev*	præventiv
medicine	*medi-seen*	medicin
menstruation	*mehnsdrua-shoon*	menstruation
nausea	*kvalme*	kvalme
oxygen	*'ghsü-ghen*	oxygen
vitamins	*vita-mee-n'*	vitaminer

At the Chemist

I need medication for ...
 yai be-her-v' ed medika- Jeg behøver et medikament
 mehn dee i-mooð...   imod ...
I have a prescription.
 yai haa reh-sehbd   Jeg har recept.

At the Dentist

I have a toothache.
 yai haa tan-peene   Jeg har tandpine.

I've lost a filling.

yai haa taabd en plām-be — Jeg har tabt en plombe.

I've broken a tooth.

yai haa bra-gheð en tan — Jeg har brækket en tand.

My gums hurt.

mid tan-kerð gorR ānd — Mit tandkød gør ondt.

I don't want it extracted.

yai vel eghe haave dehn trā-gheð — Jeg vil ikke have den trukket.

Please give me an anaesthetic.

mā yai fā en lo-kaal be-der-velse? — Må jeg få en lokal bedøvelse?

Time & Dates

What date is it today?

vað f' en daato ehR de ee daa? — Hvad for en dato er det i dag?

What time is it?

vað ehR kl'-ghen? — Hvad er klokken?

It is ... am/pm.

kl'-ghen ehR ... 'm mor-nen/aaf-denen — Klokken er ... om morgenen/aftenen.

in the morning	*'m mor-nen*	om morgenen
in the afternoon	*'m ehfd'-medaa-en*	om eftermiddagen
in the evening	*'m aaf-denen*	om aftenen

Days of the Week

Monday	*man-daa*	mandag
Tuesday	*teers-daa*	tirsdag
Wednesday	*ohns-daa*	onsdag
Thursday	*tors-daa*	torsdag
Friday	*fre-daa*	fredag

| Saturday | *lerR-daa* | lørdag |
| Sunday | *sern-daa* | søndag |

Months

January	*janu-aa*	januar
February	*febru-aa*	februar
March	*maads*	marts
April	*a-preel*	april
May	*maay*	maj
June	*yoo-ni*	juni
July	*yoo-li*	juli
August	*aaw-gāsð*	august
September	*sehb-tehm-b'*	september
October	*ogh-too-b'*	oktober
November	*no-vehm-b'*	november
December	*de-sehm-b'*	december

Seasons

summer	*s'm'*	sommer
autumn	*ehfd'-or*	efterår
winter	*ven-d'*	vinter
spring	*f'-or*	foraår

Present

today	*ee daa*	i dag
this morning	*ee mor-ors*	i morges
tonight	*ee nad*	i nat
this week/this year	*dehne ooe/ee or*	denne uge/i år
now	*nu*	nu

DANISH

Past

yesterday	*ee gor*	i går
day before yesterday	*ee for-**ghors***	i forgårs
yesterday morning	*ee gor **mor**-ors*	i går morges
last night	*ee gor nad*	i går nat
last week/last year	*foree-e ooe/i **fyoo**-R*	forrige uge/i fjor

Future

tomorrow	*ee **mor**-orn*	i morgen
day after tomorrow	*ee 'ow'-**mor**-orn*	i overmorgen
tomorrow morning	*ee **mor**-orn tiðlid*	i morgen tidligt
tomorrow afternoon/evening	*ee **mor**-orn ehfd'-medaa/aafden*	i morgen eftermiddag/aften
next week	*nehsde ooe*	næste uge
next year	*nehsde ā*	næste år

During the Day

afternoon	*ehfd'-medaa*	eftermiddag
dawn	*daaow-grü*	daggry
day	*daa*	dag
early	*tiðli*	tidlig
midnight	*mi**ð**-nad*	midnat
morning	*mor-orn*	morgen
night	*nad*	nat
noon	*mi**ð**-daa*	middag
sundown	*sool- neð-ghaang*	solnedgang
sunrise	*sool-'b-ghaang*	solopgang

Numbers & Amounts

0	*nāl*	nul
1	*en*	en
2	*too*	to
3	*treh*	tre
4	*fee'*	fire
5	*fehm*	fem
6	*sehghs*	seks
7	*süw*	syv
8	*āde*	otte
9	*nee*	ni
10	*tee*	ti
11	*ehlve*	elve
12	*t'l*	tolv
13	*traden*	tretten
14	*fyoRden*	fjorten
15	*fehmden*	femten
16	*saaysden*	seksten
17	*serden*	sytten
18	*aden*	atten
19	*neden*	nitten
20	*tüve*	tyve
21	*en-'-tüve*	enogtyve
30	*traðve'*	tredve
40	*for'*	fyrre
50	*hal-**trehs***	halvtreds
60	*trehs*	tres
70	*hal-**fyaRs***	halvfjedrs
80	*fiRs*	firs
90	*hal-**fehms***	halvfems
100	*hun-r'ðe*	hundrede

1000	*tu-sene*	tusinde
one million	*en mili-oon*	en million
1st	*forRsd*	først
2nd	*anen*	anden
3rd	*trehð-ye*	tredje
¼	*en fyeh'-del*	en fjerdedel
⅓	*en trehð-ye-del*	en tredjedel
½	*en hal*	en halv
¾	*treh fyeh'-dele*	tre firedele

Some Useful Words

a little (amount)	*en li-le smoole*	en lille smule
double	*d'b-eld*	dobbelt
a dozen	*ed du-seen*	et dusin
Enough!	*n'gh*	Nok!
few	*fã*	få
less	*mendr'*	mindre
many	*maang-e*	mange
more	*me'*	mere
once	*en-ghaang*	engang
a pair	*ed paa*	et par
percent	*pro-sehnd*	procent
some	*noo-le*	nogle
too much	*f' maay-eð*	for meget
twice	*to ghaange*	to gange

Abbreviations

0800/2000	am/pm
a/s	Ltd., Inc.
BZ – besittere	squatters

DSB – Danske Statsbaner	the Danish National Railways
DUH – Danske Ungdomsherberger	Danish Youth Hostel Association
DVH – Danske Vandrehjem	Danish Youth Hostel Association
dagl. – dagligt	daily (Monday to Saturday)
e.kr./f.kr.	AD/BC
EF – Europæiske Fellesmarked	EEC, the Common Market
FN	UN
frk. – frøken	Miss
fr – fredag	Friday
fru	Mrs
Gd/V	St/Rd/etc
hel. – hellig	holy (as in holiday)
hlp. – holdeplass	bus/tram stop
Hr. – herr	Mr/Sir
jb – jernbane	railway
jrbst – jernbane station	railway station
Kbhvn – København	Copenhagen
KDAK	the Royal Danish Automobile Association
kgl. – kongelig	royal
kl. – klasse	class (on trains and airplanes)
km/t – kilometer pr. time	kilometres per hour
kr – krone	crown (Danish monetary unit)
lø – lørdag	Saturday

m. – med	with
ma – mandag	Monday
moms	VAT, sales tax (included in the price on all goods and services)
ndf. – nedenfor	below (used in notices, timetables, etc)
Ndr. – nordre	to the north (pertaining to place names)
on – onsdag	Wednesday
SAS	Scandinavian Airline System
Sdr. – søndre	to the south (pertaining to place names)
sø – søndag	Sunday
t.h. – til høire	to the right (used in addresses)
ti – tirsdag	Tuesday
tlf – telefon	telephone
to – torsdag	Thursday
t.v. – til venstre	to the left (used in addresses)
x, excl. – eksklusive	excluded, except

Finnish

Introduction

Finnish, or *suomi* as it is called in Finland, is almost unique. It is not closely related to any language other than Estonian and Karelian and a handful of other rare languages. Linguistically, Finnish belongs to the Finnic (or more widely, Finno-Ugric) group of languages. Hungarian is the most widely spoken of the Finno-Ugric languages, but similarities with Finnish are extremely few.

Finnish is spoken by some five million people. It is not related to any Indo-European languages. There are, however, many loan words from Baltic, Slavonic and Germanic languages, and many words that derive from French and, especially, English.

The main difficulties with Finnish are the suffixes added to noun and verb roots, which often alter in this process, and the habit of constructing long words by putting several small words together.

Outside the big towns of Finland, few people speak fluent English, so it is advisable to learn some phrases in Finnish to make your visit more rewarding. Finns appreciate any effort made by a non-native speaker and are eager to help further. Finnish is by no means an easy language to master, but it is easy to read out loud and the phonetics are not difficult – and mistakes made by foreigners are usually disregarded. There is also a notable Swedish-speaking minority in Finland, and all Finns do learn Swedish in school, so you may need your Swedish vocabulary in Finland from time to time.

Pronunciation
Vowels
Finnish has eight vowels. The alphabet also includes Swedish *å* which is pronounced as the 'au' in 'caught'. It's probably worth noting that the **å**, **ä** and **ö** are the last three letters of the alphabet. So, while *Aatami* would be one of the first entries in a telephone book, *Äänehodi* would be one of the last.

a	as the 'u' in 'sun'
e	as the 'e' in 'fell'
i	as 'i' in 'in'
o	as the 'o' in 'pot'
u	as the 'u' in 'pull'
y	as the German *ü*
ä	as the 'a' in 'act'
ö	as the 'e' in 'summer'

Vowel Harmony
Finnish divides vowels into two groups: those formed 'in the front of the mouth' (**e, i, y, ä, ö**) and those formed 'in the back of the mouth' (**a, o, u**). This distinction is very important when forming words with suffixes, because the vowels in the suffixes must be of the same type as the vowels in the root word. For example, *koulussa*, 'in school', is formed by adding -*ssa*, not -*ssä*, to the root.

Double Vowels
Double vowels are tricky to pronounce, so follow the pronunciation guide carefully. You will find that some double vowels are pronounced as one sound within one syllable, others as diphthongs, and some as separate syllables.

For example, **ää** is pronounced as a long **a**, as in American 'fast', but **aa** is pronounced as in British 'can't'. To indicate the difference, **ää**, as one syllable, is written *ÿ* in the pronunciation guide in this chapter.

Consonants

There are only 13 consonants in Finnish, although the alphabet includes English consonants. The letter **x** can be written as **ks**, and **z** can be written, and is pronounced, as **ts**. Finns consider **v** and **w** more or less as the same letter, and in phone books you will find both under 'V'. In literature of a certain type, **w** makes a word look 'older'. *Vanha* is 'old', but *wanha* is 'definitely old'.

h	weak, except at end of a 'closed' syllable, when it is almost as strong as the German *ch* in *machen*
j	as the 'y' in 'yellow'
k	soft, as the 'k' in 'skate'
p	soft, as the 'p' in 'spirit'
r	rolled
s	weak
t	soft, as the 't' in 'steak'
v	as in 'vain'

Double Consonants

Double consonants like **kk** in *viikko*, 'week', or **mm** in *summa*, 'sum', are held longer, and they always split the word into two syllables. Note that **ng** and **nk** both make two syllables, and are pronounced as **-ng-ng-** and **-ng-k-**. For example, vangit, 'prisons', is *vahng-ngit*. Note also that **np** is pronounced as **mp**, as in olenpa, *o-lehm-pah*, 'I am'.

Greetings & Civilities

Finns use *Päivää!*, literally 'Day!', as a general greeting during most of the day.

Top Useful Phrases

Hello.
hay, tehr-veh (moy) — Hei, terve. (Moi. – inf)

Goodbye.
na-keh-meen (moy) — Näkemiin. (Moi. – inf)

Excuse me.
ahn-teehk-si — Anteeksi.

May I? Do you mind?
sai-sin-ko? — Saisinko?

Sorry.
o-lehn pah-hoyl-lah-ni (so-ri) — Olen pahoillani. (Sori. – inf)

Thank you.
kee-toss (keet-ti) — Kiitos. (Kiitti. – inf)

Many thanks.
pahl-yon kee-tok-si-ah — Paljon kiitoksia.

That's fine. You're welcome.
o-leh hü-va (ay-pa kehs-ta) — Ole hyvä. (Eipä kestä – inf)

There isn't any frequently used word in Finnish for 'please'. Often *kiitos* is used. Another useful expression is 'could you', *voisitteko*, plus a verb. If you assume equality, or generally deal with informal situations, you are free to use less formal expressions. If you speak to a young clerk at a ticket booth or in a bank, you can say *voitko*, or even *voitsä*, 'are you able to', whereas an elderly lady would like to hear *voisitteko*, 'could you'. When buying a pack of cigarettes or a beer, you just state the merchandise. *Pitkä!* means 'Could you give me a large glass of beer, please!'

FINNISH

Greetings

Good morning.
hü-vÿ hu-o-mehn-tah — Hyvää huomenta.
hu-o-mehn-tah — Huomenta. (inf)
Good afternoon.
hü-vÿ pa-i-vÿ — Hyvää päivää.
pa-i-vÿ — Päivää. (inf)
Good evening/night.
hü-vÿ il-taa/ü-er-ta — Hyvää iltaa/yötä.
How are you?
mi-ta koo-loo? — Mitä kuuluu?
Well, thanks.
kee-toss hü-vÿ — Kiitos hyvää.

Forms of Address

Madam/Mrs	*rohv-vah*	Rouva
Sir/Mr	*hehr-rah*	Herra
Miss	*nay-ti*	Neiti
companion,	*üs-ta-va*	ystävä
friend	*kah-veh-ri*	kaveri (inf)

Small Talk

When you ask for a favour, use the most polite word: *Te* ('you' in the plural). Thus you place yourself below the person you are speaking to. Traditionally Finns had to make a deal, *sinunkaupat*, to call each other *sinä* instead of *Te*. The deal involved an exchange of names and a formal handshake, after which you were friends forever.

Minä means 'I', *sinä* is 'you'. Not everyone uses these words, however. In southern Finland, especially in Helsinki, most people say *mä* and *sä*. In Turku, Tampere and Oulu it is *mää*, for 'I', and *sää* for 'you' *(nää* in Oulu). In southern Savo they say *mie* and *sie*. In Helsinki it would be better to use *mä* instead of *minä*, to express that you don't place yourself above the other. In northern Savo and places in Karelia, people still use *minä* – elsewhere you may sound rather egoistic if you use it. There is an asterisk (*) in cases when you could consider using some other form, as you tour Finland. *Minä* is still the only correct word for 'I'.

FINNISH

Meeting People

What is your name?

mi-ka tay-dan ni-mehn-neh on? — Mikä Teidän nimenne on?

mi-ka sun ni-mi on? — Mikä sun nimi on? (inf)

My name is ...

mi-nun ni-mehn-ni on ... — Minun nimeni on ...

mun ni-mi on ... — Mun nimi on ... (inf)

I'd like to introduce you to ...

hah-lu-ai-sin eh-si-tehl-la si-nut ... — Haluaisin esitellä sinut ...-lle

I'm pleased to meet you.

hows-kah tah-vah-tah — Hauska tavata.

Nationalities

Where are you from?

mis-ta si-na o-leth ko-toy-sin? — Mistä sinä* olet kotoisin?

I am from ...

o-lehn ... — Olen ...

Australia	*owst-rah-li-ahs-tah*	Australiasta
Canada	*kah-nah-dahs-tah*	Kanadasta

England	*ehng-lahn-nis-tah*	Englannista
Finland	*su-o-mehs-tah*	Suomesta
Ireland	*ir-lahn-nis-tah*	Irlannista
New Zealand	*oo-dehs-tah*	Uudesta-
	seeh-lahn-nis-tah	Seelannista
Scotland	*scot-lahn-nis-tah*	Skotlannista
the USA	*üch-düs-vahl-loys-tah/*	Yhdysvalloista/
	ah-meh-ri-kahs-tah	Amerikasta
Wales	*wayl-sis-ta*	Walesistä

Age

How old are you?
ku-in-kah vahn-hah si-na o-leht?　　Kuinka vanha sinä* olet?

I am ... years old.
o-lehn ... vu-o-ti-ahs　　Olen ...-vuotias.

Occupations

What work do you do?
mi-ta si-na teeht tüh-erk-seh-si?　　Mitä sinä* teet työksesi?

I am (a/an) ...
o-lehn ...　　Olen ...

artist	*tai-tay-li-yah*	taiteilija
businessperson	*lee-keh-mi-ehs*	liikemies
engineer	*in-si-ner-ri*	insinööri
farmer	*maan vil-yeh-li-ja*	maanviljelijä
journalist	*yohr-nah-lis-ti/*	journalisti/lehtim-
	lech-ti mi-ehs	ies
lawyer	*yu-ris-ti/lah-ki mi-ehs*	juristi/lakimies
manual worker	*tü-er-la-i-nehn*	työläinen

mechanic	**meh-kaa-nik-ko**	mekaanikko
doctor	**lÿ-ka-ri**	lääkäri
nurse	**sai-raan hoy-tah-yah**	sairaanhoitaja
office worker	**toy-mis-to tü-ern teh-ki-ya**	toimistotyöntekijä
scientist	**tut-ki-yah/ti-eh-deh mi-ehs**	tutkija/tiedemies
student	**o-pis-keh-li-yah**	opiskelija
teacher	**o-peht-tah-yah**	opettaja
waiter	**tahr-yoy-li-yah**	tarjoilija
writer	**kihr-yai-li-yah**	kirjailija

Religion

What is your religion?

    mi-ka on si-nun us-kon-to-si? ·   Mikä on sinun uskontosi?

I am not religious.

    ehn o-leh us-kon-nol-li-   En ole uskonnollinen/
    nehn/us-ko-vai-nehn   uskovainen.

I am (a/an) ...

    o-lehn ...   Olen ...

Buddhist	**bud-hah-lai-nehn**	buddhalainen
Catholic	**kah-to-li-nehn**	katolinen
Christian	**kris-tit-tü**	kristitty
Hindu	**hin-du-lai-nehn**	hindulainen
Jewish	**yoo-tah-lai-nehn**	juutalainen
Lutheran	**lu-teh-ri-lai-nehn**	luterilainen
Muslim	**mus-li-mi**	muslimi

Family

Are you married?

    o-leht-ko nai-mi-sis-sah?   Oletko naimisissa?

I am single. I am married.
   o-lehn nai-mah-ton — Olen naimaton.
   o-lehn nai-mi-sis-sah — Olen naimisissa.

How many children do you have?
   ku-in-kah mon-tah lahs-tah sul-lah on? — Kuinka monta lasta sinulla on?

I don't have any children.
   mul-lah ay o-leh lahp-si-ah — Minulla ei ole lapsia.

I have a daughter/a son.
   mul-lah on tü-tar (tüt-ter)/poy-kah — Minulla on tytär (tyttö – inf)/poika.

How many brothers/sisters do you have?
   ku-in-kah mon-tah vehl-yeh-a/sis-ko-ah si-nul-lah on? — Kuinka monta veljeä/siskoa sinulla on?

Is your husband/wife here?
   on-ko si-nun mi-eh-heh-si/vai-mo-si tÿl-la? — Onko sinun miehesi/vaimosi täällä?

Do you have a boyfriend/girlfriend?
   on-ko sul-lah poy-kah üs-ta-vÿ/üt-ter üs-ta-vÿ? — Onko sinulla poikaystävää/tyttöystävää?

brother	*veh-li*	veli
children	*lahp-set*	lapset
daughter	*tü-tar*	tytär
family	*pehr-heh*	perhe
father	*i-sa*	isä
grandfather	*i-so i-sa/vaa-ri/uk-ki*	isoisä/vaari/ukki

grandmother	*i-so a-i-ti/mum-mi*	isoäiti/mummi
husband	*ah-vi-o mi-es*	aviomies
mother	*a-i-ti*	äiti
sister	*sis-ko*	sisko
son	*poy-kah*	poika
wife	*vai-mo*	vaimo

FINNISH

Feelings

I like …
   pi-dan …-sta/stah   Pidän …-sta/stä.
I don't like …
   ehn pi-da …-sta/stah   En pidä …-sta/stä.
I am cold/hot.
   mi-nul-lah on kül-ma/   Minulla on kylmä/kuuma.
   koo-mah
I am hungry/thirsty.
   mi-nun on nal-ka/yah-no   Minun on nälkä/jano.
I am in a hurry.
   mi-nul-lah on kee-reh   Minulla on kiire.
I am right.
   o-lehn oy-keh-ahs-sah   Olen oikeassa.
I am sleepy.
   o-lehn u-ni-nehn   Olen uninen.
I am angry.
   o-lehn vi-hai-nehn   Olen vihainen.
I am happy/sad.
   o-lehn i-loy-nehn/su-rul-li-   Olen iloinen/surullinen.
   nehn
I am tired.
   o-lehn va-sü-nüt   Olen väsynyt.

FINNISH

I am well.
  voyn hü-vin   Voin hyvin.
I am worried.
  o-lehn hu-o-lis-sah-ni   Olen huolissani.
I am sorry. (condolence)
  o-tahn o-saa, o-lehn   Otan osaa, olen pahoillani.
  pah-hoyl-lah-ni
I am grateful.
  o-lehn kee-tol-li-nehn   Olen kiitollinen.

Language Difficulties

Do you speak English?
  pu-hut-ko ehng-lahn-ti-ah? Puhutko englantia?
Does anyone speak English?
  pu-hoo-ko ku-kaan   Puhuuko kukaan englantia?
  ehng-lahn-ti-ah?
I speak a little ...
  pu-hun va-han ...   Puhun vähän ...
I don't speak ...
  ehn pu-hu ...   En puhu ...
I understand.
  üm-mar-ran   Ymmärrän.
I don't understand.
  ehn üm-mar-ra   En ymmärrä.
Could you speak more slowly
please?
  voy-sit-ko pu-hu-ah   Voisitko puhua hitaammin?
  hi-taam-min?
Could you repeat that?
  voyt-ko toys-taa   Voitko toistaa.

How do you say …?
   *mi-tehn **sah**-no-taan …?*   Miten sanotaan …?
What does … mean?
   *mi-ta … **tahr**-koyt-taa?*   Mitä … tarkoittaa?

I speak …
   pu-hun …   Puhun …

English	***ehng**-lahn-ti-ah*	englantia
Finnish	*su-o-meh-ah*	suomea
French	***rahns**-kaa*	ranskaa
German	***sahk**-saa*	saksaa

Some Useful Phrases

Just a minute.
   ***heth**-ki-nehn*   Hetkinen.
It's (not) important.
   *seh on (ay o-leh) **tar**-keh-ÿ*   Se on (ei ole) tärkeää.
It's (not) possible.
   seh on (ay o-leh)   Se on (ei ole) mahdollista.
   ***mahch**-dol-lis-tah*
Wait!
   o-do-tah!   Odota!
Good luck!
   on-neh-ah (lükh-kü-a   Onnea! (Lykkyä tykö!)
   tüh-ker)

Signs

BAGGAGE COUNTER	MATKATAVARAT
CHECK-IN COUNTER	LÄHTÖSELVITYS
CUSTOMS	TULLI

EMERGENCY EXIT	VARAULOSKÄYNTI
ENTRANCE	SISÄÄN
EXIT	ULOS
FREE ADMISSION	VAPAA PÄÄSY
HOT/COLD	KUUMA/KYLMÄ
INFORMATION	OPASTUS, NEUVONTA
NO ENTRY	PÄÄSY KIELLETTY
NO SMOKING	TUPAKOINTI KIELLETTY
OPEN/CLOSED	AUKI/SULJETTU
PROHIBITED	KIELLETTY
RESERVED	VARATTU
TELEPHONE	PUHELIN
TOILETS	WC

Emergencies

POLICE	POLIISI
POLICE STATION	POLIISIASEMA

Help!
   ah-pu-ah! — Apua!

It's an emergency!
   ta-ma on ha-ta-tah-pows! — Tämä on hätätapaus!

There's been an accident!
   nüt on tah-pah-tu-nut on-neht-to-moos! — Nyt on tapahtunut onnettomuus!

Call a doctor!
   kut-su-kaa lü-ka-ri! — Kutsukaa lääkäri!

Call an ambulance!
   soyt-tah-kaa ahm-bu-lahns-si! — Soittakaa ambulanssi!

FINNISH

I've been raped.
mi-nut on rais-kaht-tu   Minut on raiskattu.

I've been robbed.
mi-nut on rü-ers-teht-tü   Minut on ryöstetty.

Call the police!
soyt-tah-kaa po-lee-si!   Soittakaa poliisi!

Where is the police station?
mis-sa on po-lee-si
ah-seh-mah?   Missä on poliisiasema?

Go away!
meh-neh poys (ha-i-vü)!   Mene pois! (Häivy! – inf)

I'll call the police!
mi-na kut-sun po-lee-sin!   Minä* kutsun poliisin!

Thief!
vah-rahs!   Varas!

I am/My friend is ill.
mi-na o-lehn/mun üs-ta-va   Minä* olen/Minun ystäväni
on sai-rahs   on sairas.

I am lost.
mi-na o-lehn ehk-sük-sis-sa   Minä* olen eksyksissä.

Where are the toilets?
mis-sa on vehs-sah?   Missä on vessa?

Could you help me please?
voyt-teh-ko (voyt-ko)   Voitteko (voitko) auttaa.
owt-taa

Could I please use the
telephone?
saan-ko ka-üt-tÿ pu-heh-   Saanko käyttää puhelinta?
lin-tah?

FINNISH

I'm sorry. I apologise.
oh-lehn pah-hoyl-lah-ni.
püü-dan ahn-teehk-si

Olen pahoillani. Pyydän anteeksi.

I didn't realise I was doing anything wrong.
ehn tah-yun-nut teh-keh-va-ni mi-tÿn vÿ-rin

En tajunnut tekeväni mitään väärin.

I didn't do it.
ehn teh-nüt si-ta

En tehnyt sitä.

I wish to contact my embassy/consulate.
hah-lu-ahn ot-taa üch-teh-üt-ta soor-la-heh-tüs-ter-ni/ kon-su-laat-teen

Haluan ottaa yhteyttä suurlä-hetystööni/konsulaattiin.

I speak English.
pu-hun ehng-lahn-ti-ah

Puhun englantia.

I have medical insurance.
mul-lah on vah-koo-tus

Minulla on vakuutus.

My possessions are insured.
mun tah-vah-raht on vah-koo-teht-tu

Minun tavarat on vakuutettu.

My ... was stolen.
mul-tah on vah-rahs-teht-tu

Minulta on varastettu ...

I've lost ...
mi-na o-lehn hu-kahn-nut ...

Minä* olen hukannut ...

my bags	*lowk-ku-ni*	laukkuni
my handbag	*ka-si lowk-ku-ni*	käsilaukkuni
my money	*rah-hah-ni*	rahani
my travellers' cheques	*maht-kah shehk-ki-ni*	matkashekkini
my passport	*pahs-si-ni*	passini

Paperwork

name	*ni-mi*	nimi
address	*o-soy-teh*	osoite
date of birth	*sün-tü-ma ai-kah/*	syntymäaika/
	hen-ki-ler tun-nus	henkilötunnus
place of birth	*sün-tü-ma paik-kah*	syntymäpaikka
age	*i-ka*	ikä
sex	*su-ku pu-o-li*	sukupuoli
nationality	*kahn-sah-lai-soos*	kansalaisuus
religion	*us-kon-to*	uskonto
reason for travel	*maht-kahn tahr-koy-tus*	matkan tarkoitus
profession	*ahm-maht-ti*	ammatti
marital status	*si-vee-li sÿ-tü*	siviilisääty
passport	*pahs-si*	passi
passport number	*pahs-sin nu-meh-ro*	passin numero
visa	*vee-su-mi*	viisumi
identification	*hehn-ki-ler pah-peh-rit*	henkilöpaperit
birth certificate	*sün-tü-ma to-dis-tus*	syntymätodistus
driver's licence	*ah-yo-kort-ti*	ajokortti
car registration	*ow-ton mehrk-ki*	auton merkki
customs	*tul-li*	tulli
border	*rah-yah*	raja

FINNISH

FINNISH

Getting Around

As you look for places, visit them and leave them, you will use different words in each case, and a little grammar is needed to gain understanding on how words are constructed. Finnish grammar is extremely complicated. With all possible suffixes and meanings, you can construct over 450 different words from any noun root.

• -ssa or -ssä, 'in something': *koulu-ssa*, 'in school'
• -sta or -stä, 'from something': *koulu-sta*, 'from school'
• -double vowel plus *n*, 'to something': *koulu-un*, 'to school'
• -lla or -llä, 'on', 'at' or 'in something' or 'somebody': *koulu-lla*, 'at school'
• -lta or -ltä, 'from something' or 'somebody': *koulu-lta*, 'from school'
• -lle, 'to something' or 'somebody': *koulu-lle*, 'to school'

Consider following examples of expressing 'in ...', and 'to ... a town':

• *Helsinki: Helsingi-ssä, Helsinki-in*
• *Turku: Turu-ssa, Turku-un*
• *Varkaus: Varkaude-ssa, Varkaute-en*
• *Tampere: Tamperee-lla, Tamperee-lle*
• *Rovaniemi: Rovanieme-llä, Rovanieme-lle* (and others ending -*niemi*)
• *Seinäjoki: Seinäjoe-lla, Seinäjoe-lle* (and others ending -*joki*)
• *Kemijärvi: Kemijärve-llä, Kemijärve-lle* (and others ending -*järvi*)

To express being inside a vehicle, hotel etc, the -*ssa* suffix is used for 'in', and a double vowel plus **n** for 'to': *juna-ssa/juna-an, hotelli-ssa/hotelli-in*. When you use a vehicle, you use the *-lla* suffix, as *matkustaa juna-lla*, 'to travel by train'.

FINNISH

ARRIVALS	SAAPUVAT
BUS STOP	PYSÄKKI
DEPARTURES	LÄHTEVÄT
STATION	ASEMA
SUBWAY	ALIKULKUKÄYTÄVÄ
TICKET OFFICE	LIPPUTOIMISTO
TIMETABLE	AIKATAULU
TRAIN STATION	RAUTATIEASEMA

What time does …leave/ arrive?
   mi-hin ai-kaan …   Mihin aikaan …
   lach-teeh/saa-poo?   lähtee/saapuu?

the (air)plane	**lehn**-to ko-neh	lentokone
the boat	**lai**-vah	laiva
the bus (city)	**bus**-si	bussi
the bus (intercity)	**bus**-si/**lin**-yah ow-to	bussi/linjauto
the train	**yu**-nah	juna
the tram	**rai**-ti-o vow-nu	raitiovaunu
	(rait-sik-kah)	(raitsikka)

Directions
Where is …?
   mis-sa on …?   Missä on …?
How do I get to …?
   mi-ten mi-na pÿ-sen …?   Miten minä* pääsen …?

FINNISH

Is it far from/near here?
on-ko seh kow-kah-nah/ la-hehl-la? Onko se kaukana/lähellä?

Can I walk there?
voy-ko sin-neh ka-vehl-la? Voiko sinne kävellä?

Can you show me (on the map)?
voyt-ko na-üt-tÿ mul-leh (kahr-tahs-tah)? Voitko näyttää minulle (kartasta)?

Are there other means of getting there?
pÿ-seeh-ker sin-neh yol-lah-kin mool-lah tah-vahl-lah? Pääseekö sinne jollakin muulla tavalla?

I want to go to …
hah-lu-ahn men-na … Haluan mennä …

Go straight ahead.
kul-yeh su-o-raan Kulje suoraan.

It's two blocks down.
seh on kahch-den kort-teh-lin pÿs-sa Se on kahden korttelin päässä.

Turn left …
kÿn-nü vah-sehm-paan … Käänny vasempaan …

Turn right …
kÿn-nü oy-keh-aan … Käänny oikeaan …

at the next corner
seh-u-raa-vahs-tah kah-dun kul-mahs-tah seuraavasta kadunkulmasta

at the traffic lights
lee-kehn-neh vah-loys-sah liikennevaloissa

behind	...-*n tah-kah-nah*	...-n takana
far	*kow-kah-nah*	kaukana
near	*la-hehl-la*	lähellä
in front of	*eh-dehs-sa*	en edessä
opposite	*vahs-tah pÿ-ta* ... *ta/tah*	vastapäätä ... -ta/-tä

Buying Tickets

Excuse me, where is the ticket office?

ahn-teehk-si, mis-sa on lip-pu toy-mis-to?

Anteeksi, missä on lipputoimisto?

Where can I buy a ticket?

mis-ta voy os-taa li-pun?

Mistä voi ostaa lipun?

I want to go to ...

ha-lu-ahn men-na ...

Haluan mennä ...lle/ ...vowel + n

Do I need to book?

ta-ü-tüü-ker vah-rah-tah?

Täytyykö varata?

You need to book.

si-nun ta-ü-tüü vah-rah-tah

Sinun täytyy varata.

I would like to book a seat to ...

ha-lu-ai-sin vah-rah-tah is-tu-mah pai-kahn ...

Haluaisin varata istumapaikan ...lle/...vowel + n

I would like ...

saan-ko ...

Saanko ...

a one-way ticket	*meh-no li-pun*	menolipun
a return ticket	*meh-no pa-loo li-pun*	menopaluulipun
two tickets	*kahk-si lip-pu-ah*	kaksi lippua
tickets for all of us	*li-put mayl-leh kai-kil-leh*	liput meille kaikille

a student's fare	*o-pis-keh-li-ya li-pun*	opiskelijalipun
a child's/pensioner's fare	*lahs-tehn li-pun/eh-la-keh-la-is-tehn li-pun*	lastenlipun/eläkeläisten lipun
1st class	*en-sim-ma-i-nehn lu-ok-kah*	ensimmäinen luokka
2nd class	*toy-nehn lu-ok-kah*	toinen luokka

It is full.
   seh on ta-ün-na   Se on täynnä.
Is it completely full?
   on-ko se ai-vahn ta-ün-na?   Onko se aivan täynnä?
Can I get a stand-by ticket?
   voyn-ko saa-dah li-pun   Voinko saada lipun ilman
   il-mahn paik-kah-vah-rows-   paikkavarausta?
   tah?

Air

CHECKING IN	LÄHTÖSELVITYS

Is there a flight to …?
   on-ko … len-to-ah?   Onko …-lle/…(vowel + n)
                                              lentoa?
When is the next flight to …?
   mil-loyn on seh-u-raa-vah   Milloin on seuraava lento
   len-to …?   …vowel + n/ …-lle?
How long does the flight take?
   kow-ahn-ko len-to kehs-tÿ?   Kauanko lento kestää?
What is the flight number?
   mi-ka on len-non nu-meh-ro?   Mikä on lennon numero?

You must check at …
   tay-dan (sun) taü-tüü cheh-kah-tah … -la

Teidän (sun) täytyy tsekata …-lla

airport tax	*lehn-to kehnt-ta veh-ro*	lentokenttävero
boarding pass	*tahr-kahs-tus kort-ti*	tarkastuskortti
customs	*tul-li/tul-li tahr-kahs-tus*	tulli/tullitarkastus

Bus

BUS/TRAM STOP	PYSÄKKI

Where is the bus/tram stop?
   mis-sa on bus-si/rait-sik-kah pü-sak-ki?

Missä on bussi/raitsikka-pysäkki?

Does this bus go to …?
   meh-neeh-ker ta-ma bus-si …?

Meneekö tämä bussi … vowel + n / …lle?

How often do buses pass by?
   ku-in-kah u-sayn tas-ta kul-keeh bus-si?

Kuinka usein tästä kulkee bussi?

Could you let me know when we get to …?
   voyt-ko sah-no-ah, mil-loyn on jÿ-ta-va poys …-n lu-o-nah?

Voitko sanoa, milloin on jäätävä pois …-n luona?

I want to get off!
   mi-na hah-lu-ahn jÿ-da poys!

Minä* haluan jäädä pois!

What time is the ... bus?
mi-hin ai-kaan on ...   Mihin aikaan on ... bussi?
bus-si?

next	*seh-u-raa-vah*	seuraava
first	*ehn-sim-ma-i-nehn*	ensimmäinen
last	*vee-may-nehn*	viimeinen

Train

DINING CAR	RAVINTOLA
EXPRESS	PIKAJUNA
PLATFORM NO	RAIDE
SLEEPING CAR	MAKUUVAUNU
LONG-DISTANCE	KAUKOLIIKENNE
TRAFFIC	
LOCAL TRAIN TICKETS	LÄHILIIKENNELIPPUJA
TRAVEL SERVICE	VR MATKAPALVELU
LOST AND FOUND	LÖYTÖTAVARAT

Is this the right platform
for ...?
on-ko ta-ma oy-keh-ah   Onko tämä oikea raide ...
rai-deh ...?   vowel + n/...lle?
Passengers must ...
maht-kus-tah-yi-ehn on ...   Matkustajien on ...
change trains
vaich-deht-tah-vah yu-naa   vaihdettava junaa
The train leaves from
platform ...
yu-nah lach-teeh   Juna lähtee raiteelta ...
rai-teehl-tah ...

dining car	*rah-vin-to-lah vow-nu*	ravintolavaunu
express	*pi-kah yu-nah*	pikajuna
local	*pai-kahl-lis yu-nah*	paikallisjuna
sleeping car	*mah-koo vow-nu*	makuuvaunu

Metro

CHANGE (for coins)	KOLIKOT
PLATFORM AREA	LAITURIALUE
(for ticket check)	
WAY OUT	ULOS

Which direction takes me
to …?
  kum-paan soon-taan   Kumpaan suuntaan pääsee
  pÿ-seeh …?   …lle / vowel + n?
What is the next station?
  mi-ka on seh-u-raa-vah   Mikä on seuraava asema?
  ah-seh-mah?

Taxi

People usually just say their destination without any civilities.

Can you take me to …?
  voyt-teh-ko vi-eh-da   Voitteko viedä minut …?
  mi-nut …?
How much does it cost to go
to …?
  pahl-yon-ko mahk-saa   Paljonko maksaa matka
  maht-kah …?   …vowel + n/…lle?

Instructions

Here is fine, thank you!
  tas-sa on hü-va, kee-toss!   Tässä on hyvä, kiitos!

The next corner, please.
seh-u-raa-vaan ris-teh-ük-seehn
Seuraavaan risteykseen.

Continue!
yaht-kah vi-eh-la!
Jatka vielä!

The next street to the left/right.
seh-u-raa-vaa kah-tu-ah vah-sehm-mahl-leh/oy-keh-ahl-leh
Seuraavaa katua vasemmalle/oikealle.

Stop here!
pü-sa-ü-ta tas-sa!
Pysäytä tässä!

Please slow down.
hi-das-tah va-han
Hidasta vähän.

Please wait here.
voyt-ko o-dot-taa tas-sa va-han
Voitko odottaa tässä vähän.

Some Useful Phrases

The train is delayed/cancelled.
yu-nah on mü-er-has-sa/ peh-roo-teht-tu
Juna on myöhässä/ peruutettu.

How long will it be delayed?
kow-ahn-ko seh on mu-er-has-sa?
Kauanko se on myöhässä?

There is a delay of ... hours.
seh on ... tun-ti-ah mu-er-has-sa
Se on ... tuntia myöhässä.

Can I reserve a place?
voyn-ko vah-rah-tah pai-kahn?
Voinko varata paikan?

How long does the trip take?
*kow-ahn-ko **maht**-kah **kehs**-tÿ?*

Kauanko matka kestää?

Is it a direct route?
***on**-ko se **su-o-**rah **rayt**-ti?*

Onko se suora reitti?

Is that seat taken?
***on**-ko toy **paik**-kah **vah-raht**-tu?*

Onko tuo paikka varattu?

I want to get off at ...
mi-na jÿn poys ...-ssa/lla

Minä* jään pois ...-ssa/-lla.

Excuse me.
*ahn-**teehk**-si*

Anteeksi.

Where can I hire a bicycle?
***mis**-ta **mi**-na voyn **vu-ok**-rah-tah **pol**-ku **pü-er**-ran?*

Mistä minä* voin vuokrata polkupyörän?

Is there room for the bicycle?
***mach**-too-ko **pol**-ku **pü-er**-ra?*

Mahtuuko polkupyörä?

Car

BAD ROAD	KELIRIKKO
DETOUR	KIERTOTIE
FREEWAY	MOOTTORITIE
GARAGE	HUOLTOASEMA
MECHANIC	KORJAAMO
NO ENTRY	KIELLETTY AJOSUUNTA
NO PARKING	PYSÄKÖINTI KIELLETTY
NORMAL LEADED	97 OKTAANIA
ONE WAY	YKSISUUNTAINEN AJOTIE
REPAIRS	TIETYÖ
ICE ON ROAD	JÄÄTIE

FINNISH

SELF SERVICE	ITSEPALVELU
STOP	STOP
SUPER LEADED	99 OKTAANIA
UNLEADED	LYIJYTÖN 95E

Where can I rent a car?
mis-ta mi-na voy-sin vu-ok-rah-tah ow-ton?
Mistä minä* voisin vuokrata auton?

daily/weekly
pehr pa-i-va/pehr veek-ko
per päivä/per viikko

Does that include insurance/mileage?
koo-loo-ko see-hen vah-koo-tus/rah-yoyt-tah-mah-ton ki-lo-meht-ri mÿ-ra?
Kuuluuko siihen vakuutus/rajoittamaton kilometrimäärä?

Where's the next petrol station?
mis-sa on la-hin ben-sah ah-seh-mah?
Missä on lähin bensäsema?

Please fill the tank.
tahnk-ki ta-ü-teehn, kee-toss
Tankki täyteen, kiitos.

I want ... litres of petrol (gas).
mi-na hah-lu-ai-sin ... lit-raa ben-saa
Minä* haluaisin ... litraa bensaa.

Please check the oil and water.
voyt-ko tahr-kis-taa erl-yün ya yÿch-dü-tüs nehs-teehn
Voitko tarkistaa öljyn ja jäähdytysnesteen.

How long can I park here?
kow-ahn-ko tas-sa saa park-keeh-rah-tah?
Kauanko tässä saa parkkeerata?

Does this road lead to …?
meh-neeh-ker ta-ma ti-eh …?

Meneekö tämä tie … vowel + n / …lle?

air (for tyres)	*il-mah*	ilma
battery	*ahk-ku*	akku
brakes	*yahr-rut*	jarrut
clutch	*küt-kin*	kytkin
driver's licence	*ah-yo kort-tih*	ajokortti
engine	*mort-to-ri, ko-neh*	moottori, kone
lights	*vah-lot*	valot
oil	*erl-yü*	öljy
puncture	*rehng-ngahs rik-ko*	rengasrikko
radiator	*yüch-dü-tin*	jäähdytin
road map	*ti-eh-kahrt-tah*	tiekartta
tyres	*rehn-kaat*	renkaat
windscreen	*too-li lah-si*	tuulilasi

FINNISH

Car Problems

I need a mechanic.
mi-na tar-vin kor-yaa-yaa
Minä* tarvitsen korjaajaa.

What make is it?
mi-ta mehrk-ki-a se on?
Mitä merkkiä se on?

The battery is flat.
ahk-ku on tüch-ya
Akku on tyhjä.

The radiator is leaking.
yüch-dü-tin vu-o-taa
Jäähdytin vuotaa.

I have a flat tyre.
rehng-ngahs on tüch-ja
Rengas on tyhjä.

It's overheating.
seh koo-meh-neeh lee-kaa
Se kuumenee liikaa.

It's not working.
seh ay toy-mi
Se ei toimi.

Accommodation

CAMPING GROUND	LEIRINTÄALUE
GUESTHOUSE	MATKAILIJAKOTI
HOTEL	HOTELLI
MOTEL	MOTELLI
YOUTH HOSTEL	RETKEILYMAJA

I am looking for …
   mi-na eht-sin   Minä* etsin …
Where is …?
   mis-sa o-li-si …?   Missä olisi …?

a cheap hotel	*hahl-pah ho-tehl-li*	halpa hotelli
a good hotel	*hü-va ho-tehl-li*	hyvä hotelli
a nearby hotelli	*la-hin ho-tehl-li*	lähin hotelli

What is the address?
   mi-ka on o-soy-teh?   Mikä on osoite?
Could you write the address,
please?
   voy-sit-teh-ko kir-joyt-taa
   o-soyt-teen   Voisitteko kirjoittaa osoit-
                          teen.

At the Hotel
Do you have any rooms
available?
   on-ko tayl-la vah-paa-tah
   hu-o-neht-tah?   Onko teillä vapaata
                          huonetta?

I would like …
ha-*lu-ai-sin* … Haluaisin …

a single room	**üch**-*dehn* **hehng-ngehn hu-o-neehn**	yhden hengen huoneen
a double room	**kahch**-*dehn* **hehng-ngehn hu-o-neehn**	kahden hengen huoneen
a room with a bathroom	**hu-o**-*neehn* **kül-pü hu-o-neehl-lah**	huoneen kylpyhuoneella
to share a dorm	**mah-koo** *sah-lin* **san-kü pai-kahn**	makuusalin sänkypaikan
a bed	**sang-ngün**	sängyn

I want a room with a …
mi-*na* **hah-lu-ahn hu-o-neehn** … Minä* haluan huoneen …

bathroom	**kül-pü hu-o-neehl-lah**	kylpyhuoneella
shower	**su-ih-kul-lah**	suihkulla
television	**yos-sah on teh-leh-vi-si-o**	jossa on televisio
window	**yos-sah on ik-ku-nah**	jossa on ikkuna

I'm going to stay for …
mi-*na* **ai-on vee-pü-a** … Minä* aion viipyä …

one day	**üch-dehn pai-van**	yhden päivän
two days	**kahk-si pai-vÿ**	kaksi päivää
one week	**vee-kon**	viikon

Do you have identification?
on-ko tayl-la (sul-lah)
hehn-ki-ler pah-peh-ray-tah? Onko Teillä (sulla – inf) henkilöpapereita?

Your membership card, please.
saan-ko ya-sehn kort-tin Saanko jäsenkortin.

Sorry, we're full.
vah-li-teht-tah-vahs-ti Valitettavasti meillä on
mayl-la on ta-üt-ta täyttä.

How long will you be staying?
ku-in-kah kow-ahn si-na Kuinka kauan sinä* aiot
ai-ot vee-pü-a? viipyä?

How many nights?
ku-in-kah mon-tah u-er-ta? Kuinka monta yötä?

It's … per day/per person.
se on … pa-i-val-ta/hehng- Se on … päivältä/hengeltä.
ngehl-ta

How much is it per night/per person?
pahl-yon-ko seh on Paljonko se on yöltä/
ü-erl-ta/hehng-ngehl-ta? hengeltä?

Can I see it?
voyn-ko mi-na nach-da Voinko minä* nähdä sen?
sehn?

Are there any others?
on-ko mi-tÿn mu-i-tah? Onko mitään muita?

Are there any cheaper rooms?
on-ko hahl-vehm-paa Onko halvempaa huonetta?
hu-o-neht-tah?

Can I see the bathroom?
voyn-ko mi-na nach-da Voinko minä* nähdä
kül-pü hu-o-neehn? kylpyhuoneen?

Is there a reduction for
students/children?
*saa-ko o-pis-keh-li-yah/
lahp-si ah-lehn-nus-tah?*
Saako opiskelija/lapsi
alennusta?

Does it include breakfast?
*koo-loo-ko aa-mi-ai-nehn
hin-taan?*
Kuuluko aamiainen hintaan?

It's fine, I'll take it.
*se on hü-va, mi-na o-tahn
sen*
Se on hyvä, minä* otan sen.

I'm not sure how long I'm
staying.
*mi-na ehn ti-eh-da ku-in-
kah kow-ahn mi-na o-lehn
tÿl-la*
Minä* en tiedä kuinka
kauan minä* olen täällä.

Is there a lift?
on-ko tÿl-la his-si-a?
Onko täällä hissiä?

Where is the bathroom?
*mis-sa on kül-pü hu-o-neh
(vehs-sah)?*
Missä on kylpyhuone
(vessa)?

Is there hot water all day?
*on-ko koo-maa veht-ta
ko-ko pai-van?*
Onko kuumaa vettä koko
päivän?

Do you have a safe where I
can leave my valuables?
*on-ko taal-la yos-sain
pehs-ta vaat-tat-tah*
Onko teillä säilytyslokeroa
arvotavaralle?

Is there somewhere to wash
clothes?
*voy-ko tÿl-la yos-sain
pehs-ta vaat-tay-tah?*
Voiko täällä jossain pestä
vaatteita?

FINNISH

FINNISH

Can I use the kitchen?
voyn-ko ka-üt-tÿ
kayt-ti-er-ta?

Voinko käyttää keittiötä?

Can I use the telephone?
voyn-ko ka-üt-tÿ pu-heh-
lin-tah?

Voinko käyttää puhelinta?

Is your sauna warm?
on-ko tay-dan sow-nah
lam-pi-ma-na?

Onko teidän sauna
lämpimänä?

Do you have a smoke sauna?
on-ko tayl-la sah-vu
sow-naa?

Onko teillä savusaunaa?

Requests & Complaints

Please wake me up at ...
voyt-teh-ko heh-rat-tÿ
mi-nut kehl-lo ...

Voitteko herättää minut
kello ...

The room needs to be cleaned.
hu-o-neh ta-ü-tü-i-si
see-vo-tah

Huone täytyisi siivota.

Please change the sheets.
voyt-teh-ko vaich-taa
lah-kah-naht

Voitteko vaihtaa lakanat.

I can't open/close ...
ehn saa ... ow-ki/keen-ni   En saa ... auki/kiinni.
window   **ik-ku-naa**   ikkunaa
door   **o-veh-ah**   ovea
heating   **paht-teh-ri-ah**   patteria

I left my key in the room.
   mun a-vain ya-i hu-o-neeh-   Minun avain jäi huoneeseen.
   seehn
The toilet won't flush.
   vehs-sah ay veh-da   Vessa ei vedä.
I don't like this room.
   mi-na ehn oy-kayn pi-da   Minä* en oikein pidä tästä
   tas-ta hu-o-neehs-tah   huoneesta.
It's too small.
   se ohn lee-ahn pi-eh-ni   Se on liian pieni.
It's noisy.
   si-ehl-la on meh-lu-ah   Siellä on melua.
It's too dark.
   se ohn lee-ahn pi-meh-a   Se on liian pimeä.
It's expensive.
   se ohn kahl-lis   Se on kallis.

Some Useful Words & Phrases
I am/We are leaving …
   mi-na lah-dehn/meh   Minä* lähden/Me
   lach-deh-tÿn …   läh-detään …
now/tomorrow
   nüt/hu-o-mehn-nah   nyt/huomenna
I would like to pay the bill.
   mi-na mahk-sai-sin   Minä* maksaisin laskun.
   lahs-kun

name	*ni-mi*	nimi
given names	*eh-tu ni-meht*	etunimet
surname	*su-ku ni-mi*	sukunimi
room number	*hu-o-neehn nu-meh-ro*	huoneen numero

FINNISH

address	*o-soy-teh*	osoite
air-conditioned	*il-mahs-toy-tu*	ilmastoitu
balcony	*pahr-veh-keh*	parveke
bathroom	*kül-pü hu-o-neh*	kylpyhuone
bed	*san-kü*	sänky
bill	*lahs-ku*	lasku
blanket	*payt-to*	peitto
candle	*künt-ti-la*	kynttilä
chair	*tu-o-li*	tuoli
clean	*puh-dahs*	puhdas
cupboard	*kaap-pi*	kaappi
dark	*pi-meh-a*	pimeä
dirty	*li-kai-nehn*	likainen
double bed	*kahk-soys vu-o-deh*	kaksoisvuode
electrity	*sach-ker*	sähkö
excluded	*ay koo-lu hin-taan*	ei kuulu hintaan
included	*koo-loo hin-taan*	kuuluu hintaan
key	*ah-vain*	avain
lift (elevator)	*his-si*	hissi
light bulb	*heh-ku lahmp-pu*	hehkulamppu/
	lahmp-pu	lamppu
lock (n)	*luk-ko*	lukko
mattress	*paht-yah*	patja
mirror	*pay-li*	peili
padlock	*mu-nah luk-ko*	munalukko
pillow	*tüü-nü*	tyyny
quiet	*hil-jai-nehn*	hiljainen
room (in hotel)	*hu-o-neh/ho-tehl-li*	huone/
	hu-o-neh	hotellihuone
sauna	*sow-nah*	sauna
sheet	*lah-kah-nah*	lakana

shower	*su-ih-ku*	suihku
soap	*saip-pu-ah*	saippua
suitcase	*maht-kah lowk-ku*	matkalaukku
swimming pool	*u-i-mah ahl-lahs*	uima-allas
table	*per-ü-ta*	pöytä
toilet	*veeh-seeh/vehs-sah*	WC/vessa
toilet paper	*vehs-sah pah-peh-ri*	vessapaperi
towel	*püü-heh*	pyyhe
(some) water	*veht-ta*	vettä
cold water	*kül-mah vesi...*	kylmä vesi
hot water	*koo-mah vettÿ*	kuumaa vettää
window	*ik-ku-nah*	ikkuna

FINNISH

Around Town

I'm looking for .../
Where is ...?

mi-na eht-sin/mis-sa on ...?   Minä* etsin .../Missä on ...?

the art gallery	*tai-deh gahl-leh-ri-aa/tai-deh gahl-leh-ri-ah*	taidegalleriaa/tai-degalleria
a bank	*pahnk-ki-ah/pahnk-ki*	pankkia/pankki
the church	*kirk-ko-ah/kirk-ko*	kirkkoa/kirkko
the city centre	*kehs-kus-taa/kehs-kus-tah*	keskustaa/keskusta
the ...embassy	*soor la-heh-tüs-ter-a/soor la-heh-tüs-ter*	...-n suurlähety-stöä/suurlähetystö
my hotel	*mi-nun ho-tehl-li-ah/mi-nun ho-tehl-li*	minun hotellia/minun hotelli
a mail box	*pos-ti laa-tik-ko-ah/pos-ti laa-tik-ko*	postilaatikkoa/posti laatikko
the market	*to-ri-ah/to-ri*	toria/tori

the museum	*mu-seh-o-tah/mu-seh-o*	museota/museo
the police	*po-lee-si-ah/po-lee-si*	poliisia/poliisi
the post office	*pos-ti-ah/pos-ti*	postia/posti
a public toilet	*ü-lays-ta vehs-saa/ ü-lay-nehn vehs-sah*	yleistä vessaa/ yleinen vessa
the telephone centre	*pu-heh-lin-tah/ pu-heh-lin*	puhelinta/puhelin
the tourist information office	*maht-kay-lu toy-mis-to-ah*	matkailutoimistoa/ matkailutoimisto

What time does it open?
   mil-loyn seh ah-vah-taan?   Milloin se avataan?
What time does it close?
   mil-loyn seh sul-jeh-taan?   Milloin se suljetaan?
What ... is this?
   mi-ka ... ta-ma on?   Mikä ... tämä on?

street	*kah-tu*	katu
suburb	*kow-pung-ngin o-sah/ eh-si kow-pung-ki*	kaupunginosa/ esikaupunki

For directions, see the Getting Around section, page 89.

At the Bank

I want to exchange some
money/traveller's cheques.
   hah-lu-ai-sin vaich-taa rah-haa/maht-kah shehk-keh-ja   Haluaisin vaihtaa rahaa/matkashekkejä.
What is the exchange rate?
   mi-ka on vah-loot-tah kurs-si?   Mikä on valuuttakurssi?

How many marks per dollar?
pahl-yon-ko dol-lah-ril-lah saa mahrk-ko-yah?

Paljonko dollarilla saa markkoja?

Can I have money transferred here from my bank?
voyn-ko mi-na saadah rah-haa seer-reht-tü-a o-mahs-tah pahn-kis-tah-ni?

Voinko minä* saada rahaa siirrettyä omasta pankistani?

How long will it take to arrive?
kow-ahn-ko sehn tu-lo kehs-tÿ?

Kauanko sen tulo kestää?

Has my money arrived yet?
on-ko mi-nun rah-hah-ni saa-pu-nut vi-eh-la?

Onko minun rahani saapunut vielä?

(some) banknotes	*seh-teh-leh-i-ta*	seteleitä
cashier	*kahs-sah*	kassa
some coins	*ko-li-koy-tah*	kolikoita
credit card	*lu-ot-to kort-ti*	luottokortti
exchange	*rah-hahn vaich-to*	rahanvaihto
loose change	*pik-ku rah-haa, vaich-to rah-haa*	pikkurahaa, vaihtorahaa
money transfer	*ti-li seer-to*	tilisiirto
signature	*ahl-leh kir-yoy-tus*	allekirjoitus

At the Post Office

I would like to send …
hah-lu-ai-sin la-heht-tÿ …

Haluaisin lähettää …

a fax	*fahk-sin*	faksin
a letter	*kir-yeehn*	kirjeen
a postcard	*pos-ti kor-tin*	postikortin

FINNISH

| a parcel | *pah-keh-tin* | paketin |
| a telegram | *sach-keehn* | sähkeen |

I would like some stamps.
hah-lu-ai-sin pos-ti   Haluaisin postimerkkejä.
mehrk-keh-ja
How much is the postage?
pahl-yon-ko on pos-ti   Paljonko on postimaksu?
mahk-su?
How much does it cost to
send this to ...?
pahl-yon-ko mahk-saa   Paljonko maksaa lähettää
la-heht-tÿ ta-ma ...?   tämä ...vowel + n?

an aerogram	*ah-eh-ro-grahm-mi*	aerogrammi
air mail	*lehn-to pos-ti-nah*	lentopostina
envelope	*kir-jeh*	kirje
parcel	*pah-keht-ti*	paketti
registered mail	*kir-jaht-tu kir-jeh*	kirjattu kirje
surface mail	*maa pos-ti-nah*	maapostina

Telephone

I want to ring ...
hah-lu-ai-sin soyt-taa ...   Haluaisin soittaa ...
The number is ...
pu-heh-lin nu-meh-ro on ...   Puhelinnumero on ...
I want to speak for three
minutes.
hah-lu-ahn pu-hu-ah   Haluan puhua kolme
kol-meh mi-noot-ti-ah   minuuttia.

FINNISH

How much does a three-minute call cost?

pahl-yon-ko mahk-saa kol-mehn mi-noo-tin pu-heh-lu?

Paljonko maksaa kolmen minuutin puhelu?

How much does each extra minute cost?

pahl-yon-ko mahk-saa jo-kai-nehn li-sa mi-noot-ti?

Paljonko maksaa jokainen lisäminuutti?

I would like to speak to Mr Nieminen.

hah-lu-ai-sin pu-hu-ah hehr-rah ni-eh-mi-sehn kahns-sah

Haluaisin puhua herra Nieminen kanssa.

I want to make a reverse-charges phone call.

hah-lu-ahn soyt-taa vahs-tah pu-heh-lun

Haluan soittaa vastapuhelun.

It's engaged.

seh on vah-raht-tu

Se on varattu.

I've been cut off.

pu-heh-lu kaht-keh-si

Puhelu katkesi.

Sightseeing

Do you have a guidebook/local map?

on-ko si-nul-lah maht-kah o-pahs-tah/kahrt-taa?

Onko sinulla matkaopasta/karttaa?

What are the main attractions?

mit-ka o-vaht tar-kaym-mat nach-ta-vüü- deht?

Mitkä ovat tärkeimmät nähtävyydet?

FINNISH

What is that?
   mi-ka tu-o on?   Mikä tuo on?
How old is it?
   ku-in-kah vahn-hah seh on?   Kuinka vanha se on?
Can I take photographs?
   voyn-ko mi-na ot-taa vah-lo
   ku-vi-ah?   Voinko minä* ottaa
                  valokuvia?
What time does it open/close?
   mil-loyn seh ow-keh-aa/
   sul-yeh-taan?   Milloin se aukeaa/suljetaan?

ancient	*vahn-hah*	vanha
archaeological	*ahr-keh-o-lo-gi-nehn*	arkeologinen
beach	*u-i-mah rahn-tah*	uimaranta
building	*rah-kehn-nus*	rakennus
castle	*lin-nah*	linna
cathedral	*tu-o-mi-o kirk-ko,*	tuomiokirkko,
	kah-tehd-raa-li	katedraali
church	*kirk-ko*	kirkko
concert hall	*kon-sehrt-ti hahl-li*	konserttihalli
library	*kir-jahs-to*	kirjasto
main square	*kehs-kus to-ri*	keskustori
market	*to-ri/kowp-pah to-ri/*	tori, kauppatori,
	mahrk-ki-naht	markkinat
monastery	*lu-os-tah-ri*	luostari
monument	*mu-is-to mehrk-ki/*	muistomerkki/
	mo-nu-mehnt-ti	monumentti
mosque	*mos-kay-yah*	moskeija
old city	*vahn-hah kow-pun-ki*	vanhakaupunki
palace	*pah-laht-si*	palatsi
opera house	*orp-peh-rah tah-lo*	oopperatalo

ruins	*row-ni-ot*	rauniot
stadium	*stah-di-on*	stadion
some statues	*paht-sai-tah*	patsaita
synagogue	*sü-nah-gor-gah*	synagooga
temple	*tehmp-peh-li*	temppeli
university	*ü-li o-pis-to, kor-keh-ah koh-lu*	yliopisto, korkeakoulu

Entertainment

What's there to do in the evening?

mi-ta tÿl-la voy teh-da il-tai-sin?

Mitä täällä voi tehdä iltaisin?

Are there any discos?

on-ko tÿl-la üch-tÿn dis-ko-ah?

Onko täällä yhtään diskoa?

Are there places where you can hear local folk music?

voy-ko tÿl-la mis-sÿn kool-lah pai-kal- lis-tah kahn-sahn mu-seek-ki-ah?

Voiko täällä missään kuulla paikallista kansanmusiikkia?

How much does it cost to get in?

pahl-yon-ko on pÿ-sü mahk-su?

Paljonko on pääsymaksu?

cinema	*eh-lo-ku-vah teh-aht-teh-ri*	elokuvateatteri
concert	*kon-sehrt-ti*	konsertti
discotheque	*dis-ko*	disko
theatre	*teh-aht-teh-ri*	teatteri

114 Finnish

In the Country
Weather
What's the weather like?

mi-ka on sÿ ti-lah,   Mikä on säätila?
mil-lai-nehn sÿ on?   Millainen sää on?

The weather is ... today.
ta-nÿn on ...   Tänään on ...
Will it be ... tomorrow?
on-ko hu-o-mehn-nah?   Onko huomenna... ?

cloudy	*pil-vis-ta*	pilvistä
cold	*kül-mÿ*	kylmää
foggy	*su-mu-is-tah*	sumuista
forest fire alert	*meht-sa pah-lo vah-roy-tus*	metsäpalovaroitus
frosty	*pahk-kahs-tah*	pakkasta
hot	*koo-mah*	kuuma
raining	*sah-deht-tah*	sadetta
snowing	*lun-tah/lu-mih sah-deht-tah*	lunta/lumisadetta
summer night frost	*hahl-laa*	hallaa
sunny	*ow-rin-koys-tah*	aurinkoista
thunderstorm	*uk-kos-tah*	ukkosta
wet snowfall	*ran-tÿ*	räntää
windy	*too-lihs-tah*	tuulista

Camping
Am I allowed to camp here?
saa-ko tÿl-la lay-ri-ü-tü-a?   Saako täällä leiriytyä?

Is there a campsite nearby?
on-ko tÿl-la yos-sain la-hehl-la?

Onko täällä jossain lähellä leirintäaluetta?

backpack	*rehp-pu*	reppu
can opener	*pur-kin ah-vaa-yah*	purkinavaaja
compass	*kom-pahs-si*	kompassi
some firewood	*polt-to poo-tah*	polttopuuta
foam mattress	*mah-koo ah-lou-tah*	makuualusta
gas cartridge	*kaa-su sa-i-li-er*	kaasusäiliö
hammock	*reep-pu maht-to*	riippumatto
mattress	*paht-yah*	patja
penknife	*link-ku vayt-si*	linkkuveitsi
rope	*ker-ü-si*	köysi
tent	*tehlt-tah*	teltta
torch (flashlight)	*tahs-ku lahmp-pu*	taskulamppu
sleeping bag	*mah-koo pus-si*	makuupussi
stove	*reht-ki kay-tin*	retkikeitin
water bottle	*veh-si pul-lo*	vesipullo

Food

breakfast	*aa-mi-ai-nehn*	aamiainen
lunch	*loh-nahs*	lounas
early/late dinner	*pa-i-val-li-nehn/ il-lahl-li-nehn*	päivällinen/ illallinen

Table for ..., please.
saa-daan-ko meh per-ü-ta ...?

Saadaanko me pöytä ...lle?

Can I see the menu please?
voyn-ko mi-na nach-da meh-nun?

Voinko minä* nähdä menun?

FINNISH

I would like the set lunch,
please.
   saan-ko pa-i-van loh-naan   Saanko päivän lounaan.
What does it include?
   mi-ta see-hehn koo-loo?   Mitä siihen kuuluu?
Service is included in the bill.
   tahr-yoy-lu koo-loo   Tarjoilu kuuluu hintaan.
   hin-taan

Some Useful Words

ashtray	*tuh-kah kup-pi*	tuhkakuppi
the bill	*lahs-ku*	lasku
a cup	*kup-pi*	kuppi
dessert	*yal-ki ru-o-kah*	jälkiruoka
a drink	*yu-o-mah*	juoma
a fork	*haa-ruk-kah*	haarukka
fresh	*tu-o-reh*	tuore
a glass	*lah-si*	lasi
a knife	*vayt-si*	veitsi
a plate	*low-tah-nehn*	lautanen
spicy	*mows-teht-tu*	maustettu
spoiled	*pi-laan-tu-nut*	pilaantunut
a spoon	*lu-sik-kah*	lusikka
sweet	*mah-keh-ah*	makea
teaspoon	*teeh lu-sik-kah*	teelusikka
toothpick	*hahm-mahs tik-ku*	hammastikku

Vegetarian Meals

I am a vegetarian.
   o-lehn kahs-vis sü-er-ya   Olen kasvissyöjä.
I don't eat meat.
   ehn sü-er li-haa   En syö lihaa.

I don't eat chicken, fish, or
ham.
   ehn sü-er kah-naa, kah-laa   En syö kanaa, kalaa enkä
   ehn-ka kink-ku-ah   kinkkua.

Staples
bread   *leipä*
cheese   *juusto*
macaroni   *makaroni*
oats   *kaura*
rice   *riisi*
rye   *ruis*

Meat
chicken   *kana/broileri*
beef   *naudan/härkä*
ham   *kinkku*
liver   *maksa*
meat   *liha*
minced meat   *jauheliha*
pork   *porsaan/possun*
reindeer   *poron*
sausage   *makkara*
steak   *pihvi*

Seafood
Baltic herring   *silakka*
fish   *kala*
herring   *silli*
salmon   *lohi*
seafood (not fish)   *äyriäis*
shrimp   *katkarapu*

Vegetables

cabbage	*kaali*
carrot	*porkkana*
garlic	*valkosipuli*
mushroom	*sieni*
onion	*sipuli*
pea	*herne*
potato	*peruna*
swede	*lanttu*
tomato	*tomaatti*
vegetable	*vihannes*
vegetable/vegetarian	*kasvis*

Prepared Food

berry or fruit soup	*kiisseli*
filled bread	*kukko*
minced vegetables and/or meat, baked in an oven	*laatikko*
omelette	*munakas*
open sandwich	*voileipä*
pan-fried food	*pannu*
pie	*piiras*
porridge	*puuro*
roll	*sämpylä*
salad	*salaatti*
sauce	*soosi/kastike*
scalloped food or pie	*paistos*
soup	*keitto/soppa*
thin barley bread, like chappati	*rieska*
titbit	*herkku*

Grilli Food

Grilli can also be called *katukeittiö*, *snägäri* or *nakkikioski*. Enormously popular, they prepare real junk food by order till early hours when everything else is closed. You can also find local specialities, such as *mikkeliläinen* in Mikkeli.

atomi	Meat pie with ham or fried egg.
camping	Sausage.
hampurilainen	Hamburger.
kalapuikot	Finger-shaped fried fish.
kebakko	Finger-shaped meat ball
kuumakoira	Hot dog.
lihapiirakka	Pie with meat & rice filling.
makkaraperunat	Sausage with French fries.
munakukkaro	Hamburger with fried egg.
nakki/nakit	Small sausage.
nakkipiiras	Small sausage inside a pie.
porilainen	Thick *lauantai* sausage in a burger bread.
publiski	Kind of hot dog.
ranskalaiset	French fries.
reissumies	Two slices of rye bread with filling.
vety	Meat pie with ham and eggs.

Other Meals

janssonin kiusaus	Potato and herring prepared in oven.
kaalikääryleet	Minced meat covered with cabbage leaves.
kesäkeitto	Vegetable soup/'summer soup'.
lihamureke	Seasoned minced meat prepared in oven.
lihapullat	Meatballs.
lipeäkala	Lutefish.

metsästäjänpihvi   'Hunter's steak' – minced meat with mushroom sauce.
pyttipannu   Ham and potatoes fried in butter.

Local Specialities

karjalanpiirakka   Rye pie with rice, barley or potato filling. (Eastern)
lanttusupikas   Kind of rye pita bread with swede filling. (Savo)
lörtsy   Thin pancake-shaped doughnut with apple or meat filling. (Eastern)
kukko   Large rye bread loaf with filling, either pork and vegetable, such as swede, *lanttukukko*, or potato, *perunakukko;* or pork and fish, *kalakukko*, specifically small whitefish, *muikkukukko*, or perch, *ahvenkukko*. (Eastern)
kukkonen   Rice porridge on bread. (Karelian)
leipäjuusto   Cheese bread. (Pohjanmaa & Kainuu)
loimulohi   Salmon prepared at open fire. (Eastern)
mustamakkara   Rice-filled black sausage. (Tampere)
muurinpohjalettu   Thin large fried pancake. (Eastern)
neulamuikut   Small whitefish. (Karelian)
poronkäristys   Reindeer casserole. (Lapland)
sultsina   Kind of chappati bread stuffed with porridge. (Karelian)
rönttönen   Round pie with filling made of rye, potato and lingon. (Kuhmo)
vatruska   Thick pancake made of mashed potato and wheat flour. (Karelian)

Methods of Cooking & Preparation

BBQ'd	*grillattu*
cooked	*keitetty*
cutlet	*leike*
dipped in flour & fried	*paneerattu*
fried	*käristetty*
frozen	*pakastettu/jäädyke*
gravy-salted	*graavisuolattu*
heated in microwave oven	*kuumennettu mikrossa*
prepared in oven	*paistettu*
salted	*suolattu*
smoked	*savustettu*
steamed	*höyrytetty*
stuffed	*täytetty*
sugar added	*sokeroitu*
sweetened or malted	*imelletty*

Fruit

blueberry	*mustikka*
cranberry	*puolukka*
pineapple	*ananas*
strawberry	*mansikka*

Drinks – Nonalcoholic

A *kahvila* is a normal café, whereas a *kahvio* serves coffee in say, a fuel station or a supermarket, but basically these two are similar places, also called *kuppila*.

A *baari* serves beer and soft drinks, no strong alcohol, and is also called *kapakka*. Restaurants, *ravintola*, that have permission to serve strong alcohol have *A-oikeudet*, or 'full rights'. With *B-oikeudet* you have less choice.

berry drink	*mehu*
coffee	*kahvi*
drinking water	*juomavesi*
fresh juice	*tuoremehu*
hot chocolate	*kaakao*
ice water	*jäävesi*
milk	*maito*
soft drink	*limonadi/limu/limppari/limsa*
soft drink, literally 'refreshing drink'	*virvoitusjuoma*
sour milk	*piimä*
tea	*tee*
water	*vesi*

Drinks – Alcoholic

drinkki	Cocktail drink.
huurteinen	Cold beer, literally 'frosty'.
kossu	Another name for strong Koskenkorva spirit.
kotikalja	Literally 'home-brewed malt drink'.
lonkero	Another name for a long gin.
pitkä	Literally 'long', large glass of strong beer.

beer	*olut*
beer, literally 'malt drink'	*kalja*
light beer	*I-olut/ykkös olut*
medium strong beer	*keskikalja/kolmonen/III-olut*
red wine	*punaviini*
strong alcohol, vodka	*viina*
strong beer	*IV A-olut/nelos olut*
white wine	*valkoviini*
wine	*viini*

Shopping

How much is it?
   pahl-yon-ko seh mahk-saa?   Paljonko se maksaa?

bookshop	*kir-yah kowp-pah*	kirjakauppa
camera shop	*vah-lo ku-vows lee-keh*	valokuvausliike
clothing store	*vaa-teh kowp-pah*	vaatekauppa
delicatessen	*hehrk-ku kowp-pah*	herkkukauppa
general store, shop	*kowp-pah*	kauppa
laundry	*peh-su-lah*	pesula
market	*kowp-pah to-ri/ mahrk-ki-naht/ bah-saa-ri*	kauppatori/mark-kinat/basaari
newsagency/ stationers	*lech-ti ki-os-ki/pah-peh-ri kowp-pah*	lehtikioski/paperika uppa
pharmacy	*ahp-teehk-ki*	apteekki
shoeshop	*kehn-ka kowp-pah*	kenkäkauppa
souvenir shop	*maht-kah mu-is-to müü-ma-la*	matkamuisto-myymälä
supermarket	*su-pehr mahr-keht*	supermarket
vegetable shop	*vi-hahn-nehs kowp-pah*	vihanneskauppa

I would like to buy …
   hah-lu-ai-sin os-taa …   Haluaisin ostaa …
Do you have others?
   on-ko tayl-la mu-i-tah?   Onko teillä muita?
I don't like it.
   ehn oy-kayn pi-da see-ta   En oikein pidä siitä.

Can I look at it?
voyn-ko mi-na **kaht**-so-ah
si-ta?
                                         Voinko minä* katsoa sitä?

I'm just looking.
mi-na **vain** kaht-seh-lehn
                                         Minä* vain katselen.

Can you write down the price?
voyt-teh-ko **kir**-yoyt-taa
hin-nahn?
                                         Voitteko kirjoittaa hinnan?

Do you accept credit cards?
voy-ko **mahk**-saa lu-ot-to-
kort-til-lah?
                                         Voiko maksaa luottokortilla?

Could you lower the price?
voyt-ko lahs-keh-ah **hin**-taa?
                                         Voitko laskea hintaa?

I don't have much money.
mul-lah ay o-leh **pahl**-yon
rah-haa
                                         Mulla ei ole paljon rahaa.

Can I help you?
voyn-ko **owt**-taa?
                                         Voinko auttaa?

Will that be all?
yah tu-leeh-ko **moo**-tah?
                                         Ja tuleeko muuta?

Would you like it wrapped?
pis-teh-tÿn-ker pah-keht-
teen?
                                         Pistetäänkö pakettiin?

Sorry, this is the only one.
ta-ma on **may**-dan ai-no-ah
                                         Tämä on meidän ainoa.

How much/many do you
want?
pahl-yon-ko si-na **hah**-lu-
aht/**ku**-in-kah mon-tah pis-
teh-tÿn?
                                         Paljonko sinä* haluat?/
Kuinka monta pistetään?

FINNISH

Souvenirs

some earrings	*kor-vah ko-ru-yah*	korvakoruja
some handicrafts	*ka-si ter-i-ta*	käsitöitä
necklace	*kow-lah ko-ru*	kaulakoru
pottery	*keh-rah-meek-kah*	keramiikka
ring	*sor-mus*	sormus
rug	*maht-to, raa-nu*	matto, raanu

Clothing

clothing	*vaat-teeht*	vaatteet
coat	*tahk-ki*	takki
dress	*pu-ku*	puku
jacket	*tahk-ki*	takki
jumper (sweater)	*pu-seh-ro/yump-peh-ri*	pusero/jumpperi
shirt	*pai-tah*	paita
shoes	*kehng-ngat*	kengät
skirt	*hah-meh*	hame
trousers	*hoh-sut*	housut

It doesn't/They don't fit.
 ta-ma/na-ma ay mahch-du   Tämä/Nämä ei mahdu.

It is too …
 seh on lee-ahn …   Se on liian …

big/small	*i-so/pi-eh-ni*	iso/pieni
short/long	*lü-hüt/peet-ka*	lyhyt/pitkä
tight/loose	*ki-reh-a/ler-ü-sa*	kireä/löysä

FINNISH

Materials

cotton	*poo-vil-laa*	puuvillaa
handmade	*ka-sin teh-tüh/ka-si-tü-er-ta*	käsintehty/käsityötä
leather	*nahch-kaa*	nahkaa
of brass	*mehs-sin-ki-a*	messinkiä
of gold	*kul-taa*	kultaa
of silver	*ho-peh-aa*	hopeaa
flax	*pehl-lah-vaa*	pellavaa
pure alpaca	*ahl-pahk-kaa*	alpakkaa
silk	*silk-ki-a*	silkkiä
wool	*vil-laa*	villaa

Toiletries

comb	*kahm-pa*	kampa
some condoms	*kon-do-meh-yah*	kondomeja
deodorant	*deh-o-do-rahnt-ti*	deodorantti
hairbrush	*hi-us hahr-yah*	hiusharja
moisturising cream	*kos-te-us voy-deh*	kosteusvoide
razor	*pahr-tah teh-ra*	partaterä
sanitary napkins	*tehr-veh-üs si-deh/pik-ku hoh-sun su-o-yah*	terveysside/pikkuhousunsuoja
shampoo	*shahmp-por*	shampoo
shaving cream	*pahr-tah vaah-to*	partavaahto
some tampons	*tahm-po-neh-yah*	tamponeja
tissues	*neh-na lee-nah*	nenäliina
toilet paper	*vehs-sah pah-peh-ri*	vessapaperi
toothbrush	*hahm-mahs hahr-yah*	hammasharja
toothpaste	*hahm-mahs tah-nah*	hammastahna

Stationery & Publications

map	*kahrt-tah*	kartta
newspaper	*sah-no-mah lech-ti*	sanomalehti
newspaper in English	*ehng-lahn-nin ki-eh-li-nehn sah-no-mah lech-ti*	englannin kieli-nen sanomalehti
novels in English	*ehng-lahn-nin ki-eh-li-si-a ro-maa-neh-yah*	englannin kielisiä romaaneja
paper	*pah-peh-ri*	paperi
pen (ballpoint)	*kü-na (koo-lah kü-na)*	kynä (kuulakynä)
scissors	*sahk-seht*	sakset

Photography

How much is it to process this film?

pahl-yon-ko mahk-saa keh-hit-tÿ ta-ma fil-mi? — Paljonko maksaa kehittää tämä filmi?

When will it be ready?

kos-kah seh on vahl-mis? — Koska se on valmis?

I'd like a film for this camera.

mi-na hah-lu-ai-sin fil-min ta-han kah-meh-raan — Minä* haluaisin filmin tähän kameraan.

B&W (film)	*mus-tah vahl-koy-nehn*	mustavalkoinen
camera	*kah-meh-rah*	kamera
colour (film)	*va-ri fil-mi*	värifilmi
film	*fil-mi*	filmi
flash	*sah-lah-mah*	salama
lens	*ob-yehk-tee-vi/lins-si*	objektiivi/linssi
light meter	*vah-lo-tus mit-tah-ri*	valotusmittari

FINNISH

Smoking

A packet of cigarettes, please.
saan-ko tu-pahk-kah ahs-kin, kee-toss   Saanko tupakka-askin, kiitos.

Are these cigarettes strong/mild?
o-vaht-ko na-ma tu-pah-kaht vach-vo-yah/mi-eh-to-yah?   Ovatko nämä tupakat vahvoja/mietoja?

Do you have a light?
on-ko sul-lah tul-tah?   Onko sinulla tulta?

cigarette papers	*sah-vu-keh pah-peh-ri-ah*	savukepaperia
some cigarettes	*tu-pahk-kaa*	tupakkaa
filtered	*filt-teh-ri*	filtteri
lighter	*sü-tü-tin*	sytytin
	süt-ka	sytkä (inf)
matches	*tu-li ti-kut*	tulitikut
	ti-kut	tikut (inf)
menthol	*menth-tor-li*	menthol
pipe	*peep-pu*	piippu
tobacco	*tu-pahk-kah*	tupakka

Colours

black	*mus-tah*	musta
blue	*si-ni-nehn*	sininen
brown	*rus-keeh*	ruskea
green	*vih-reeh*	vihreä
orange	*o-rahns-si*	oranssi
pink	*vaa-leh-ahn pu-nai-nehn (pink-ki)*	vaaleanpunainen (pinkki)

purple	*vi-o-leht-ti*	violetti
red	*pu-nah-nehn*	punainen
white	*vahl-ko-nehn*	valkoinen
yellow	*kel-tah-nehn*	keltainen

Sizes & Comparisons

small	*pi-eh-ni*	pieni
big	*soo-ri/i-so*	suuri/iso
heavy	*pai-nah-vah*	painava
light	*keh-vüt*	kevyt
more	*eh-neh-man*	enemmän
less	*va-hehm-man*	vähemän
too much/many	*lee-kaa/lee-ahn mon-tah*	liikaa/liian monta
many	*mon-tah*	monta
enough	*tahr-peehk-si*	tarpeeksi
also	*mü-ers*	myös
a little bit	*va-han*	vähän

Health

Where is ...?
   mis-sa on ...?   Missä on ...?

the doctor	*la-a-ka-ri*	lääkäri
the hospital	*sai-raa-lah*	sairaala
the chemist	*ahp-teehk-ki*	apteekki
the dentist	*hahm-mahs lÿ-ka-ri*	hammaslääkäri

I am sick.
   o-lehn sai-rahs   Olen sairas.
My friend is sick.
   üs-ta-va-ni on sai-rahs   Ystäväni on sairas.

Could I see a female doctor?
*on-ko mahch-dol-lis-tah tah-
vah-tah nais lÿ-ka-ri?*
Onko mahdollista tavata
naislääkäri?

What's the matter?
mi-ka on ha-ta-na?
Mikä on hätänä?

Where does it hurt?
mis-ta saht-too?
Mistä sattuu?

It hurts here.
saht-too tÿl-ta
Sattuu täältä.

My ... hurts.
mi-nun ... on ki-peh-a
Minun ... on kipeä.

Parts of the Body

ankle	*nilk-kah*	nilkka
arm	*ka-si*	käsi
back	*sehl-ka*	selkä
chest	*rin-tah/rin-tah keh-ha*	rinta/rintakehä
ear	*kor-vah*	korva
eye	*sil-ma*	silmä
finger	*sor-mi*	sormi
foot	*yahl-kah*	jalka
hand	*ka-si*	käsi
head	*pÿ*	pää
heart	*sü-dan*	sydän
leg	*sÿ-ri*	sääri
mouth	*soo*	suu
nose	*neh-na*	nenä
ribs	*kül-ki loot*	kylkiluut
skin	*i-ho*	iho
stomach	*vaht-sah/mah-hah*	maha/vatsa
teeth	*hahm-paat*	hampaat
throat	*kurk-ku*	kurkku

Ailments

I have ...

mul-lah on ...   Minulla on ...

an allergy	*ahl-lehr-gi-ah*	allergia
anaemia	*ah-neh-mi-ah*	anemia
a blister	*rahk-ko*	rakko
a burn	*pah-lo vahm-mah*	palovamma
a cold	*fluns-sah*	flunssa
constipation	*um-meh-tus-tah*	ummetusta
a cough	*üs-ka*	yskä
diarrhoea	*ri-pu-li*	ripuli
fever	*koo-meht-tah*	kuumetta
a headache	*pÿn sar-kü*	päänsärky
hepatitis	*mahk-sah tu-leh-dus/heh-pah-teet-ti*	maksatulehdus/hepatiitti
indigestion	*roo-ahn su-lah-tos ha-i-ri-er*	ruuansulatushäiriö
an infection	*tu-leh-dus*	tulehdus
influenza	*in-flu-ehns-sah*	influenssa
lice	*ta-i-ta*	täitä
low/high blood pressure	*mah-tah-lah/kor-keh-ah veh-rehn pai-neh*	matala/korkea verenpaine
sore throat	*kurk-ku ki-peh-a*	kurkku kipeä
sprain	*nilk-kah nür-yach-ta-nüt*	nilkka nyrjähtänyt
a stomachache	*mah-hah ki-pu*	mahakipu
sunburn	*i-ho pah-lah-nut*	iho palanut
a venereal disease	*su-ku pu-o-li tow-ti*	sukupuolitauti
worms	*mah-to-yah*	matoja

FINNISH

Some Useful Words & Phrases

I'm pregnant.
*o-lehn **rahs**-kaa-nah* — Olen raskaana.

I'm on the pill.
*o-lehn **lÿ**-keh koo-ril-lah* — Olen lääkekuurilla.

I haven't had my period for ... months
***mul**-lah **ay** o-leh ol-lut koo-kow-ti-si-ah ... koo-kow-teehn* — Minulla ei ole ollut kuukautisia ...vowel + n kuukauteen.

I have been vaccinated.
***mut** on ro-ko-teht-tu* — Minut on rokotettu.

I have my own syringe.
mul**-lah **on** o-mah **ru**-is-keh **neh-u-lah — Minulla on oma ruiskeneula.

I feel better/worse.
***voyn**-ti-ni **on** pah-**rehm**-pi/hu-o-nom-pi* — Vointini on parempi/huonompi.

I'm ...
o-lehn ... — Olen ...

diabetic	*di-**ah**-beeh-tik-ko*	diabeetikko
epileptic	*eh-pi-**lehp**-tik-ko*	epileptikko
asthmatic	*ahst-**maa**-tik-ko*	astmaatikko

I'm allergic to ...
***mi**-na o-lehn ahl-**lehr**-gi-nehn ...* — Minä* olen allerginen ...

antibiotics	***ahn**-ti-bi-or-tayl-leh*	antibiooteille
penicillin	***peh**-ni-sil-lee-nil-leh*	penisilliinille

accident	*on-neht-to-moos*	onnettomuus
addiction	*reep-pu-voos*	riippuvuus
some antibiotics	*ahn-ti-bi-ort-teh-yah*	antibiootteja
antiseptic	*ahn-ti-sehp-ti-nehn*	antiseptinen
aspirin	*ahs-pi-ree-ni*	aspiriini
bandage	*si-deh*	side
blood test	*veh-ri ko-eh*	verikoe
contraceptive	*ech-ka-i-sü va-li-neh*	ehkäisyväline
injection	*ru-is-keh*	ruiske
injury	*vahm-mah*	vamma
medicine	*lü-keh*	lääke
menstruation	*koo-kow-ti-seht*	kuukautiset
nausea	*pah-hoyn voyn-ti*	pahoinvointi
oxygen	*hahp-pi*	happi
some vitamins	*vi-tah-mee-neh-yah*	vitamiineja

FINNISH

At the Chemist
I need medication for ...
   tahr-vit-sen lü-ki-tüs-ta ...   Tarvitsen lääkitystä ...-a/ä
   -ah/a vahr-tehn   varten.
I have a prescription.
   mi-nul-lah on reh-sehp-ti   Minulla on resepti.

At the Dentist
I have a toothache.
   mun hahm-mahs-tah   Minun hammasta särkee.
   sar-keeh
I've lost a filling.
   mi-nul-tah on ir-ron-nut   Minulta on irronnut paikka.
   paik-kah

I've broken a tooth.

mi-nul-tah on loh-yehn-nut hahm-mahs	Minulta on lohjennut hammas.

My gums hurt.

i-keh-ni-a sar-keeh	Ikeniä särkee.

I don't want it extracted.

ehn hah-lu-ah eht-ta hahm-mahs poys-teh-taan	En halua, että hammas poistetaan.

Please give me an anaesthetic.

voyt-teh-ko poo-dut-taa	Voitteko puuduttaa.

Time & Dates

What date is it today?

mi-ka pa-i-va ta-nŷn on?	Mikä päivä tänään on?

What time is it?

pahl-yon-ko kehl-lo on?	Paljonko kello on?

It is ...

kehl-lo on ...		Kello on ...
in the morning	*aa-mul-lah*	aamulla
in the afternoon	*il-tah pa-i-val-la*	iltapäivällä
in evening	*il-lahl-lah*	illalla

Days of the Week

Monday	*maa-nahn-tai*	maanantai
Tuesday	*tees-tai*	tiistai
Wednesday	*kehs-ki veek-ko*	keskiviikko
Thursday	*tors-tai*	torstai
Friday	*pehr-yahn-tai*	perjantai
Saturday	*low-ahn-tai*	lauantai
Sunday	*sun-nun-tai*	sunnuntai

Months

January	*tahm-mi-koo*	tammikuu
February	*hehl-mi-koo*	helmikuu
March	*maa-lis-koo*	maaliskuu
April	*huh-ti-koo*	huhtikuu
May	*toh-ko-koo*	toukokuu
June	*keh-sa-koo*	kesäkuu
July	*hay-na-koo*	heinäkuu
August	*eh-lo-koo*	elokuu
September	*süüs-koo*	syyskuu
October	*lo-kah-koo*	lokakuu
November	*mahr-rahs-koo*	marraskuu
December	*yoh-lu-koo*	joulukuu

Seasons

summer	*keh-sa*	kesä
autumn	*sük-sü*	syksy
winter	*tahl-vi*	talvi
spring	*keh-vat*	kevät

Present

today	*ta-nÿn*	tänään
this morning	*ta-na aa-mu-nah*	tänä aamuna
tonight	*ta-na il-tah-nah*	tänä iltana
this week	*tal-la vee-kol-lah*	tällä viikolla
this year	*ta-na vu-on-nah*	tänä vuonna
now	*nüt*	nyt

Past

yesterday	*ay-lehn*	eilen
day before yesterday	*toys-sah pa-i-va-na*	toissapäivänä

FINNISH

FINNISH

yesterday morning	*ay-lehn aa-mul-lah*	eilen aamulla
last night	*vee-meh ü-er-na*	viime yönä
last week	*vee-meh vee-kol-lah*	viime viikolla
last year	*vee-meh vu-on-nah*	viime vuonna

Future

tomorrow	*hu-o-mehn-nah*	huomenna
day after tomorrow	*ü-li hu-o-mehn-nah*	ylihuomenna
tomorrow morning	*hu-o-mehn aa-mu-nah*	huomenaamuna
tomorrow after-noon/evening	*hu-o-mehn-nah il-tah pa-i-val-la/hu-o-mehn il-tah-nah*	huomenna iltapäivällä/huomen iltana
next week	*ehn-si vee-kol-lah*	ensi viikolla
next year	*ehn-si vu-on-nah*	ensi vuonna

During the Day

afternoon	*il-tah pa-i-val-la*	iltapäivällä
dawn, very early morning	*aa-mun koyt-to, aa-mul-lah vahr-hain*	aamunkoitto, aamulla varhain
day	*pa-i-va*	päivä
early	*ai-kai-sin*	aikaisin
midnight	*kehs-ki ü-er*	keskiyö
morning	*aa-mu*	aamu
night	*ü-er*	yö
noon	*kehs-ki pa-i-va*	keskipäivä
sundown	*ow-ring-ngon lahs-ku*	auringonlasku
sunrise	*ow-ring-ngon noh-su*	auringonnousu

Numbers & Amounts

0	*nol-lah*	nolla
1	*ük-si*	yksi (yks – inf)
2	*kahk-si*	kaksi (kaks – inf)
3	*kol-meh*	kolme
4	*nehl-ya*	neljä
5	*vee-si*	viisi (viis – inf)
6	*koo-si*	kuusi (kuus – inf)
7	*sayt-seh-man*	seitsemän (seittemän – inf)
8	*kahch-dehk-sahn*	kahdeksan (kaheksan – inf)
9	*üch-dehk-san*	yhdeksän (yheksän – inf)
10	*küm-meh-nehn*	kymmenen
11	*ük-si toys-tah*	yksitoista
12	*kahk-si toys-tah*	kaksitoista
13	*kol-meh toys-tah*	kolmetoista
14	*nehl-ya toys-tah*	neljätoista
15	*vee-si toys-tah*	viisitoista
20	*kahk-si küm-mehn-ta*	kaksikymmentä
30	*kol-meh küm-mehn-ta*	kolmekymmentä
40	*nehl-ya küm-mehn-ta*	neljäkymmentä
50	*vee-si küm-mehn-ta*	viisikymmentä
60	*koo-si küm-mehn-ta*	kuusikymmentä
70	*sayt-seh-man küm-mehn-ta*	seitsemänkym-mentä
80	*kahch-dehk-sahn-küm-mehn-ta*	kahdeksankym-mentä
90	*üch-dehk-san-küm-mehn-ta*	yhdeksänkym-mentä

FINNISH

FINNISH

100	*sah-tah*	sata
1000	*tu-haht*	tuhat
one million	*mihl-yor-nah*	miljoona
1st	*ehn-sin-ma-i-nehn*	ensimmäinen
	eh-kah	(eka – inf)
2nd	*toy-nehn*	toinen
	to-kah	(toka – inf)
3rd	*kol-mahs*	kolmas
¼	*nehl-yas o-sah/*	neljäsosa/
	nehl-yan-nehs	neljännes
⅓	*kol-mahs o-sah/*	kolmasosa/
	kol-mahn-nehs	kolmannes
½	*pu-o-leht*	puolet
¾	*kol-meh nehl-yas*	kolme neljäsosaa
	o-saa	

Some Useful Words

a little	*va-han*	vähän
double	*tup-laht*	tuplat
a dozen	*tu-si-nah*	tusina
Enough!	*yo reet-tÿ*	Jo riittää!
few	*hahr-vah*	harva
less	*va-hehm-man*	vähemmän
many	*mon-tah/mo-ni-ah*	monta/monia
more	*eh-nehm-man*	enemmän
once	*kehr-rahn*	kerran
a pair	*pah-ri*	pari
percent	*pro-sehnt-ti*	prosentti
some	*yo-tah-kin/va-han/*	jotakin/vähän/
	yon-kin vehr-rahn	jonkin verran

| too much | *lee-kaa/lee-ahn pahl-yon* | liikaa/liian paljon |
| twice | *kahch-dehs-ti/ kahk-si kehr-taa* | kahdesti/kaksi kertaa |

Abbreviations

ALE – alennusmyynti		sale
ark – arkisin		on weekdays (Monday to Saturday)
as. – asema		station
eiL – ei lauantaisin		not on Saturdays
EP – erikoispikajuna		special express train
EY – Euroopan Yhteisöt		European Communities(EC)
Hki		Helsinki
k. – katu		Street
ke – keskiviikko		Wednesday
-kj. – -kuja		alley
kpl – kappaletta		amount of something, or pieces
la – lauantai		Saturday
ma – maanantai		Monday
mk – markka*		Finnish marks (currency)
n:o, nro – numero		number
pe – perjantai		Friday
PL – Postilokero		PO Box
puh., p. – puhelinnumero		telephone number
-t. – -tie		Road
SF – Suomi Finland		Finland – Official abbreviation of Finland, in Finnish and Swedish

SRM – Suomen Retkeilymajajärjestö — Finnish YHA

SS — (in timetables only) when there are two consecutive holidays, buses run on the second holiday only

su – sunnuntai — Sunday
ti – tiistai — Tuesday
Tku — Turku
to – torstai — Thursday
Tre — Tampere
v. – vuonna — year
VR – Valtion Rautatiet — National Railways

Icelandic

Icelandic

Introduction

Icelandic is a North Germanic language. Iceland was settled primarily by Norwegians in the 9th and 10th centuries. By the 14th century Icelandic (Old Norse) and Norwegian had grown apart considerably. This was due to changes in Norwegian, whereas Icelandic remained largely unchanged. In fact, it has an unbroken literary tradition, dating from about 1100, and the language has changed remarkably little through the centuries. The treasures of the *Sagas* and the poetic *Edda*, written about 700 years ago, can be enjoyed by a modern-day speaker of Icelandic.

Icelanders are proud of their literary heritage. They are particulary conservative when it comes to the written word; borrowed vocabulary is ill tolerated and the policy of keeping the language pure is very strong. After all, Icelandic is spoken by a mere 250,000 people, and outside pressures on the language, in these times of easy travel and worldwide communications, are enormous.

The practice of creating neologisms (new words), instead of adopting foreign words is well established in Iceland. Neologisms, such as *útvarp*, 'radio', *sjónvarp*, 'television', *tölva*, 'computer', and *þota*, 'jet', are just a few that have become part of the Icelandic vocabulary in the last 50 years.

Icelandic is a highly inflected language. Nouns are inflected in four cases: nominative, accusative, dative and genitive, in singular and plural. Most pronouns and adjectives are also inflected. Prepositions and certain verbs determine cases. Nouns

142

change their endings with each case. The plural is formed with still different endings.

There are three genders; masculine, feminine and neuter. Objects may be defined as any of the three.

Icelandic has no indefinite article ('a/an' in English), only a definite article ('the'). The article changes according to gender. *Hinn* (masculine), *hin* (feminine), *hið* (neuter). It is normally attached to the end of a noun. When attached to a noun it drops the *h*: *maðurinn*, 'the man'. The definite article also declines with the noun. Verbs are inflected in three persons (1st, 2nd, and 3rd), singular and plural.

Icelanders are a rather informal people. A person is very rarely addressed by title and/or surname. Family names are illegal in Iceland, unless they were adopted before the Personal Names Act which was passed by Iceland's parliament, *Alþing*, in 1925. Icelanders use the ancient patronymic system, where *son*, 'son' or *dóttir*, 'daughter' is attached to the genitive form of the father's or, less commonly, the mother's, first name. The telephone book entries are listed according to first names.

All this will, no doubt, be quite daunting to an outsider. As one might expect, most Icelanders speak English, and often as many as three or four other languages, although among themselves they only converse in Icelandic. Your efforts to speak Icelandic will most certainly be met with great enthusiasm.

Pronunciation

Stress is generally on the first syllable. Double consonants are pronounced as such. The Icelandic alphabet consists of 33 letters: a, á, b, d, ð, e, é, f, g, h, I, í, j, k, l, m, n, o, ó, p, r, s, t, u, ú, v, x, y, ý, z, þ, æ, ö.

Icelandic	Pronunciation Guide	Sounds
a	*aa*	as the 'a' in 'father'
a	*ah*	as in the Italian *pasta*
e	*ea*	as in 'fear'
e	*eh*	as in 'get', 'bet'
i, y	*i*	as the 'e' in 'pretty'
í, ý	*ee*	as the 'e' in 'see', 'evil'
o	*o*	as in 'pot'
u	*ü*	there is no equivalent sound in English. It sounds a bit like the vowel sound in the French word *peur*. The pronunciation guide is *ü*, although it is not a good phonetic translation for this sound. The *u* in *Guð* 'God', is always pronounced as 'v'.
ú	*u*	as the 'o' in 'moon', 'woman'
ö	*er*	as in 'fern', 'turn', but without a trace of 'r'

Diphthongs

á	*ow*	as in 'out'
ei, ey	*ay*	as in 'paid', 'day'
ó	*oh*	as in 'note'
æ	*ai*	as in 'eye', 'dive'
au	*eü*	there is no equivalent sound in English

Semiconsonants

é	*yeh*	as in 'yet', 'yes'

Consonants

ð	*ð*	as in 'lather'
f	*f*	as in English. When between vowels or at the end of a word it is pronounced as 'v'. When followed by l or n it is pronounced as 'b'.

g	*g*	as in 'good'. When between vowels or before **r** or **ð**, (*sagt*, 'said'), it has a guttural sound as in the Scottish *loch*, rendered as *gh* in pronunciation guide
h	*h*	as in English, except when followed by 'v', when it is pronounced as 'k'
j	*y*	as in 'yes', 'yellow'
l	*l*	as in English, except when double 'l' occurs, when it is pronounced as 'dl' (*kalla*, 'call')
n	*n*	as in English, except when double 'n' forms an end to a word, when it is pronounced as 'dn', (*einn*, 'one'), but never when double 'n' forms part of the article *hinn*
p	*p*	as in English, except before 's' or 't', when it is pronounced as 'f' (skipta, *skift-ah*, 'exchange')
r	*r*	always trilled
þ	*th*	as in 'thin', 'three'

Greetings & Civilities
Top Useful Phrases

Hello.
   hahl-loh   Halló.

Goodbye.
   blehs   Bless.

Yes.
   yow   Já.

No.
   nay   Nei.

Excuse me. (forgive me)
   ahf-saak-ið   Afsakið.

Sorry.
  myehr thi-kir thaað layt   Mér þykir það leitt.
Please.
  gyer-ðü svo veal   Gjörðu svo vel.
Thank you.
  tahk fir-ir   Takk fyrir.
That's fine.
  ahlt ee lai-i   Allt í lagi
You're welcome.
  ehk-ehrt aað thahk-ah   Ekkert að þakka.

Greetings

Good morning.
  gohð-ahn dai-in   Góðan daginn.
Good afternoon.
  gohð-ahn dai-in   Góðan daginn.
Good evening/night.
  ghot kverld/ghoh-ð-ah noht   Gott kvöld.

How are you?
  *kvehrn-ikh heahv-ür thu   Hvernig hefur þú það?
  thaað?*
Well, thanks.
  ghot, tahk   Gott, takk.

Forms of Address

Madam/Mrs	*froo*	Frú
Sir/Mr	*hehr-rah*	Herra
Miss	*frer-kehn*	Fröken
companion,	*vin-ür*	vinur (m)
friend	*vin-ko-nah*	vinkona (f)

Small Talk
Meeting People
What is your name?
kvaað hay-tir-thu?   Hvað heitir þú?

My name is ...
yehgh hay-ti ...   Ég heiti ...

I'm pleased to meet you.
kon-dü saidl/sail   Kondu sæll (m)/sæl (f).

Nationalities
Where are you from?
kvaað-ahn ehrt thu?   Hvaðan ert þú?

I am from ...
yehgh ehr frow ...   Ég er frá....

Australia	*owst-rah-lee-ü*	Ástralíu
Canada	*kaaa-naa-dah*	Kanada
England	*ayngh-laan-di*	Englandi
Ireland	*eer-laan-di*	Írlandi
New Zealand	*nee-aa syow-laan-di*	Nýja Sjálandi
Scotland	*skot-laan-di*	Skotlandi
the USA	*baand-ah-ree-kyü-nüm*	Bandaríkjunum

Age
How old are you?
kvaað ehr-dü gaam-ahdl/ ger-mül?   Hvað ertu gamall (m)/ gömul?(f)

I am ... years old.
yehgh ehr ... ow-rah   Ég er ... ára.

Occupations

What do you do?
kvaað geh-ir thu? Hvað gerir þú?

I am (a/an) ...
yehgh ehr ... Ég er ...

business person/ in business	*keüp-sees-lü-maað-r/ ee við-skift-üm*	kaupsýslumaður/ í viðskiptum (in business)
journalist	*fryeht-ah-maað-ür*	fréttamaður
manual worker	*vehrk-ah-maað-ür*	verkamaður
nurse	*hyook-rün-ahr-fraið- ing-ür*	hjúkrunarfræðingur
office worker	*skrif-stof-ü-maað-ür*	skrifstofumaður
scientist	*vee-sin-dah-maað-ür*	vísindamaður
student	*nowms-maað-ür*	námsmaður
teacher	*kehn-ah-ri*	kennari
waiter	*thyohdn/thyohn-üs- dü-stul-kah*	þjónn/þjónus- tustúlka
writer	*rit-herf-ünd-ür*	rithöfundur

Religion

What is your religion?
kvehr-ahr tru-ahr ehrt thu? Hverrar trúar ert þú?

I am not religious.
yehgh ehr ehk-i Ég er ekki trúaður (m)/
tru-aað-ür/tru-üð trúuð (f)

I am ...
yehgh ehr ... Ég er ...

Buddhist	*bu-dah-tru-ahr*	Búddatrúar
Catholic	*Kaa-thohl-skür*	Kaþólskur (m)
	Kaa-tholsk	Kaþólsk (f)

Christian	*krist-in-ahr tru-ahr*	Kristinnar trúar.
Hindu	*hin-du tru-ahr*	Hindú trúar.
Jewish	*gið-ing-ür*	Gyðingur
Muslim	*mu-haa-meðs-tru-ahr*	Múhameðstrúar

Family

Are you married?
ehrt-ü gift-ür/gift? Ert þú giftur (m)/gift (f)?

I am single. I am married.
yehgh ehr ayn-hlayp-ür/ayn-hlayp. Ég er einhleypur (m)/einhleyp (f).
yehgh ehr gift-ür/gift Ég er giftur (m)/gift (f).

How many children do you have?
kvaað owt thu merg berdn? Hvað átt þú mörg börn?

I don't have any children.
yehgh ow ayn-gin berdn Ég á engin börn.

Is your husband/wife here?
ehr maað-ür-in thin/kon-ahn theen hyehr? Er maðurinn þinn/konan þín hér?

Do you have a boyfriend/girlfriend?
owt thu kair-ahs-dah/kair-üs-dü? Átt þú kærasta/kærustu?

brother	*broh-ðir*	bróðir
children	*berdn*	börn
daughter	*doht-ir*	dóttir
family	*fyerl-skil-dah*	fjölskylda
father	*faað-ir*	faðir
grandfather	*aa-vi*	afi

ICELANDIC

grandmother	*aam-mah*	amma
husband	*ay-in-maað-ür*	eiginmaður
mother	*mohð-ir*	móðir
sister	*sist-ir*	systir
son	*son-ür*	sonur
wife	*ay-in-ko-nah*	eiginkona

Feelings

I (don't) like ...
   yehgh ehr (ehk-i) hri-vin   Ég er (ekki) hrifinn af ...
   av ...

I am ...
   myehr ehr ...   Mér er ...

cold/hot	*kahlt/hayt*	kalt/heitt
sleepy	*siv-yaað-ür*	syfjaður

I am ...
   yehgh ehr ...   Ég er ...

angry	*rayð-ür/rayð*	reiður (m)/reið (f)
grateful	*thahk-law-tür*	þakklátur (m)
	thahk-lowt	þakklát (f)
happy	*aw-naighð-ür*	ánægður (m)
	ow-naighð	ánægð(f)
hungry	*svown-gür*	svangur (m)
	sveüngh	svöng (f)
sad	*hrig-gür*	hryggur (m)
	hrig	hrygg (f)
tired	*thrayt-ür/thrayt*	þreyttur (m)
		þreytt (f)
well	*frees-gür*	frískur (m)
	freesk	frísk (f)

I am worried.
yehgh heaf ow-hig-yür
Ég hef áhyggjur.

I am sorry. (condolence)
myehr thik-ir layt
Mér þykir leitt.

Language Difficulties

Do you speak English?
taa-laar thu ean-skü?
Talar þú ensku?

Does anyone speak English?
taa-laar ayn-kvehr ean-skü?
Talar einhver ensku?

I speak a little Icelandic.
yehgh taa-lah svo lit-lah
ees-lehn-skü
Ég tala svolitla íslensku.

I don't speak ...
yehgh taa-lah ...
Ég tala ...

I (don't) understand.
yehgh skil ehk-i
Ég skil ekki.

Could you speak more slowly
please?
gai-tir thu taa-lahð
svo-lee-tið haigh-ahr?
Gætir þú talað svolítið
hægar?

Could you repeat that?
gai-tir thu ean-dür-tehk-ið
theht-ah?
Gætir þú endurtekið þetta?

How do you say ...?
kvehr-nigh say-ir
maað-ür ...?
Hvernig segir maður ...?

What does ... mean?
kvaað theeð-ir ...?
Hvað þýðir ...?

I speak ...
yehgh taa-lah ...   Ég tala ...

English	*ean-skü*	ensku
French	*frern-skü*	frönsku
German	*thees-kü*	þýsku
Italian	*ee-terl-skü*	ítölsku
Spanish	*spern-skü*	spönsku

Some Useful Phrases

Sure.
  viss-ü-leagh-ah   Vissulega.
Just a minute.
  Bee-dü aað-ayns   Bíddu aðeins.
Good luck!
  gown-gi theehr veahl   Gangi þér vel!

Signs

BAGGAGE COUNTER	FARANGUR
CHECK-IN COUNTER	INNRITUN
CUSTOMS	TOLLUR
EMERGENCY EXIT	NEYÐARÚTGANGUR
ENTRANCE	INNGANGUR or INN
EXIT	ÚTGANGUR or ÚT
FREE ADMISSION	ÓKEYPIS
HOT/COLD	HEITT/KALT
INFORMATION	UPPLÝSINGAR
NO ENTRY	AÐGANGUR BANNAÐUR
NO SMOKING	REYKINGAR BANNAÐAR
OPEN/CLOSED	OPIÐ/LOKAÐ

ICELANDIC

PROHIBITED	BANNAÐ
RESERVED	FRÁTEKIÐ
TELEPHONE	SÍMI
TOILETS	SNYRTING
LADIES/GENTLEMEN	KONUR/KARLAR

Emergencies

POLICE	LÖGREGLA
POLICE STATION	LÖGREGLUSTÖÐ

Help!
hyowlp!   Hjálp!

There's been an accident!
thaað hehf-ür orð-ið slis!   Það hefur orðið slys!

Call a doctor!
now-ið ee laik-ni!   Náið í lækni!

Call an ambulance!
now-ið ee syuk-rah beel!   Náið í sjúkrabíl!

I've been raped.
myehr vaar neüð-gaað   Mér var nauðgað.

I've been robbed!
yehgh vaar rain-dür/raind!   Ég var rændur (m)/rænd (f)!

Call the police!
nowið ee lerg-rehgl-ün-ah!   Náið í lögregluna!

Where is the police station?
kvaar ehr lergh-rehgh-lü-   Hvar er lögreglustöðin?
sterð-in?

Go away!
faar-ðü!   Farðu!

ICELANDIC

Thief!
thyoh-vür!

Þjófur!

I am/My friend is ill.
yehgh ehr/vin-ür min ehr vay-kür

Ég er/vinur minn er veikur.

I am lost.
yehgh erh vilt- ür

Ég er villtur.

Where are the toilets?
kvaar ehr snirt-ingh-in?/ kvaar ehr kloh-seht-ið?

Hvar er snyrtingin?/Hvar er klósettið?

Could you help me please?
gai-tir thu hyowlp-ahð myehr?

Gætir þú hjálpað mér?

Could I please use the telephone?
gai-ti yehgh fayn-ghið ahð hrin-gyah?

Gæti ég fengið að hringja?

I'm sorry.
myehr thik-ir thaað layt.

Mér þykir það leitt.

I didn't realise I was doing anything wrong.
yehgh vi-si ehk-i ahð yehgh vai-ri ahð gea-rah row-nt

Ég vissi ekki að ég væri að gera rangt.

I didn't do it.
yehgh gyer-ði thaað ehk-i

Ég gerði það ekki.

I wish to contact my embassy/consulate.
yehgh vil haa-vah saam-baand við sehndi-rowð mit/raið-is-mahn min

Ég vil hafa samband við sendiráð mitt/ræðismann minn.

I speak English.
   yehgh taa-lah ean-skü   Ég tala ensku.
I have medical insurance.
   yehgh hehf syuk-raa-trigh- Ég hef sjúkratryggingu.
   ing-ü
My possessions are insured.
   aygh-ür meen-aar ehr-ü   Eigur mínar eru tryggðar.
   trighð-ahr

... was stolen.
   ... vaar sto-lið   ... var stolið.
I've lost ...
   yehgh teen-di   Ég týndi ...

my bags	*ter-skü-nüm mee-nüm*	töskunum mínum
my handbag	*haand-tersk-ün-i mi-ni*	handtöskunni minni
my money	*pehn-ing-ün-üm mee-nüm*	peningunum mínum
my travellers' cheques	*ferð-aa-tye-kü-nüm mee-nüm*	ferðatékkunum mínum
my passport	*vehg-aa-breef-in-ü mee-nü*	vegabréfinu mínu

Paperwork

name	*nahbn*	nafn
address	*hay-mil-is-fowng*	heimilisfang
date of birth	*faið-ing-ahr-daagh-ür*	fæðingardagur
place of birth	*faið-ing-aar-staað-ür*	fæðingarstaður
age	*aald-ür*	aldur
sex	*kin*	kyn

nationality	*thyohð-ehr-ni*	þjóðerni
religion	*tru*	trú
reason for travel	*ow-staið-ah fehrð-ah-laaghs-ins*	ástæða ferðalagsins
profession	*aat-vin-ah*	atvinna
passport	*veagh-ah-bryehv*	vegabréf
passport number	*veagh-ah-bryehvs-nu-mehr*	vegabréfsnúmer
visa	*veagh-ah-bryehvs-ow-rit-ün*	vegabréfsáritun
tourist card	*fehrð-ah-mahn-ah-spyaald*	ferðamannaspjald
identification	*skil-ree-ki*	skilríki
birth certificate	*faið-ing-ahr-vot-orð*	fæðingarvottorð
driver's licence	*er-kü-skeer-tay-ni*	ökuskýrteini
car owner's title	*ayg-nahr-voth-orð*	eignarvottorð
car registration	*biv-rayð-ah-skoð-ün*	bifreiðaskoðun
customs	*todl-skoð-ü*	tollskoðun
immigration	*vehgh-ah-bryehvs-skoð-ün*	vegabréfsskoðun

Getting Around

ARRIVALS	KOMA
BUS STOP	BIÐSTÖÐ
DEPARTURES	BROTTFÖR
STATION	STÖÐ
TICKET OFFICE	MIÐASALA
TIMETABLE	TÍMAÁÆTLUN
TRAIN STATION	LESTARSTÖÐ

What time does ...
leave/arrive?
    kveh-nayr....fehr/keh-mür   Hvenær .....fer/kemur?

the aeroplane	*flügh-vyehl-in*	flugvélin
the boat	*bow-tür-in*	báturinn
the bus	*vahgn-in*	vagninn (city bus)
the train	*lehst-in*	lestin
the tram	*spor-vahgn-in*	sporvagninn

Directions

Where is ...?
    kvaar ehr ...?   hvar er ...?

How do I get to ...?
    kvehr-nigh kehmst yehgh   Hvernig kemst ég til ...?
    til ...?

Is it far from/near here?
    ehr thaað lowngt hyehð-   Er það langt héðan?
    ahn?

Can I walk there?
    ehr thaað ee gern-gü fai-ri?   Er það í göngufæri?

Can you show me (on the map)?
    geh-tür thu seent myer (ow   Getur þú sýnt mér (á
    kort-in-ü)?   kortinu)?

I want to go to ...
    migh lown-gahr aað faa-   Mig langar að fara til ...
    rah til ...

Go straight ahead.
    faar-ðü baynt aav eügh-üm   Farðu beint af augum.

ICELANDIC

It's two blocks down.
thaað ehr tvaym-ür gert-üm nehð-ahr

Það er tveimur götum neðar.

Turn left ...
baygh-ðü til vinst-ri ...

Beygðu til vinstri.

Turn right ...
baygh-ðü til haigh-ri ...

Beygðu til hægri ...

at the next corner
við nais-dah hordn

við næsta horn

at the traffic lights
við üm-fehrð-aar-ljohs-in

við umferðarljósin

behind	*fir-ir ahft-ahn*	fyrir aftan
in front of	*fir-ir fraam-ahn*	fyrir framan
far	*lownght ee bür-dü*	langt í burtu
near	*now-laight*	nálægt
opposite	*ow moh-ti*	á móti

Buying Tickets

Where is the ticket office?
kvaar ehr mið-ah-saal-ahn?

Hvar er miðasalan?

Where can I buy a ticket?
kvaar geht yehgh kayft mið-ah?

Hvar get ég keypt miða?

I want to go to ...
yehgh vil faa-rah til ...

Ég vil fara til ...

Do I need to book?
thaarf yehgh aað pahn-tah?

Þarf ég að panta?

You need to book.
thu thahrft aað pahn-tah

Þú þarft að panta.

I'd like to book a seat to ...
gai-ti yehgh pahn-tahð faar   Gæti ég pantað far til ...
til ...

I would like ...
gai-ti yehgh fayn-ghið ...   Gæti ég fengid ...

a one-way ticket	*mið-ah, aað-rah layð-in-ah*	miða, aðra leiðina
a return ticket	*mið-ah, bowð-ahr layð-ir*	miða, báðar leiðir
two tickets	*tvo mið-ah*	tvo miða
tickets for all of us	*mið-ah fir-ir ok-ür erdl*	miða fyrir okkur öll
a student's fare	*nowms-mahn-ah-mið-ah*	námsmannamiða
1st class	*first-ah faar-reem-i*	fyrsta farrými
2nd class	*ahn-aað faar-reem-i*	annað farrými

It is full.
thaað ehr fült   Það er fullt.
Is it completely full?
ehr aal-vehgh fült?   Er alveg fullt?
Can I get a stand-by ticket?
gyeht yehgh fayn-gið   Get ég fengið forfallamiða?
for-fahd-lah-mið-ah?
Can I have a refund?
gyeht yehgh fayn-gið   Get ég fengið endurgreiðslu?
ehnd-ür-grayð-lü?

Bus

BUS STOP	STRÆTISVAGN/BIÐSTÖÐ

160 Icelandic

Where is the bus stop?
kvaar ehr bið-sterð-in? — Hvar er biðstöðin?
Which bus goes to ...?
kvaað-ah vaaghn fehr til ...? — Hvaða vagn fer til ...?
Does this bus go to ...?
fehr theh-si vaagn til ...? — Fer þessi vagn til ...?
How often do buses pass by?
kvaað ko-mah vahgn-aar-nir oft? — Hvað koma vagnarnir oft?
What time is the ... bus?
kveh-nair kehm-ür ... vaagn-in? — Hvenær kemur ... vagninn?

next	*naist*	næst
first	*first*	fyrst
last	*seeð-ahst*	síðast

Could you let me know when we get to ...?
gai-tir thu low-tið migh vi-tah thehgh-aar við kom-üm til ... — Gætir þú látið mig vita þegar við komum til ...?
I want to get off!
yehgh vil faa-rah ut ur! — Ég vil fara út úr!

Taxi
Please take me to ...
gai-tir thoo ekið myehr til ... — Gætir þú ekið mér til ...?
How much does it cost to go to ...?
kvaað kost-ahr aað faa-rah til ...? — Hvað kostar að fara til ...?

ICELANDIC

Instructions

Here is fine, thank you.
heehr-nah ehr ow-gait, tahk   Hérna er ágætt, takk.

The next corner, please.
nais-tah hodn, tahk   Næsta horn, takk.

Continue.
hahl-dü ow-frahm   Haltu áfram.

The next street to the left/right.
nais-tah gaa-tah til   Næsta gata til vinstri/hægri.
vinst-ri/haigh-ri

Stop here!
staan-sah hyehr-nah!   Stansa hérna!

ICELANDIC

Car

GARAGE	VERKSTÆÐI
GIVE WAY	BIÐSKYLDA
MECHANIC	VÉLVIRKI
NO ENTRY	ALLUR AKSTUR BANNAÐUR
NO PARKING	ENGIN BÍLASTÆÐI
NORMAL	EÐLILEGT
ONE WAY	EINSTEFNA
REPAIRS	VIÐGERÐIR
SELF SERVICE	SJÁLFSAFGREIÐSLA
STOP	STANS
SUPER	SUPER
UNLEADED	BLÝLAUST

Where's the next petrol station?
kvaar ehr nais-dah behn-seen-sterð?
Hvar er næsta bensínstöð?

Please fill the tank.
gyer-ið svo vehl aað fid-lah town-kin
Gjörið svo vel að fylla tankinn.

I want ... litres of petrol (gas).
yehgh thaarf ... leet-rah aaf behn-seen-i
Ég þarf ... lítra af bensíni.

Please check the oil and water.
gyer-ið svo vehl aað aat-hugh-ah o-lee-ü ogh vahtn
Gjörið svo vel að athuga olíu og vatn.

air (for tyres)	*loft (ee dehk)*	loft (í dekk)
battery	*raaf-gay-mir*	rafgeymir
brakes	*brehm-sür*	bremsur
clutch	*kup-leeng*	kúplíng
driver's licence	*er-kü-skeer-tay-ni*	ökuskírteini
engine	*vyehl*	vél
lights	*lyohs*	ljós
radiator	*vahss-kahss-i*	vatnskassi
road map	*vehgh-ah-kort*	vegakort
tyres	*dehk*	dekk
windscreen	*fraam-ruð-ah*	framrúða

Car Problems

The battery is flat.
gaym-ir-in ehr raav-mahgns-leüs
Geymirinn er rafmagnslaus.

The radiator is leaking.
vahss-kahss-in leh-kür
Vatnskassinn lekur.

I have a flat tyre.
thaað ehr sprun-ghið hyow myer   Það er sprungið hjá mér.

It's overheating.
hahn heh-vür of-hit-nað   Hann hefur ofhitnað.

It's not working.
hahn virk-ahr ehk-i   Hann virkar ekki.

Accommodation

CAMPING GROUND	TJALDSTÆÐI
GUESTHOUSE	GISTIHEIMILI
HOTEL	HÓTEL
MOTEL	GISTIHÚS
YOUTH HOSTEL	FARFUGLAHEIMILI

I am looking for ...
yehgh ehr aað lay-tah aað ...   Ég er að leita að ...

Where is a... hotel?
kvaar ehr ... ho-tehl?   Hvar er ... hótel?

cheap	*oh-deert*	ódýrt
nearby	*now-laight*	nálægt
clean	*hraynt*	hreint

What is the address?
kvaað ehr hay-mil-is-fown-gið?   Hvað er heimilisfangið?

ICELANDIC

Could you write the address, please?
gai-tir thu skrif-aað nið-ür hay-mil-is fown-gið?

Gætir þú skrifað niður heimilisfangid?

At the Hotel

Do you have any rooms available?
ehr-ü hehr-behr-ghi leüs?

Eru herbergi laus?

I would like ...
gai-ti yehgh fayn-ghið ...

Gæti ég fengid ...

a single room	*ayn-stahk-lings-hehr-behr-ghi*	einstaklingsher-bergi
a double room	*tveh-yaa-mahn-ah-hehr-behr-gi*	tveggjamannaher bergi
a room with a bathroom	*hehr-behr-ghi mehð baað-i*	herbergi með baði.
to share a dorm	*aað day-lah hehr-behr-ghi meað erð-rüm*	að deila herbergi með öðrum
a bed	*rum*	rúm

I'm going to stay for ...
yehgh vehrð ee ...

Ég verð í ...

one day	*aydn daagh*	einn dag
two days	*tvo daagh-ah*	tvo daga
one week	*ay-nah vi-kü*	eina viku

Do you have identification?
ehrt thu mehð skil-ree-ki?

Ert þú með skilríki?

Sorry, we're full.
meer thi-kir thaað layt,
thaað ehr füdl boh-kahð

Mé þykir það leitt, það er
fullbókað.

How long will you be staying?
kvaað ait-lahr thu aað
veh-ra layn-gi?

Kvað ætlar þú að vera lengi?

How many nights?
kvaað maar-gahr nai-tür?

Hvað margar nætur?

It's ... per day/per person.
thaað kost-ahr ... ow daagh
fir-ir mahn-in

Það kostar ... á dag fyrir
manninn.

How much is it per night/per
person?
kvaað kost-ahr noht-in
fir-ir mahn-in?

Hvað kostar nóttin fyirir
manninn?

Can I see it?
mow yehgh syow thaað?

Má ég sjá það?

Are there any others?
eh-rü nok-ür ern-ür?

Eru nokkur önnur?

Are there any cheaper rooms?
eh-rü nok-ür oh-deer-ah-ri
hehr-behr-gi?

Eru nokkur ódýrari
herbergi?

Can I see the bathroom?
mow yehgh syow baað-
hehr-behr-gið?

Má ég sjá herbergið?

Is there a reduction for
students/children?
ehr ahf-slowt-ür fir-ir
nowms-mehn/berdn?

Er afsláttur fyrir
námsmenn/börn?

Does it include breakfast?
ehr morgh-ün-maat-ür in-i-faal-in?

Er morgunmatur innifalinn?

It's fine, I'll take it.
thaað er ow-gait, yehgh fai thaað

Það er ágætt, ég fæ það.

I'm not sure how long I'm staying.
yehgh ehr ehk-i viss üm kvaað yehgh vehð layn-gi

Ég er ekki viss um hvað ég verð lengi.

Where is the bathroom?
kvaar ehr baað-hehr-behr-giö?

Hvar er baðherbergið?

Is there hot water all day?
ehr hayt vahtn ahd-lahn dai-in?

Er heitt vatn allan daginn?

May I leave these in your safe?
mow yehgh gay-mah theh-dah ee er-igh-is-hohl-vi?

Má ég geyma þetta í öryggishólfi?

Is there somewhere to wash clothes?
ehr ayn-kvehrs-staað-ahr haight aað thvo thvot?

Er einhversstaðar hægt að þvo þvott?

Can I use the kitchen?
mow yehgh no-tah ehld-hu-siö?

Má ég nota eldhúsið?

Can I use the telephone?
mow yehgh no-tah see-mahn?

Má ég nota símann?

Some Useful Words & Phrases

We are leaving now/tomorrow.

við ehr-üm aað faa-rah
nu-nah/ow mor-gun

Við erum að fara núna/á morgum.

I would like to pay the bill.

yehgh vil bor-ghah
raykn-ingh-in

Ég vil borga reikninginn.

bathroom	*baað-hehr-behr-gi*	baðherbergi
bed	*rum*	rúm
bill	*raykn-ingh-ür*	reikningur
blanket	*teh-bi*	teppi
candle	*kehr-di*	kerti
clean	*hraydn*	hreinn
dirty	*ow-hraydn*	óhreinn
double bed	*tvee-brayt rum*	tvíbreitt rúm
electricity	*raav-mahgn*	rafmagn
excluded	*fir-ir üt-ahn*	fyrir utan
fan	*vif-dah*	vifta
included	*in-i-faal-ið*	innifalið
key	*li-kidl*	lykill
lift (elevator)	*lif-dah*	lyfta
light bulb	*lyow-sah-peh-rah*	ljósapera
lock (n)	*lows*	lás
mirror	*spay-idl*	spegill
pillow	*kod-di*	koddi
quiet	*hlyoht*	hljótt
sheet	*laak*	lak
shower	*stür-dah*	sturta
soap	*sow-pah*	sápa
toilet	*kloh-seht/saal-ehr-ni*	klósett/salerni

ICELANDIC

toilet paper	*klow-seht-pah-peer*	klósettpappír
towel	*haand-klai-ði*	handklæði
water	*vahtn*	vatn
cold water	*kahlt vahtn*	kalt vatn
hot water	*hayt vahtn*	heitt vatn
window	*ghlü-ghi*	gluggi

Around Town

I'm looking for ...
   yehgh ehr aað lay-tah aað ...   Ég er að leita að ...

a bank	*bown-kah*	banka
the city centre	*mið-bai-nüm*	miðbænum
the ... embassy	*sehn-di-row-ði-nü*	sendiráðinu
my hotel	*hoh-tehl-i-nü mee-nü*	hótelinu mínu
the market	*mahrk-aað-nüm*	markaðnum
the police	*lergh-rehgl-ü-ni*	lögreglunni
the post office	*pohst-hus-i-nü*	pósthúsinu
a public toilet	*aal-mehn-inghs-saal-ehr-ni*	almenningssalerni
the telephone centre	*seem-sterðin-i*	símstöðinni
the tourist information office	*üp-lees-een-gah-thjohn-üst-ü fir-ir fehrð-ah-fohlk*	upplýsingaþjónustu fyrir ferðafólk

What time does it open?
   kveh-nair ehr op-nahð?   Hvenær er opnað?

What time does it close?
   kveh-nair ehr lo-kahð?   Hvenær er lokað?

What street/suburb is this?
kvaað-ah gaa-tah/kvehr-vi ehr theh-dah?　　　Hvaða gata/hverfi er þetta?

For directions, see the Getting Around section, page 157.

At the Bank
I want to exchange some money/traveller's cheques.
yehgh thaarf aað skif-dah pehn-ingh-üm/fehrð-ah-tyehk-üm　　　Ég þarf að skipta peningum/ferðatékkum.

What is the exchange rate?
kvehrt ehr skift-ah-hlüt-fahdl-ið?　　　Hvert er skiptahlutfallið?

How many kronas per dollar?
kvaað ehr-ü maar-gahr krohn-ür ee dol-ah-raa-nüm?　　　Hvað eru margar krónur í dollaranum?

bank notes	*sehð-lahr*	seðlar
cashier	*gyaald-kehr-i*	gjaldkeri
coins	*smow-mint*	smámynt
credit card	*grayð-slü-kort*	greiðslukort
exchange	*skif-dah*	skipta
loose change	*rayð-ü-fyeh*	reiðufé
signature	*ün-dir-skrift*	undirskrift

At the Post Office
I would like to send ...
yehgh ait-lah aað sehn-dah ...　　　Ég ætla að senda ...

ICELANDIC

a letter	*breef*	bréf
a postcard	*kort*	kort
a parcel	*pahk-ah*	pakka
a telegram	*skay-ti*	skeyti

I would like some stamps.
  yehgh aid-lah aað fow nok-ür free-mehr-gi
Ég ætla að fá nokkur frímerki.

How much is the postage?
  kvaað kos-dahr mi-kið ün-dir theh-dah
Hvað kostar mikið undir þetta?

How much does it cost to send this to ...?
  kvaað kos-dahr aað sehn-dah theh-dah til ...?
Hvað kostar að senda þetta til ...?

an aerogram	*flügh-breef*	flugbréf
air mail	*flugh-pohst-ür*	flugpóstur
envelope	*üm-slaagh*	umslag
mail box	*pohst-kahss-i*	póstkassi
parcel	*pah-gi*	pakki
registered mail	*ow-birð-ahr-pohst-ür*	ábyrgðar póstur
surface mail/sea mail	*syoh-pohst-ür*	sjópóstur

Telephone

I want to ring ...
  yehgh thaarv aað hreen-gya ...
Ég þarf að hringja ...

The number is ...
  nu-mehr-ið ehr ...
Númerið er ...

I want to speak for three minutes.

yehgh ait-lah aað taa-lah ee thryowr meen-ut-ür

Ég ætla að tala í þrjár mínútur.

How much does a three-minute call cost?

kvaað kos-dahr thri-ghjah-meen-ut-nah sahm-taal?

Hvað kostar þriggja mínútna samtal?

How much does each extra minute cost?

kvaað kos-dahr kvehr meen-u-tah?

Hvað kostar hver mínúta?

I would like to speak to Jón Pálsson.

gai-ti yehgh fayn-gið aað taalah við yohn powls-sohn

Gæti ég fengið að tala við Jón Pálsson?

I want to make a reverse-charges phone call.

yehgh ait-lah aað hreen-ghyah ogh við-taak-ahn-di bor-gaar

Ég ætla að hringja og viðtakandi borgar.

It's engaged.

thaað ehr ow taa-li

Það er á tali.

I've been cut off.

thaað slit-naað-i

Það slitnaði.

Sightseeing

Do you have a guidebook/local map?

owt-ü fehrð-ah-haand-bohk/kort aav staað-nüm?

Áttu ferðahandbók/kort af staðnum?

What are the main attractions?
   kvaað ehr mahrk-vehrt aað syow?

Hvað er markvert að sjá?

What is that?
   kvaað ehr theh-dah?

Hvað er þetta?

How old is it?
   kvaað ehr thaað gaam-ahlt?

Hvað er það gamalt?

Can I take photographs?
   mow yehgh taa-kah mind-ir?

Má ég taka myndir?

What time does it open/close?
   klük-ahn kvaað op-nahr/ lok-ahr?

Klukkan hvað opnar/lokar?

In the Country
Weather

What's the weather like?
   kvehr-nigh ehr vehð-rið?

Hvernig er veðrið?

The weather is ... today.
   vehð-rið ehr ... ee daagh

Veðrið er ... í dag.

Will it be ... tomorrow?
   thaað vehrð-ür ... ow mor-ghün

Það verður ... á morgun.

cloudy	*skee-ahð*	skýjað
cold	*kahlt*	kalt
hot	*hayt*	heitt
raining	*righ-ningh*	rigning
snowing	*snyoh-ahr*	snjóar
sunny	*sohl-skin*	sólskin
windy	*kvahst*	hvasst

Camping

Am I allowed to camp here?
mow yehgh tyaal-dah hyehr? — Má ég tjalda hér?

Is there a campsite nearby?
ehr tyaald-staið-i hyehr now-laight? — Er tjaldstæði hér nálægt?

backpack	*baak-po-ki*	bakpoki
can opener	*doh-sah-op-naa-ri*	dósaopnari
compass	*owt-ah-vi-ti*	áttaviti
firewood	*ehld-i-við-ür*	eldiviður
gas cartridge	*gaas-ku-tür*	gaskútur
mattress	*dee-nah*	dýna
penknife	*vaa-sah-hneev-ür*	vasahnífur
rope	*snai-ri*	snæri
tent	*tyaald*	tjald
tent pegs	*tyaald-hai-lahr*	tjaldhælar
torch (flashlight)	*vaa-sah-lyohs*	vasaljós
sleeping bag	*svehbn-po-ki*	svefnpoki
stove	*ehld-ah-veehl*	eldavél
water bottle	*vahs-flahs-ga*	vatnsflaska

Food

breakfast	*mor-gün-maa-tür*	morgunmatur
lunch	*how-day-is-maat-ür*	hádegismatur
dinner	*kverld-maat-ür*	kvöldmatur

Table for ..., please.
gyeht yehgh fayn-gið ..., mah-nah borð? — Get ég fengið ..., manna borð?

ICELANDIC

Can I see the menu please?
   gyeht-yehgh fayn-gið aað
   syow maat-sehð-il-in?

Get ég fengið að sjá matseðilinn?

I would like the set lunch, please.
   gai-ti yehgh fayn-gið maat
   daagh-sins?

Gæti ég fengið mat dagsins?

What does it include?
   kvaað ehr in-i-faal-ið?

Hvað er innifalið?

Is service included in the bill?
   ehr thyoh-nüs-dah
   in-i-faal-in?

Er þjónusta innifalin?

Not too spicy please.
   eh-ki of kri-dahð, tahk

Ekki of kryddað, takk.

ashtray	*ers-kü-bah-ghi*	öskubakki
the bill	*rayk-ningh-ür-in*	reikningurinn
a cup	*bod-li*	bolli
a drink	*drik-ür*	drykkur
a fork	*ghahf-adl*	gaffall
a glass	*ghlaas*	glas
a knife	*hnee-vür*	hnífur
a plate	*disk-ür*	diskur
a spoon	*skayð*	skeið
teaspoon	*teh-skayð*	teskeið

Vegetarian Meals

I am a vegetarian.
   yehgh ehr grain-meht-is-ai-tah

Ég er grænmetisæta.

I don't eat meat.
   yehgh bor-ðah ehk-i kyert

Ég borða ekki kjöt.

Staple Foods & Condiments

bread	*brauð*
butter	*smjör*
cheese	*ostur*
cream	*rjómi*
eggs	*egg*
fish	*fiskur*
fruit	*ávextir*
ham	*skinka*
honey	*hunang*
jam	*sulta*
ketchup	*tómatsósa*
lemon	*sítróna*
marmalade	*marmelaði*
meat	*kjót*
milk	*mjólk*
mustard	*sinnep*
omelette	*eggjakaka*
pepper	*pipar*
potatos	*kartöflur*
rice	*hrísgrjón*
salad	*salat*
salt	*salt*
sandwich	*samloka*
sauce	*sósa*
sausage	*pylsa*
seasonings	*bragðefni*
sugar	*sykur*
vegetables	*grænmeti*
water	*vatn*

ICELANDIC

Meat & Poultry — Kjöt og Fuglar

beef	*nautakjöt*
chicken	*kjúklingur*
lamb	*lambakjöt*
pork	*svínakjöt*
reindeer	*hreindýrakjöt*
turkey	*kalkúnn*

Fish — Fiskur

cod	*þorskur*
haddock	*ýsa*
halibut	*lúða*
herring	*síld*
lobster	*humar*
salmon	*lax*
scallop	*hörpudiskur*
shrimp	*rækja*

Fruit — Ávextir

apples	*epli*
apricots	*apríkósur*
bananas	*bananar*
blueberries	*bláber*
crowberries	*kræikiber*
grapes	*vínber*
oranges	*appelsínur*
peaches	*ferskjur*
pears	*perur*
pineapple	*ananas*
strawberries	*jarðaber*

ICELANDIC

Vegetables	**Grænmeti**
cabbage	*hvítkál*
cauliflower	*blómkál*
carrots	*gulrætir*
cucumber	*gúrka*
garlic	*hvítlaukur*
green peas	*grænar baunir*
green pepper	*græn paprika*
lettuce	*salat*
mushrooms	*sveppir*
onion	*laukur*
potatoes	*kartöflur*

Traditional Icelandic Food

Hangikjöt

Smoked lamb, leg or shoulder. Served hot or cold, with potatoes in béchamel sauce and green peas. Also popular as a luncheon meat.

Svið

Singed sheep heads. Eaten hot or cold, with either plain boiled potatoes, mashed potatos or swede turnips. The pressed and gelled variety is popular for packed lunches.

Saltkjöt

Salted lamb/mutton, served with potatoes or swede turnips and often accompanied by split pea soup.

Bjúgu

Smoked minced meat sausage. Served hot or cold with potatoes in white sauce.

Slátur

Blood and liver puddings. Prepared in the months of September and October, when slaughtering is at its peak. The blood pudding is called *Blóðmör* and the liver pudding *Lifrarpylsa*.

ICELANDIC

Eaten hot or cold, sliced. Traditionally, the *Slátur* that could not be eaten fresh, was pickled in whey and enjoyed throughout the winter months.

Harðfiskur

Dried fish; haddock, cod or catfish. It does not require cooking, but is enjoyed as snack food. Often spread with a little butter.

Skyr

A dairy product similar to yoghurt. It is very low in fat content. Eaten as dessert with sugar and milk and with fresh berries, when in season.

Seytt rúgbrauð

Cooked rye bread, moist and chewy. Popular with *Hangikjöt*.

Flatkökur

Rye pancakes, also popular with *Hangikjöt*.

Kjötsúpa

Soup, made of a small quantity of vegetables, large quantity of lamb meat and rice. Always served hot.

Methods of Cooking

baked	*bakað*
boiled	*soðið*
chopped	*saxað*
fried	*steikt*
grilled	*grillað*
jellied	*í hlaupi*
mashed	*stappað*
smoked	*reykt*
steamed	*gufusoðið*

Desserts
Ábætir

biscuits	*smákökur/kex*
cake	*kaka*
fruit	*ávextir*
ice cream	*ís/rjómaís*
pancakes	*pönnukökur*
pudding	*búðingur*
schocolate	*súkkulaði*
stewed fruit	*ávaxtagrautur*

Drinks – Nonalcoholic

coffee/white/black	*kaffi/með mjólk/svart*
fruit juce	*ávaxtasafi*
milk	*mjólk*
ice	*klaki*
soft drinks	*gosdrykkir*
tea	*te*
water	*vatn*

Drinks – Alcoholic

aqua vitae (brandy)	*brennivín*
beer	*bjór*
cognac	*koníak*
liqeur	*líkjör*
whisky	*whisky*
wine: red/white	*vín: rauðvín/hvítvín*

Shopping

general store, shop	*buð*	búð
laundry	*thvo-dah-hus*	þvottahús
market	*mahr-kaað-ür*	markaður

ICELANDIC

newsagency/ stationers	*blaa-ðaa-saa-lah/ boh-kah-buð*	blaðasala/bókabúð
pharmacy	*aap-oh-tehk*	apótek
supermarket	*stohr-mahr-kaað-ür*	stórmarkaður
vegetable shop	*grain-meht-is-buð*	grænmetisbúð

I would like to buy ...
   migh lown-ghahr aað keü-pah ... — Mig langar að kaupa ...
Can you write down the price?
   gyeht-ür-ü skri-vaað nið-ür verðið — Gætir þú skrifað niður verðið?

Toiletries

comb	*gray-ðah*	greiða
condoms	*smok-ahr*	smokkar
deodorant	*svi-tah-likt-ahr-ay-ðir*	svitalyktareyðir
razor	*raak-veehl*	rakvél
sanitary napkins	*der-mü-bin-di*	dömubindi
shampoo	*syaam-poh*	sjampó
shaving cream	*raak-krehm*	rakkrem
soap	*sow-pah*	sápa
tampons	*vaht-tahp-ahr/ tahm-poh-nahr*	vatttappar/ tampónar
tissues	*breehf-thür-kür*	bréfþurkur
toilet paper	*kloh-seht-pah-peer*	klósettpappír
toothbrush	*tahn-büs-di*	tannbursti
toothpaste	*tahn-krehm*	tannkrem

Stationery & Publications

map	*kort*	kort
newspaper	*daagh-blaað*	dagblað
newspaper in English	*dagh-blaað ow ean-skü*	dagblað á ensku
paper	*pah-peer*	pappír
pen (ballpoint)	*pehn-ni/ku-lü-pehn-ni*	penni/kúlupenni

Smoking

A packet of cigarettes, please.
aydn see-gaar-eh-dü-pahk-ah, tahk   Einn sígarettupakka, takk.

Do you have a light?
ow-dü ehld?   Áttu eld?

cigarette papers	*see-gaar-eh-dü-breehf*	sígarettubréf
cigarettes	*see-gaar-eh-dür*	sígarettur
filtered	*mehð see-ü/mehð feel-tehr*	með síu/með fílter
lighter	*kvay-kyah-ri*	kveikjari
matches	*ehld-speet-ür*	eldspýtur
menthol	*mehnt-ohl*	mentól
tobacco	*toh-baak*	tóbak

Colours

black	*svahrt*	svart
blue	*blowt*	blátt
brown	*brunt*	brúnt
green	*graint*	grænt
red	*reüt*	rautt
white	*kveet*	hvítt
yellow	*gült*	gult

Sizes & Comparisons

small	*lee-tið*	lítið
big	*stohrt*	stórt
heavy	*thunt*	þúngt
light	*lyeht*	létt
more	*may-rah*	meira
less	*mi-nah*	minna
too much/many	*ov mi-kið/maar-gir*	of mikið/margir

Health

Where is ...?
    kvaar ehr ...?   Hvar er?

a doctor	*laik-nir*	læknir
a hospital	*syuk-rah-hus*	sjúkrahús
a chemist	*aa-po-tehk*	apótek
a dentist	*tahn-laik-nir*	tannlæknir

Could I see a female doctor?
    gay-ti yehgh fayn-gið aað   Gæti ég fengið að tala við
    taa-lah við kvehn layk-ni?   kvenlækni?
What's the matter?
    kvaað ehr aað?   Hvað er að?
Where does it hurt?
    kvaar fin-ür thu til?   Hvar finnur þú til?
It hurts here.
    migh vehrk-yahr hyehr   Mig verkjar hér.
I have ...
    yehgh ehr mehð ...   Ég er með ...

Ailments

a cold	*kvehf*	kvef
constipation	*haarð-lee-vi*	harðlífi
diarrhoea	*nið-ür-gowng*	niðurgang
fever	*hi-tah*	hita
a headache	*her-vüð-vehrk*	höfuðverk
indigestion	*mehlt-ing-ahr-trüb-lün*	meltingartruflun
influenza	*flehn-sü*	flensu
low/high blood pressure	*low-ahn/how-ahn blohð-threest-ing*	lágan/háan blóðþrýsting
sore throat	*howls-bohl-gü*	hálsbólgu
sprain	*togh-nün*	tognun
a stomachache	*maagh-ah-vehrk*	magaverk
sunburn/I am sunburnt.	*sohl-brü-ni/yehgh ehr sohl-brün-in*	sólbruni/Ég er sólbrunninn.

ICELANDIC

Some Useful Words & Phrases

I'm ...
   yehgh ehr ...   Ég er ...

diabetic	*sik-ür-syu-kür*	sykursjúkur
epileptic	*flogh-ah-vay-kür*	flogaveikur
asthmatic	*mehð ahs-mah*	með asma

I'm allergic to antibiotics/penicillin.
   yehgh ehr mehð ov-nai-mi fir-ir fu-kah-liv-yüm/pehn-si-lee-ni   Ég er með ofnæmi fyrir fúkalyfjum/pensilíni.

I'm pregnant.
   yehgh ehr thun-güð   Ég er þunguð

I have been vaccinated.
yehgh fyehk oh-nai-mis-spreü-tü   Ég fékk ónæmissprautu.

I have my own syringe.
yehgh ehr með mee-nah ay-in spreü-tü   Ég er með mína eigin sprautu.

I feel better/worse.
meehr leeð-ür beh-tür/vehr   Mér líður betur/verr.

antibiotics	*fu-kah-lif*	fúkalyf
antiseptic	*soht-hrayns-aandi*	sótthreinsandi
blood pressure	*blohð-threest-ing-ür*	blóðþrýstingur
blood test	*blohð-prüvah*	blóðprufa
contraceptive	*gyeht-naað-ahr-verdn*	getnaðarvörn
injection	*spreü-tah*	sprauta
medicine	*lif*	lyf
menstruation	*blaið-ing-ahr*	blæðingar
nausea	*oh-ghleh-ði*	ógleði
toothache	*tahn-pee-nah*	tannpína

At the Chemist

I need medication for ...
yehgh thaarf lif við ...   Ég þarf lyf við ...

I have a prescription.
yehgh ehr með lif-sehð-il   Ég er með lyfseðil.

Time & Dates

What date is it today?
kvaað-ah daagh-ür ehr ee daagh?   Hvaða dagur er í dag?

What time is it?
kvaað er klük-ahn?   Hvað er klukkan?

It is ... am/pm.
hoon ehr ... fir-ir how-day-i/   Hún er ... fyrir hádegi/eftir
ehf-dir how-day-i   hádegi.

in the morning	*aað mo-dni*	að morgni
in the afternoon	*ehft-ir how-day-i*	eftir hádegi
in the evening	*aað kverl-di*	að kvöldi

Days of the Week

Monday	*mow-nü-daagh-ür*	mánudagur
Tuesday	*thrið-yü-daagh-ür*	þriðjudagur
Wednesday	*mið-vik-ü-daagh-ür*	miðvikudagur
Thursday	*fim-tü-daagh-ür*	fimmtudagur
Friday	*fers-dü-daagh-ür*	föstudagur
Saturday	*leügh-ah-daagh-ür*	laugardagur
Sunday	*sün-ü-daagh-ür*	sunnudagur

Months

January	*yaa-nu-ahr*	janúar
February	*fehb-ru-ahr*	febrúar
March	*mahrs*	mars
April	*aa-preel*	apríl
May	*mahee*	maí
June	*yu-nee*	júní
July	*yu-lee*	júlí
August	*ow-gust*	ágúst
September	*sehft-ehm-behr*	september
October	*okt-oh-behr*	október
November	*noh-vehm-behr*	nóvember
December	*dehs-ehm-behr*	desember

Seasons

summer	*sü-maar*	sumar
autumn	*heüst*	haust
winter	*veh-tür*	vetur
spring	*vor*	vor

Present

today	*ee daagh*	í dag
this morning	*ee mor-gün*	í morgun
tonight	*ee kverld*	í kvöld
this week	*thes-ah vi-kü*	þessa viku
this year	*theht-ah owr*	þetta ár
now	*nu-nah*	núna

Past

yesterday	*ee gair*	í gær
(two) days ago	*fir-ir tvay-mür*	fyrir tveimur
	dergh-üm	dögum

Future

tomorrow	*ow mor-gün*	á morgun
in (two) days	*ehf-dir tvo daag-ah*	eftir tvo daga

During the Day

afternoon	*ehf-dir how-day-i*	eftir hádegi
day	*daagh-ür*	dagur
midnight	*miðnait-i*	miðnætti
morning	*mor-gün*	morgun
night	*noht*	nótt
noon	*how-day-i*	hádegi
sundown	*sohl-ahr-laagh*	sólarlag
sunrise	*sohl-ahr-üp-rows*	sólarupprás

Numbers & Amounts

0	*nul*	núll
1	*aydn*	einn
2	*tvayr*	tveir
3	*threer*	þrír
4	*fyoh-rir*	fjórir
5	*fimm*	fimm
6	*sehks*	sex
7	*syer*	sjö
8	*owt-dah*	átta
9	*nee-ü*	níu
10	*tee-ü*	tíu
20	*tü-tülgh-ü*	tuttugu
100	*ayt hün-drahð*	eitt hundrað
1000	*ayt thus-ünd*	eitt þúsund
one million	*ayn mil-yohn*	ein milljón
a little (amount)	*lee-tið*	lítið
few	*fow-ir*	fáir
more	*may-rah*	meira
some	*nok-rir*	nokkrir
too much	*ov mi-kið*	of mikið

Abbreviations

fyrsti	1st
annar	2nd
þriðji	3rd
eftir/fyrir Krist	AD/BC
áunnin ónæmisbæklun	AIDS
fyrir hádegi/eftir hádegi	am/pm
doktor	Dr

aðalpósthús	GPO
nafnskírteini	ID
Hr/Frú/Frk	Mr/Mrs/Ms
norður/suður	Nth/Sth
gata/vegur	St/Rd

Norwegian

Norwegian

Introduction

Norway has two official written language forms. They are quite alike, and every Norwegian learns both at school. Bokmål, literally 'book-language', hereafter referred to as BM, is the urban-Norwegian variety of Danish, the language of the former rulers of Norway. BM, also called Dano-Norwegian, has high prestige in some circles. It is written by more than 80% of the population, but not widely spoken. Nonetheless, many business people, officials and others do speak it.

The other written langage is Nynorsk, or 'New Norwegian' – as opposed to Old Norwegian, the language in Norway before 1500 AD, that is, before Danish rule. Nynorsk, hereafter referred to as NN, is a kind of common denominator of everyday speech in all its widely spoken dialects. It is therefore very appropriate for the traveller who wants to communicate with Norwegians all over the country, although it must be noted that NN is disliked by some members of society, especially class-conscious people. You may even come across those who claim that NN doesn't really exist!

In speech the distinction between BM and NN is no problem, since Norwegians understand either. Both are used in the media, although BM is predominant in the daily papers and is used exclusively in the gutter press. The towns and villages in the tourist areas, fjords and mountains have NN as their working written language, the cities often use BM. However, the Norwegian language situation is far more complicated than it looks from the sketch given above.

A striking feature of both written languages is that many words
have two or more officially authorised forms of spelling in either
language. One can choose according to one's speech or social
aspirations. In many cases it is possible to choose spellings which
are common to either language. Although many speak their Norwegian more or less as if it were a mingling of NN and BM, they
generally frown upon a written rendering of this cocktail.

In the rural (and therefore mostly NN) areas you may come
across people who hardly speak a word of English, and if you
show an effort to speak their tongue, it will help a great deal to
establish contact. Many Norwegians will answer you in English,
as they are only too eager to show off their knowledge. It seems
as if they generally feel ill at ease with the fact that they belong
to a small language community.

Quite a few Norwegians, especially those engaged in com-
merce, like to make you believe that you are travelling in an
English-speaking country. They give their shops, restaurants,
companies and products English names, and use signs and
billboards expressed in English. The fact that this English, let
alone its spelling, sometimes makes little sense to the English
speaker, doesn't appear to bother these people in the least.

Pronunciation
Vowels
Length, as a distinctive feature of vowels, is very important in
the pronunciation of Norwegian. Almost every vowel has a
(very) long and a (very) short counterpart, when appearing in a
stressed syllable. Generally, it is long when followed by one
consonant, and short when followed by two or more consonants.

A few words, mainly function words like pronouns and
auxiliaries, are 'misspelt': the vowel is short in spite of the fact
that it is followed by only one consonant.

Norwegian	Pronunciation Guide	Sound
a	*ah*	as in 'cut'
a long	*aa*	as in 'father'
å	*o*	as in British English 'pot'
å long	*or*	as in British English 'lord'
æ		has the same pronunciation as the first four varieties of e
e	*a*	before r, as in British English 'bat'
e	*ã*	before r, as in British English 'bad'
e	*eh*	as in 'bet'
e long	*ē*	as in posh British 'day'; close to German *sehen*
e	*uh*	as the 'u' in 'lettuce', always unstressed
i	*ee*	like 'beat', but very short, as the French *si, il*
i long	*ēē*	as in 'seethe'
o	*u*	as in British 'pot'
o long	*oo*	like the American 'zoo', but more like the German *u* in *suchen*
o	*u*	as the 'u' in 'put'
o long	*or*	as in 'lord'
ø	*er*	as in German *zwölf*, or French *boeuf*
ø long	*ør*	as in British 'fern'
u	*ü*	as in French *sud*
u long	*üü*	like British 'soon', but more like German *süss*
u	*u*	as in 'put'
y	*ÿ*	between French *sud* and *si*
y	*ÿÿ*	long between 'seethe' and German *süss*

Diphthongs

ai	*ai*	as in 'dive'
ei	*ay*	similar to Australian English 'day'
au	*ohw*	similar to Australian English 'shown'
øy	*öy*	as the French *eui* in *fauteuil*

Consonants & Semivowels

d at the end of a word, or between two vowels, it is often silent

g as in 'get', but before the letters or combinations **ei, i, j, øy**, and **y** it is, in most cases, pronounced like the 'y' in 'yard'. The combination **gn** is pronounced as the 'ng' of 'sing', followed by an 'n'.

h like the 'h' in 'her', but before **v** and **j** it is silent

j always like the 'y' in 'yard'

k a hard sound as in 'kin', but before the letters or combinations **ei, i, j, øy**, and **y**, it is, in most words, pronounced as the 'ch' in 'chin'. In many areas though, these combinations are pronounced like the 'h' in 'huge', or like the German *ch* in the word *ich*.

l pronounced thinly, as in 'list', except after the phonetic *ah, aa, o* and *or* sounds, when it becomes the 'l' sound of 'all'.

ng in most areas, like the 'ng' sound in 'sing'

r trilled, as in Spanish (rendered as **rr** in our pronunciation guide). In south-west Norway, however, the **r** is pronounced gutturally, as in French.

The combinations **rd, rl, rn, rt** sound a bit like American 'weird', 'earl', 'earn' and 'start', but with a much weaker 'r'. The resulting consonants are made with the tip of the tongue curled well behind the teeth, and the preceding vowel is lengthened. These

NORWEGIAN

consonants occur even when the **r** is the last letter of one word and the **d, l, n,** or **t** is the first letter of the next word. In some words, however, where the **d** in the combination **rd** is silent, the preceding vowel is often lengthened but the **r** trilled: for example, the word gard, meaning farm, is pronounced *gaarr*, not *gahrd*.

The combination **rs** is pronounced 'sh' as in 'fish'.

s always voiceless, like the 's' in 'us'. The combination **sk** followed by **ei, i, j, øy** and **y** is pronounced as 'sh': so the Norwegian word ski sounds like the English 'she'.

t like the English 't', except in two cases where it is silent: in the Norwegian word det (meaning 'it', that'), roughly pronounced like British English 'dare'; and in the definite singular ending -et of Norwegian neutral nouns

v is nearly always pronounced like the English 'w' but without rounding the lips – rather like a German speaker would pronounce a 'w'

Greetings & Civilities
Top Useful Phrases
Hello.
   gud-daag   Goddag.
Goodbye.
   mo-rnah   Morna.
Yes.
   yaa.   Ja.
No.
   nay   Nei.

Excuse me.
ün-shȳl   Unnskyld.
May I? Do you mind?
  for-rr eh lorv? haa rdü   Får eg lov? Har du noko
  nor-ko i-moot deh?   imot det? (NN)
  for-rr yeh lorv? haa rdü   Får jeg lov? Har du noe
  noo-uh i-moot deh?   imot det? (BM)
Sorry. (excuse me, forgive me)
  ün-shȳl (ēg ā rlay fo rdē)   Unnskyld. (eg er lei for det)
                                             (NN)
  om fo-rlaa-dl-suh   Om forlatelse. (BM)
Please.
  vä sho sneel   Ver så snill. (NN)
  vä sho sneel   Vær så snill. (BM)
Thank you.
  tahk   ⊱ Takk.
Many thanks.
  tüüsn tahk   Tusen takk.
That's fine. You're welcome.
  eeng-ah or-shaak   Inga årsak. (NN)
  eeng-uhn or-shaak   Ingen årsak. (BM)

Greetings
Good morning.
  gu mo-rr-gon   God morgon. (NN)
  gu mor-rn   God morgen. (BM)
Good afternoon.
  gud-daag   Goddag.
Good evening/night.
  gu kveh-l/gu nah-t   God kveld./God natt.

NORWEGIAN

How are you?
*ku-rleys **haa** rdü deh?* — Korleis har du det? (NN)
*vu-rdahn **haa** rdü deh?* — Hvordan har du det? (BM)
Well, thanks.
brraa tahk. — Bra, takk.

Forms of Address

madam/Mrs	*gud **daag**/frrüü ...*	goddag/fru ...
sir/Mr	*gud **daag**/harr ...*	goddag/herr ...
Miss	*gud **daag**/düü/**frrēr**-kuhn*	goddag/du/frøken
companion, friend (m)	*kah-mah-**rraat**, vehn*	kamerat, venn
companion, friend (f)	*vehn-**neen**-nuh*	venninne

Small Talk
Meeting People

What is your name?
*kaa **hey**-tuh rdü?* — Kva heiter du? (NN)
*vaa **hē**-tuh rdü?* — Hva heter du? (BM)
My name is ...
*eh **hey**-tuhrr ...* — Eg heiter ... (NN)
*ya **hē**-tuhrr ...* — Jeg heter ... (BM)
I'd like to introduce you to ...
deh-tuh ärr ... — Dette er ...
I'm pleased to meet you.
*h**ÿg**-guh-leh o **trreh**-fuh dēg* — hyggeleg å treffe deg. (NN)
*h**ÿg**uh-lee o **trreh**-fuh day* — hyggelig å treffe deg (BM)

Nationalities

Where are you from?

kvaar ä rdü frror? — Kvar er du frå? (NN)

vurr ä rdü frraa? — Hvor er du fra? (BM)

I am from …

ēg ärr frror … — Eg er frå … (NN)

ya ärr frrah … — Jeg er fra … (BM)

Australia	*ohw-strraa-lee-ah*	Australia
Canada	*kah-nah-dah*	Kanada
England	*ehng-lahn*	England
Ireland	*ēē-rlahn*	Irland
New Zealand	*nӯӯ sē-lahn*	Ny Zealand
Norway	*nor-rrehg/norr-guh*	Noreg/Norge (NN)
	norr-guh	Norge (BM)
Scotland	*skot-lahn*	Skottland
the USA	*sahm-bahn-staa-tah-nuh, üü-wehs-saa*	Sambandsstatane, USA (NN)
	dee forr-ēn-tuh staa-tuhrr, üü-wehs-saa	De Forente Stater, USA (BM)
Wales	*vehls*	Wales

Age

How old are you?

kurr gahm-mahl ä rdüü? — Kor gammal er du? (NN)

vurr gahm-mahl ä rdüü? — Hvor gammel er du? (BM)

I am … years old.

ēg ärr … — Eg er … (NN)

ya ärr … — Jeg er … (BM)

NORWEGIAN

Occupations

What (work) do you do?

*kaa **drrēēv** dü **mē**?*	Kva driv du med? (NN)
*vaa **drrēē**-vuh rdü **mē**?*	Hva driver du med? (BM)

I am a/an ...

*ēg **ārr** ...*	Eg er ... (NN)
*ya **ārr** ...*	Jeg er ... (BM)
artist	**künst**-nahrr	kunstnar (NN)
	künst-nuhrr	kunstner (BM)
business man/woman	*fo-**rreht**-neengs-mahn/fo-**rreht**-neengs-kveen-nuh*	forretningsmann/ forettningskvinne
doctor	**lē**-guh	lege
engineer	*eensh-uhn-**yēr**-rr*	ingeniør
farmer	**gaarr**-brrüü-kahrr	gardbrukar (NN)
	gaarr-brrüü-kuhrr	gardbruker (BM)
journalist	*shü-rnah-**leest***	journalist
lawyer	*yü-**rreest***	jurist
manual worker	**ahrr**-bay-ahrr	arbeidar (NN)
	ahrr-bay-duhrr	arbeider (BM)
mechanic	*meh-**kaa**-nee-kahrr*	mekanikar (NN)
	*meh-**kaa**-nee-kuhrr*	mekaniker (BM)
nurse	*shüü-kuh-play-ahrr*	sjukepleiar (NN)
	shüü-kuh-play-uhrr	sjukepleier (BM)
office worker	*kun-too-**rr**-ahrr-bay-ahrr*	kontorarbeidar (NN)
	*kun-too-**rr**-ahrr-bay-duhrr*	kontorarbeider (BM)
scientist	**vēēt**-skaaps-mahn	vitskapsmann (NN)
	vēē-tuhn-skaaps-mahn	vitenskapsmann (BM)

NORWEGIAN

student	*stü-deh-nt*	student
teacher	*lā-rrahrr*	lærar (NN)
	lā-rruhrr	lærer (BM)
waiter	*kehl-nuhrr/sehrr-vē-rreengs-daa-muh*	kelner/serveringsdame
writer	*fo-rr-faht-tahrr*	forfattar (NN)
	fo-rr-faht-tuhrr	forfatter (BM)

Religion

What is your religion?

| *kvaa ā deen reh-lee-gyoon?* | Kva er din religion? (NN) |
| *vaa ā deen reh-lee-gyoon?* | Hva er din religion? (BM) |

I am not religious.

| *ēg ārr eech-uh trüü-ahn-duh* | Eg er ikkje truande. (NN) |
| *ya ārr eek-kuh troo-uhn-nuh* | Jeg er ikke truende. (BM) |

I am …

ēg ārr …	Eg er … (NN)
ya ārr …	Jeg er … (BM)
Buddhist	*büd-deest*	buddhist
Catholic	*kah-tolsk*	katolsk
Hindu	*heen-dü*	hindu
Jewish	*yēr-duh*	jøde
Muslim	*müs-leem*	muslim
Protestant	*prro-teh-stahnt*	protestant

Family

Are you married?

| *ā dü yeeft?* | Er du gift? |

I am single. I am married.

| *ēg ārr ayns-leh. ēg ārr yeeft* | Eg er einsleg. Eg er gift. (NN) |
| *ya ārr ēns-lee.ya ārr yeeft* | Jeg er enslig. Jeg er gift. (BM) |

NORWEGIAN

How many children do you have?

*kurr mahng-uh **bon** haa rdü?*	Kor mange born har du? (NN)
*vurr mahng-uh **baa-rn** haa rdü?*	Hvor mange barn har du? (BM)

I don't have any children.

*eh **hahch**-uh nor-kon bon*	Eg har ikkje nokon born. (NN)
*ya **hahk**-kuh noon baa-rn*	Jeg har ikke noen barn. (BM)

I have a daughter/a son.

*eh haarr ay **dot**-tuhrr/ayn **sorn***	Eg har ei dotter/ein son. (NN)
*ya haarr ay **daht**-tuhrr/ehn **sern***	Jeg har ei datter/en sønn. (BM)

How many brothers/sisters do you have?

*kurr mahng-uh **sȳsh**-uhn haa rdü?*	Kor mange sysken har du? (NN)
*vurr mahng-uh **sers**-kuhn haa rdü?*	Hvor mange søsken har du? (BM)

Is your husband/wife here?

*ärr **mahn**-n deen härr/ärr **kor**-nah dee härr?*	Er mannen din her?/Er kona di her? (NN)
*ärr **mahn**-n deen härr/ärr **koo**-nah dee härr?*	Er mannen din her?/Er kona di her? (BM)

Do you have a boyfriend/girlfriend?

*haa rdü **fahst fer-l-yuh**?*	Har du fast fylgje? (NN)
*haa dü **fahst fer-l-luh**?*	Har du fast følge? (BM)

brother	*brroorr*	bror
children	*baa-rn*	barn
daughter	*dot-tuhrr*	dotter (NN)
	daht-tuhrr	datter (BM)
family	*fah-mēē-lee-uh*	familie
father	*faarr*	far
grandfather	**behs**-*tuh-faarr*	bestefar
grandmother	**behs**-*tuh-moorr*	bestemor
husband	*mahn*	mann
mother	*moorr*	mor
sister	*sȳs-tuhrr*	syster (NN)
	ser-s-tuhrr	søster (BM)
son	*sor-n*	son (NN)
	ser-n	sønn (BM)
wife	*kor-nuh*	kone (NN)
	koo-nuh	kone (BM)

Feelings

I (don't) like …
  eh lēē-kuhrr (eech-uh) …   Eg liker (ikkje) … (NN)
  ya lēē-kuhrr (eek-uh) …   Jeg liker (ikke) … (BM)

I feel cold/hot.	*eh frrȳȳs/eh haa rdeh vahrrnt*	Eg frys./Eg har det varmt. (NN)
	ya frrȳȳs-uhrr/ya haa rdeh vah-rnt	Jeg fryser./Jeg har det varmt. (BM)
I am hungry/ thirsty.	*ēg ā svol-tuhn/ ter-sht*	Eg er svolten/ tørst. (NN)
	ya ā shül-tuhn/ ter-sht	Jeg har sulten/ tørst. (BM)

I am in a hurry.	*eh haarr **hahst-varrk***	Eg har hastverk. (NN)
	*ya haarr **hahst-varrk***	Jeg har hastverk. (BM)
You are right.	*dü haa **rreht***	Du har rett.
I am sleepy.	*ēg ā **sher-v-nee***	Eg er søvnig. (NN)
	*ya ā **sher-v-nee***	Jeg er søvnig. (BM)

I am ...		
ēg ārr ...		Eg er ... (NN)
ya ārr ...		Jeg er ... (BM)
angry	***seen-nah***	sinna
happy/sad	***lȳk-kuh-lee/nē-forr***	lykkelig/nedfor
tired	***trrer-t***	trøtt
well	***brraa***	bra
worried	***ü-rroo-leh***	uroleg (NN)
	ü-rroo-lee	urolig (BM)

I am sorry. (condolence)
kon-du-lē-rruhrr Kondolerer.
I am grateful.
*ēg ā **tahk-sahm*** Eg er takksam. (NN)
*ya ā **tahk-nehm-lee*** Jeg er takknemlig. (BM)

Language Difficulties
Do you speak English?
*snah-kah rdü **ehng-uhlsk**?* Snakkar du engelsk? (NN)
*snah-kuh rdü **ehng-uhlsk**?* Snakker du engelsk? (BM)

Does anyone speak English?
*ä deh nor-kon som snah-kahrr **ehng**-uhlsk harr?*
*ä deh noon som snah-kuhrr **ehng**-uhlsk harr?*

Er det nokon som snakkar engelsk her? (NN)
Er det noen som snakker engelsk her? (BM)

I speak a little ...
*eh snah-kahrr **leet** ...*
*ya snah-kuh **leet** ...*

Eg snakkar litt ... (NN)
Jeg snakker litt ... (BM)

I don't speak ...
*eh snah-kahrr **ee**-chuh ...*
*ya snah-kuhrr **eek**-kuh ...*

Eg snakkar ikkje ... (NN)
Jeg snakker ikke ... (BM)

I (don't) understand.
*eh fosh-**tor-rr** (eechuh)*
*ya fosh-**tor-rr** (eekuh)*

Eg forstår (ikkje). (NN)
Jeg forstår (ikkje). (BM)

Could you speak more slowly please?
*kahn dü snah-kuh **lahng**-sah-mah-rruh?*
*kahn dü snah-kuh **lahng**-som-muh-rruh?*

Kan du snakke lang-samare? (NN)
Kan du snakke lang-sommere? (BM)

Could you repeat that?
*kahn dü **yehn**-tah dē?*

Kan du gjenta det?

How do you say ...?
kvaa hay-tuhrr ... por noshk?
vaa hē-tuhrr ... por noshk?

Kva heiter ... på norsk? (NN)
Hva heter ... på norsk? (BM)

What does ... mean?
*kvaa buh-**tӯӯrr** ...?*
*vaa buh-**tӯӯrr** ...?*

Kva betyr ...? (NN)
Va betyr ...? (BM)

I speak ...
  eh snah-kahrr ...
  ya snah-kuhrr ...

English	*ehng-ehlsk*	engelsk
French	*frrahnsk*	fransk
German	*tÿsk*	tysk
Norwegian	*noshk*	norsk
Spanish	*spahnsk*	spansk

Eg snakkar ... (NN)
Jeg snakker ... (BM)

Some Useful Phrases

Sure.
  veest — Visst.

Just a minute.
  vehnt leet — Vent litt.

It's (not) important.
  deh ärr (eech-uh) veek-tee — Det er (ikkje) viktig. (NN)
  deh ärr (eek-uh) veek-tee — Det er (ikke) viktig. (BM)

It's (not) possible.
  deh är (eech-uh) mor-gleh — Det er (ikkje) mogleg. (NN)
  deh är (eek-uh) müü-lee — Det er (ikke) mulig. (BM)

Wait!
  vehnt! — Vent!

Good luck!
  lÿk-kuh teel! — Lykke til! (BM)

Signs

BAGGAGE COUNTER	REISEGODS
CHECK-IN COUNTER	BAGASJEINNLEVERING
CUSTOMS	TOLL
EMERGENCY EXIT	NØDUTGANG

NORWEGIAN

ENTRANCE	INNGANG
EXIT	UTGANG
FREE ADMISSION	GRATIS TILGJENGE (NN)
	GRATIS ADGANG (BM)
HOT/COLD	VARM/KALD
INFORMATION	OPPLYSNINGAR (NN)
	OPPLYSNINGER (BM)
NO ENTRY	IKKJE TILGJENGE (NN)
	INGEN ADGANG (BM)
NO SMOKING	IKKJE RØYK (NN)
	RØYKING FORBUDT (BM)
OPEN/CLOSED	OPEN/STENGD (NN)
	ÅPEN/STENGT (BM)
PROHIBITED	FORBODE (NN)
	FORBUDT (BM)
RESERVED	RESERVERT
TELEPHONE	TELEFON
TOILETS	TOALETTAR (NN)
	TOALETTER (BM)

NORWEGIAN

Emergencies

| POLICE | POLITI |
| POLICE STATION | POLITISTASJON/ LENS-MANNSKONTOR |

Help!
  yehlp!   Hjelp!

It's an emergency!

deht-tuh ārr eht ah-küt-teel-fehl-luh! — Dette er eit akutt-tilfelle! (NN)

deht-tuh ārr eht ah-küt-teel-fehl-luh! — Dette er et akutt-tilfelle! (BM)

There's been an accident!

deh haa shehd ay üü-lȳk-kuh! — Det har skjedd ei ulykke!

Call a doctor!

rreeng ehn lē-guh! — Ring ein lege!

Call an ambulance!

rreeng eht-tuhr ehn shüü-kuh-bēēl! — Ring etter ein sjukebil!

I've been raped.

ēg ārr vahl-tē-kuhn. — Eg er valdteken. (NN)

ya ārr vol-taht — Jeg er voldtatt. (BM)

I've been robbed.

ēg ārr rraa-nah — Eg er rana. (NN)

ya ārr rraa-nah — Jeg er rana. (BM)

Call the police!

rreeng pu-lee-tēē-uh! — Ring politiet!

Where is the police station?

kvaarr ārr pu-lee-tēē-stah-shoon-n? — Kvar er politistasjonen? (NN)

vurr ārr pu-lee-tēē-stah-shoon-n? — Hvor er politistasjonen? (BM)

Go away!/Buzz off!

fo-shveen!/peeg-aav! — Forsvinn!/Pigg av!

I'll call the police!
eh teel-kahl-lahr pu-lee-tēē-uh!   Eg tilkallar politiet! (NN)

ya teel-kahl-luhr pu-lee-tēē-uh!   Jeg tilkaller politiet! (BM)

Thief!
chüüv!   Tjuv! (NN)

tȳȳv!   Tyv! (BM)

I am ill.
ēg ārr shüük   Eg er sjuk. (NN)

yay ā shüük   Jeg er sjuk. (BM)

I am lost.
ēg haarr got meh veel   Eg har gått meg vill. (NN)

ya haarr got meh veel   Jeg har gått meg vill. (BM)

Where are the toilets?
kvaarr ārr tuah-leht-tah-nuh?   Kvar er toalettane? (NN)

vurr ārr tuah-leht-tuh-nuh?   Hvor er toalettene? (BM)

Could you help me please?
kahn dü yehl-puh meh kahn-shuh?   Kan du hjelpe meg kanskje?

Could I please use the telephone?
kahn eh for lor-nuh t eh-leh-foon-n?   Kan eg få låne telefonen? (NN)

kahn ya for lor-nuh teh-leh-foon-n?   Kan jeg få låne telefonen? (BM)

I'm sorry.
ēg ā lay fo rdē   Eg er lei for det. (NN)

yay ā lay fo rdē   Jeg er lei for det. (BM)

I didn't realise I was doing anything wrong.

*eh vaarr eech-uh **klaarr** or-vuhrr aht eh yoo-rruh nor-ko **gaa**-luh*

Eg var ikkje klar over at eg gjorde noko gale. (NN)

*ya vaarr eek-kuh **klaarr** or-vuhrr aht ya yoo-rruh noo-uh **gaalt***

Jeg var ikke klar over at jeg gjorde noe galt. (BM)

I didn't do it.

*ēg haarr **eech**-uh yu-rt dē*

Eg har ikkje gjort det. (NN)

*ya haarr **eek**-kuh yu-rt dē*

Jeg har ikke gjort det. (BM)

I wish to contact my embassy/consulate.

*va-sho-**sneel** o laa meh for kon-**tahk**-tuh ahm-bah-**saa**-dn meen/kon-sü-**laa**-tuh meet*

Ver så snill og la meg få kontakte ambassaden min/konsulatet mitt. (NN)

*va-sho-**sneel** o laa meh for kon-**tahk**-tuh meen ahm-bah-**saa**-duh/meet kon-sü-**laat***

Vær så snill og la meg få kontakte min ambass-ade/mitt konsulat. (BM)

I speak English.

*eh snah-**kahrr** **ehng**-uhlsk*

Eg snakkar engelsk. (NN)

*ya snah-**kuhrr** **ehng**-uhlsk*

Jeg snakker engelsk. (BM)

I have medical insurance.

*ēg haa **shüü**-kuh-fo-**sheek**-rreeng*

Eg har sjukeforsikring. (NN)

*ya haa **shüü**-kuh-fo-**sheek**-rreeng*

Jeg har sjukeforsikring. (BM)

My possessions are insured.

ayg-nuh-lüüt-nuh mēē-nuh	Eignelutene mine er
ărr fo-sheek-rra	forsikra. (NN)
ay-uhn-dē-luh-nuh mēē-nuh	Eiendelene mine er
ărr fo-sheek-rruht	forsikret. (BM)

My ... was stolen.

... meen ărr stor-luhn	... min er stolen. (NN)
... meen ărr styor-luht	... min er stjålet. (BM)

I've lost ...

eh haarr mees-tah ...	Eg har mista ... (NN)
ya haarr mees-tah ...	Jeg har mista ... (BM)
my bags	*bah-gaa-shuhn meen*	bagasjen min
my handbag	*vehs-kah mē*	veska mi
my money	*pehng-ah-nuh mēē-nuh*	pengane mine
my travellers' cheques	*rray-suh-shehk-kah-nuh mēē-nuh*	reisesjekkane mine
my passport	*pahs-suh meet*	passet mitt

Paperwork

name	*nahmn*	namn (NN)
	nahvn	navn (BM)
address	*ah-drreh-suh*	adresse
date of birth	*fer-t-suhls-daa-tu*	fødselsdato
place of birth	*fēr-duh-staa*	fødestad (NN)
	fēr-duh-stē	fødested (BM)
age	*ahl-duhrr*	alder
sex	*cher-n*	kjønn
nationality	*nah-shu-nah-lee-tēt*	nasjonalitet
religion	*rreh-lee-gyoon*	religion

reason for travel	*seek-tuh-mor-luh*	siktemålet med
	meh rray-sah	reisa (NN)
	hehn-seekt meh	hensikt med
	rray-sn	reisen (BM)
profession	*ŷrr-kuh*	yrke
marital status	*see-vēēl-stahn*	sivilstand
passport	*pahs*	pass
passport number	*pahs-num-muhrr*	passnummer
visa	*vēē-süm*	visum
tourist card	*tü-rreest-ku-rt*	turistkort
identification	*lē-gē-tee-mē-rreeng*	legetimering
birth certificate	*fer-ts-ls-aht-tehst*	fødselsattest
driver's licence	*fēr-rrahrr-kurrt*	førarkort (NN)
	fēr-rruhrr-ko-rt	førerkort (BM)
car owner's title	*vong-n-ko-rt*	vognkort
car registration	*chehn-nuh-taykn*	kjenneteikn (NN)
	chehn-nuh-tayn	kjennetegn (BM)
customs	*tol*	toll
immigration	*een-vahn-drreeng*	innvandring
border	*grrehn-suh*	grense

Getting Around

ARRIVALS	INNKOMST (NN)
	ANKOMST (BM)
BUS STOP	BUSSTOPP
DEPARTURES	AVGANG
STATION	STASJON
SUBWAY	T-BANE
TICKET OFFICE	BILETTKONTOR
TIMETABLE	RUTEPLAN
TRAIN STATION	JERNBANESTASJON

NORWEGIAN

What time does ... leave/
arrive?

   kaa tēē gor-rr/cheh-m ...?   Kva tid går/kjem ...? (NN)

   norr gor-rr/kom-muhrr ...?   Når går/kommer ...? (BM)

the (air)plane	*flȳȳ-yuh*	flyet
the boat	*bor-tn*	båten
the bus (citybus)	*büsn (bȳȳ-büsn)*	bussen (bybussen)
the bus (intercity)	*büsn (leen-yuh-büsn)*	bussen (linje-bussen)
the train	*tor-guh*	toget
the tram	*trreek-kuh-n*	trikken

Directions

Where is ...?

   kurr ārr ...?   Kor er ...? (NN)

   vurr ārr ...?   Hvor er ārr ...? (BM)

How do I get to ...?

   kurr-lays chehm ēg teel ...?   Korleis kjem eg til ...? (NN)

   vu-rdahn kom-muhrr ya teel ...?   Hvordan kommer jeg til ...? (BM)

Is it far from/near here?

   ā deh lahngt hārr-ee-frror?   Er det langt herifrå? (NN)

   ā rdeh lahngt hārr-frrah?   Er det langt herfra? (BM)

Can I walk there?

   kahn eh gor dēēt?   Kan eg gå dit? (NN)

   kahn ya gor dēēt?   Kan jeg gå dit? (BM)

Can you show me (on the map)?

   kahn dü vēē-suh mā (po kah-rtuh)?   Kan du vise meg (på kartet)?

NORWEGIAN

Are there other means of
getting there?

*ā rdeh ehn **ahn**-nahn mor-tuh o kor-muh dēēt po?*	Er det ein annan måte å kome dit på? (NN)
*ā rdeh ehn **aa**-uhn mor-tuh or kom-muh dēēt po?*	Er det en annen måte å komme dit på? (BM)

I want to go to …

eh skahl teel …	Eg skal til … (NN)
ya skahl teel …	Jeg skal til … (BM)

Go straight ahead.

*deh ā **rreht** frrahm*	Det er rett fram.

It's two blocks down.

deh ā too kvah-rtaal vēē-ah-rruh	Det er to kvartal vidare. (NN)
deh ā too kvah-rtaal vēē-duh-rruh	Det er to kvartal videre. (BM)

Turn right …

*taa teel **hēr**-grruh …*	Ta til høgre. (NN)
*taa teel **höy**-rruh …*	Ta til høyre. (BM)

Turn left …

taa teel vehns-trruh …	Ta til venstre …

at the next corner

*veh **nehs**-tuh yēr-nuh*	ved neste hjørnet

at the traffic lights.

veh lȳȳs-krrȳs-suh	ved lyskrysset

behind	*bak*	bak
in front of	***frrahm**-fo-rr*	framfor
far	*lahngt*	langt
near	*nārr*	nær
opposite	*or-vuhrr-**fo-rr***	overfor

Buying Tickets

Excuse me, where is the ticket
office?

*ün-shȳl **kurr** ärr bee-leht-*
lüü-kah?

Unnskyld, kor er
billettluka? (NN)

*ün-shȳl **vurr** ärr bee-leht-*
lüü-kah?

Unnskyld, hvor er
billettluka? (BM)

Where can I buy a ticket?

***kurr** kahn eh löysuh*
bee-leht?

Kor kan eg løyse bilett?
(NN)

***vurr** kahn ya lēr-suh*
bee-leht?

Hvor kan jeg løse billett?
(BM)

I want to go to ...

eh skahl teel ...

Eg skal til ... (NN)

ya skahl teel ...

Jeg skal til ... (BM)

Do I need to book?

ä deh ner-d-vehn-dee o
buh-steel-luh plahs?

Er det nødvendig å bestille
plass?

You need to book.

*dü **mor** buhsteel-luh plahs*

Du må bestille plass.

I would like to book a seat
to ...

eh veel yā-rnuh buh-steel-
luh see-chuh-plahs teel ...

Eg vil gjerne bestille sitje-
plass til ... (NN)

ya veel yā-rnuh buh-steel-
luh see-tuh-plahs teel ...

Jeg vil gjerne bestille sitte-
plass til ... (BM)

I would like ...

eh veel yā-rnuh haa ...

Eg vil gjerne ha ... (NN)

ya veel yā-rnuh haa ...

Jeg vil gjerne ha ... (BM)

a one-way ticket   ***ehn-kehlt-bee-leht***   enkeltbillett

a return ticket   ***tüü-rruh-tüürr***   tur-retur

two tickets	*too bee-leht-tahrr*	to billettar
tickets for all of us	*beeleh-tahrr teel os ahl-luh sah-mahn*	billettar til oss alle saman
a student's fare	*stü-dehnt-rah-baht*	studentrabatt
a child's/pensioner's fare	*baa-rnuh-bee-leht/ ho-nēr-rr-bee-leht*	barnebillett/honnør-billett
1st class	*fer-sh-tuh klahs-suh*	første klasse
2nd class	*ahn-drruh klahs-suh*	andre klasse
	aa-uhn klahs-suh	annen klasse (BM)

It is full.
deh ärr fült   Det er fullt.

Is it completely full?
ä deh haylt fült?   Er det heilt fullt?

Can I get a stand-by ticket?
kahn eh for ehn shahn-suh-bee-leht?   Kan eg få ein sjansebillett? (NN)

kahn ya for uhn shahn-suh-bee-leht?   Kan jeg få en sjansebilett? (BM)

Air

| CHECK-IN | INNSJEKKING |
| LUGGAGE PICKUP | BAGASJETRALLE |

Is there a flight to …?
ä deh eht flȳȳ teel …?   Er det eit fly til …?

When is the next flight to …?
no-rr ä nehs-tuh flȳȳ-yuh til …?   Når er neste flyet til …?

How long does the flight take?
kurr lehng-uh tēk flȳȳ-yeeng-ah? — Kor lenge tek flyginga? (NN)
vurr lehng-uh taarr flȳȳ-geeng-ah? — Hvor lenge tar flyginga? (BM)

What is the flight number?
kaa ärr flait-nu-muh-rruh? — Kva er flightnummeret? (NN)
vaa ärr flait-nu-muh-rruh? — Hva er flightnummeret? (BM)

You must check in at …
dü mor shehk-kuh een veh … — Du må sjekke inn ved …

airport tax	*lüft-hahmn-aa-yeeft*	lufthamnavgift (NN)
	lüft-hahvn-aav-yeeft	lufthavnavgift (BM)
boarding pass	*um-boo-rr-stēēg(n)eeng-sko-rt*	ombordstig(n)ings-kort
customs	*tol*	toll

Bus

BUS/TRAM STOP	BUSS/TRIKKHALDEPLASS (NN) BUSS/TRIKKHOLDEPLASS (BM)

Where is the bus/tram stop?
kvaarr ärr büs/trreek-hahl-duh-plahsn? — Kvar er buss/trikkhaldeplassen? (NN)
vurr ärr büs/trreek-hol-luh-plahsn? — Hvor er buss/trikkholdeplassen? (BM)

NORWEGIAN

Which bus goes to …?
 kvaa büs gor rteel …? Kva buss går til …? (NN)
 veel-kuhn büs gor rteel …? Hvilken buss går til …? (BM)
Does this bus go to …?
 gor rdehn-nuh büsn teel …? Går denne bussen til …?
How often do buses pass by?
 kurr mahng-uh büs-sahrr Kor mange bussar går det?
 gor-rdeh?   (NN)
 vurr mahng-uh büs-suhrr Hvor mange busser går det?
 gor-rdeh?   (BM)

What time is the … bus?
 kaa tēē chehm … büsn? Kva tid kjem …-bussen? (NN)
 no-rr kom-muhr … büsn? Når kommer …-bussen? (BM)

next	**nehs-tuh**	neste
first	**fer-shtuh**	første
last	**sees-tuh**	siste

Train

DINING CAR	SPISEVOGN
EXPRESS	EKSPRESSTOG
PLATFORM NO	SPOR
SLEEPING CAR	SOVEVOGN

Is this the right platform
for …?
 ã rdeht-tuh rreht-tuh plaht- Er dette rette plattforma for
 fo-rr-mah fo-rr tor-guh toget til …?
 teel …?

The train leaves from
platform …
   tor-guh gor-rr frror   Toget går frå spor …
   spoorr …

Passengers must …
   rray-sahn-duh mor …   Reisande må … (NN)
   rray-suhn-duh mor …   Reisende må … (BM)

change trains	*bȳt-tuh tor-g*	byte tog
change platforms	*gor teel spoorr* …	gå til spor …
dining car	*spēē-suh-vong-n*	spisevogn
express	*ehks-prrehs-tor-g*	ekspresstog
local	*lu-kaal-tor-g*	lokaltog
sleeping car/	*sor-vuh-vong-n/*	sovevogn/ligge-
couchette car	*leeg-guh-vong-n*	vogn

Metro

METRO/UNDERGROUND	T-BANE
CHANGE (for coins)	VEKSLING
THIS WAY TO	(DENNE VEGEN) TIL
WAY OUT	UTGANG

Which line takes me to …?
   kvaa leen-yuh/baa-nuh mor   Kva linje/bane må eg ta til
   eh taa teel …?   …? (NN)
   veel-kuhn leen-yuh/baa-   hvilken linje/bane må eg ta
   nuh mor eh taa teel …?   til …? (BM)Taxi
What is the next station?
   kvaa ā rnehs-tuh   Kva er neste stasjon? (NN)
   stah-shoon?
   vaa ā rnehs-tuh   Hva er neste stasjon? (BM)
   stah-shoon?

Taxi

Where can I get hold of a taxi? (NN)

*korr kahn eh for **taak** ee ay drro-shuh?*
Kor kan eg få tak i ei drosje? (NN)

*vorr kahn ya for **taak** ee ay drro-shuh?*
Hvor kan jeg få tak i ei drosje? (BM)

Can you take me to …?

*kahn dü **chēr-rruh mā teel** …?*
Kan du kjøre meg til …?

Please take me to …

*veel dü **chēr-rruh mā teel** …?*
Vil du kjøre meg til …?

How much does it cost to go to …?

*korr **mȳch-uh** kos-tarr deh o chy-rruh teel …?*
Kor mykje kostar det å køyre til …? (NN)

*vorr **mȳȳ-yuh** kos-tuhrr deh o chēr-rruh teel …?*
Hvor mye koster det å kjøre til …? (BM)

Instructions

Here is fine, thank you.

*dü kahn **stop-puh hārr**, tahk*
Du kan stoppe her, takk.

The next corner, please.

*kahn dü **stop-puh** veh nehs-tuh yēr-rnuh*
Kan du stoppe ved neste hjørnet?

Continue!

***furt**-sheht bah-rruh!*
Fortsett bare!

The next street to the left/right.

*nehs-tuh gaa-tah teel **vehn-strruh/hēr-grruh** (hȫy-rruh)*
Neste gata til venstre/høgre. (BM: høyre)

Stop here!
stop härr!   Stopp her!
Please slow down.
*vä sho **sneel** o chöyrr leet   Ver så snill og køyr litt
lahng-sah-mah-rruh*   langsamare. (NN)
*vä sho **sneel** o chør-rr leet   Vær så snill og kjør litt
lahng-som-muh-rruh*   langsommere. (BM)
Please wait here.
*värr sor sneel o **vehn**-tuh   Ver så snill å vente her. (NN)
härr*
*värr sor sneel o **vehn**-tuh   Vær så snill å vente her.
härr*   (BM)

Car

DETOUR	OMKJØRING
FREEWAY	MOTORVEG
GARAGE	GARASJE
GIVE WAY	VIKEPLIKT
MECHANIC	MEKANIKAR (NN)
	MEKANIKER (BM)
NO ENTRY	INNKJØRING FORBODE (NN)
	INNKJØRING FORBUDT (BM)
NO PARKING	PARKERING FORBODE (NN)
	PARKERING FORBUDT (BM)
NORMAL	NORMAL

ONE WAY	EINVEGSKØYRING (NN)
	ENVEISKJØRING (BM)
REPAIRS	BILVERSTAD (NN)
	BILVERKSTED (BM)
SELF SERVICE	SJØLVBETJENING (NN)
	SELVBETJENING (BM)
STOP	STOPP
SUPER	SUPER
UNLEADED	BLYFRI

Where can I rent a car?
*kurr kahn eh **lay**-guh ehn **bēēl?*** — Kor kan eg leige ein bil? (NN)
*vurr kahn ya **lay**-uh uhn **bēēl?*** — Hvor kan jeg leie en bil? (BM)

How much is it …?
*korr **mȳchuh** kos-tarr deh …?* — Kor mykje kostar det …? (NN)
*vorr **mȳȳyuh** kos-tuhrr deh …?* — Hvor mye koster det …? (BM)

daily/weekly
*parr **daag**/vē-kuh* — pr. dag/veke (NN)
*parr **daag**/üü-kuh* — pr. dag/uke (BM)

Does that include insurance/mileage?
*ārr deh **mē**-rehk-nah fo-**sheek**-reengofrrēē **chēry**-rruh-aa-stahn?* — Er det medrekna forsikring og fri køyreavstand? (NN)
*ārrdeh **mē**-rehng-nah fo-**sheek**-reeng/frrēē **chēr**-rruh-aa-stahn?* — Er det medrekna forsikring og fri køjreavstand? (BM)

Where's the next petrol
station?

kurr ā *narr-mahs-tuh behn-*
sēēn-stah-shoon-n?
vurr ā *rnarr-muhs-tuh*
behn-sēēn-stah-shoon-n?

Kor er nærmaste
bensinstasjonen? (NN)
Hvor er nærmeste
bensinstasjonen? (BM)

Please fill the tank.

fül tahngk tahk

Full tank, takk.

I want ... litres of petrol (gas).

eh veel haa ... lēē-tuhrr
ben-sēēn
ya veel haa ... lēē-tuhrr
ben-sēēn

Eg vil ha ... liter bensin.
(NN)
Jeg vil ha ... liter bensin.
(BM)

Please check the oil and water.

kahn dü shehk-kuh ul-yuh
og vahtn/vahn?

Kan du sjekke olje og vatn
(BM: vann)?

How long can I park here?

kurr lehng-uh kan bēēl-n
meen stor hārr?
vurr lehng-uh kan bēēl-n
meen stor hārr?

Kor lenge kan bilen min stå
her? (NN)
Hvor lenge kan bilen min
stå her? (BM)

Does this road lead to ...?

ā dehtuh vē-yuhn teel ...?

Er dette vegen til ...?

air (for tyres)	*lüft*	luft
battery	*baht-tuh-rrēē*	batteri
brakes	*brrehm-suhrr*	bremser
clutch	*kler-ch*	kløtsj
driver's licence	*fēr-rrahrr-ko-rt*	førarkort (NN)
	fēr-rruhrr-ko-rt	førerkort (BM)
engine	*moo-turr*	motor

lights	*lȳk-tuhrr*	lykter
oil	*ul-yuh*	olje
puncture	*pung-tē-rreeng*	punktering
radiator	*rrahdee-yaa-turr*	radiator
road map	*kah-rt*	kart
tyres	*dehk*	dekk
windscreen	*frront-rrüü-tuh*	frontrute

Some Useful Phrases

The train is delayed/cancelled.

tor-guh ārr fo-sheeng-kah/een-steelt

Toget er forsinka/innstilt.

How long will it be delayed?

kurr mȳch-uh ā deh fo-sheeng-kah?

Kor mykje er det forseinka? (NN)

vurr mȳȳ-yuh ā deh fo-sheeng-kah?

Hvor mye er det forsinka? (BM)

There is a delay of … hours.

tor-guh ārr … tēē-mahrr ehtuhrr rüü-tuh

Toget er … timar etter rute. (NN)

tor-guh ārr … tēē-muhrr ehtuhrr rüü-tuh

Toget er … timer etter rute. (BM)

Can I reserve a seat?

kahn eh buh-steel-luh plass?

Kan eg bestille plass? (NN)

kahn ya buh-steel-luh plass?

Kan jeg bestille plass? (BM)

How long does the trip take?

kurr lehng-uh tēk rray-sah?

Kor lenge tek reisa? (NN)

vurr lehng-uh taarr rray-sah?

Hvor lenge tar reisa? (BM)

Is it a direct route?
   *ã deh eht dee-**rrehk**-tuh*   Er det eit direkte tog? (NN)
   tor-g?
   *ã deh eht dee-**rrehk**-tuh*   Er det et direkte tog? (BM)
   tor-g?

Is that seat taken?
   *ã **dehn**-nuh stoo-ln up-taht?*   Er denne stolen opptatt?

I want to get off at …
   eh veel gor aav ee …   Eg vil gå av i … (NN)
   ya veel gor aav ee …   Jeg vil gå av i … (BM)

Excuse me.
   ün-shȳl   Unnskyld.

Where can I hire a bicycle?
   *kvaarr kahn eh for **lay**-guh*   Kvar kan eg få leige ein
   ehn sȳk-kuhl?   sykkel? (NN)
   vurr kahn ya lay-uh uhn   Hvor kan jeg leie en
   sȳk-kuhl?   sykkel? (BM)

Car Problems

I need a mechanic.
   *eh haarr **brrüük** fo-rr ayn*   Eg har bruk for ein
   beel-meh-kaa-nee-kahrr   bilmekanikar. (NN)
   *ya haarr **brrüük** fo-rr uhn*   Jeg har bruk for en
   beel-meh-kaa-nee-kuhrr   bilmekaniker. (BM)

What make is it?
   *kvaa fo-rr **marr**-kuh ã rdeh*   Kva for merke er det det
   deh yehld?   gjeld? (NN)
   *veel-kuht **marr**-kuh ã rdeh?*   Hvilket merke er det? (BM)

The battery is flat.
   *baht-tuh-**rrēē**-uh ãrr **flaht***   Batteriet er flatt.

The radiator is leaking.
   *rrah-dee-**aa**-too-rn ã **rlehk***   Radiatoren er lekk.

I have a flat tyre.
yüü-luh ärr pung-tē-rt   Hjulet er punktert.
It's overheating.
moo-tu-rn koo-kahrr   Motoren kokar. (NN)
mootu-rn koo-kuhrr   Motoren koker. (BM)
It's not working.
deh füng-gē-rruhrr eech-uh   Det fungerer ikkje. (NN)
deh füng-gē-rruhrr eek-kuh   Det fungerer ikke. (BM)

Accommodation

CAMPING GROUND	KAMPING/LEIRPLASS
GUESTHOUSE	GJESTGIVERI/
	PENSIONAT
HOTEL	HOTELL
YOUTH HOSTEL	VANDRERHJEM

I am looking for …
eh ärr por layt ehturr …   Eg er på leit etter … (NN)
ya lay-tuhrr ehturr …   Jeg leiter etter … (BM)

Where is …?
kvaarr ärr …?   Kvar er …? (NN)
vurr ärr …?   Hvor er …? (BM)

a cheap hotel	*eht beel-lee hu-tehl*	eit (BM et) billig hotell
a good hotel	*eht got hu-tehl*	eit godt hotell (NN)
	eht got hu-tehl	et godt hotell (BM)
a nearby hotel	*eht hu-tehl ee närr-laykuhn*	eit hotell i nærleiken (NN)
	eht hu-tehl ee närr-hētah	et hotell i nærheten (BM)

| a nice/quaint hotel | *eht koo-shleh/gahm-mahl-dahks hu-tehl* | eit koseleg/gam-maldags hotell (NN) |
| | *eht koo-shlee/gahm-mahl-dahks hu-tehl* | et koselig/gam-meldags hotell (BM) |

What is the address?
| *kvaa ärr ah-drrehs-ah?* | Kva er adressa? (NN) |
| *vaa ärr ah-drrehs-ah?* | Hva er adressa? (BM) |

Could you write the address, please?
| *kahn dü vä-rruh so sneel o skrrēē-vuh up ah-drrehs-ah?* | Kan du vere (BM være) så snill å skrive opp adressa? |

At the Hotel

Do you have any rooms available?
| *haa rdü lē-dee-uh rrum?* | Har du ledige rom? |

I would like ...
| *eh veel yä-nuh ...* | Eg vil gjerne ... (NN) |
| *ya veel yä-rnuh ...* | Jeg vil gjerne ... (BM) |

a single room	*haa eht ehng-kuhlt-rrum*	ha eit enkeltrom
a double room	*haa eht dob-uhlt-rrum*	ha eit dobbeltrom
a room with a bathroom	*haa eht rrum meh baad*	ha eit rom med bad
to share a dorm	*leeg-guh por sor-vuh-saa-luhn*	ligge på sovesalen

NORWEGIAN

Do you have identification?

haa rdü lē-gee-tee-mah-shoon? — Har du legitimasjon?

Your membership card, please.

mē-lehms-ko-rtuh deet tahk — Medlemskortet ditt, takk.

Sorry, we're full.

eh ā lay fo dē men deh ārr fült — Eg er lei for det men det er fullt. (NN)

buh-klaa-guhrr deh ārr fült — Beklager, det er fullt. (BM)

How long will you be staying?

kurr lehng-yuh blēē-rr dü hārr? — Kor lengje blir du her? (NN)

vurr lehng-uh blēē-rr dü hārr? — Hvor lenge blir du her? (BM)

How many nights?

kurr mahng-uh neht-tuhr? — Kor mange netter? (NN)

vurr mahng-uh neht-tuhr? — Hvor mange netter? (BM)

It's ... per day/per person.

deh ārr ... pa rdaag/parr pa-shoon — Det er ... pr. dag/pr. person.

There are four of us.

vee ārr fēē-rruh stÿk-kuh (stÿk-kuhrr) — Vi er fire stykke (BM: stykker).

I want a room with a ...

eh veel yā-nuh haa eht rrum meh ... — Eg vil gjerne ha eit rom med ... (NN)

ya veel yā-nuh haa uht rrum meh ... — Jeg vil gjerne ha et rom med ... (BM)

bathroom	*baad*	bad
shower	*düsh*	dusj

television	**fyā-rn**-*sȳȳn*	fjernsyn
window	**veen**-*dü*	vindauge (NN)
	veen-*dü*	vindu (BM)

I'm going to stay for ...

*eh haa **tehnkt** o blēē hārr* — Eg har tenkt å bli her i ...
ee ... — (NN)
*ya haa **tehnkt** o blēē hārr* — Jeg har tenkt å bli her i ...
ee ... — (BM)

one day	**ayn daag**	ein dag
two days	**too daa**-*gahrr*	to dagar
one week	*ay **vē**-kuh*	ei veke

How much is it per night/per person?

*kurr **mȳch**-uh ā deh pa* — Kor mykje er det pr. dag/pr.
rdaag/*parr pa-shoon?* — person? (NN)
*vurr **mȳȳ**-yuh ā deh pa* — Vor mye er det pr. dag/pr.
rdaag/*parr pa-shoon?* — person? (BM)

Can I see it?

kahn eh for shor deh? — Kan eg få sjå det? (NN)
kahn ya for se deh? — Kan jeg få se det? (BM)

Are there any others?

*haa rdü **ahn**-drruh?* — Har du andre?

Are there any cheaper rooms?

*haa rdü **beel**-leh-gah-rruh* — Har du billegare rom? (NN)
rrum?
*haa rdü **beel**-lee-uh-rruh* — Har du billigere rom? (BM)
rrum?

Can I see the bathroom?

*kahn eh fo **shor** baa-duh?* — Kan eg få sjå badet? (NN)
kahn eh fo se baa-duh? — Kan eg få se badet? (BM)

Is there a reduction for
students/children?

*yēē rdü stü-**dehnt**-rrah-
baht/**baa**-rnuh-rrah-**baht**?*　　Gir du studentrabatt/
　　　　　　　　　　　　　　　barnerabatt?

Does it include breakfast?

***frrüü*-kostn mē-rrehk-nah?*　　Frukosten medrekna? (NN)
*eenklȳ-sēēv-uh **frroo**-kostn?*　　Inklusive frokosten? (BM)

It's fine, I'll take it.

***brraa** eh tēk deh*　　　　　　Bra, eg tek det. (NN)
***brraa** ya taa rdeh*　　　　　　Bra, jeg tar det. (BM)

I'm not sure how long I'm
staying.

*eh vayt ēēch-uh kurr
lehng-uh eh skah blēē
vā-rrahn-duh hārr*　　　　　　Eg veit ikkje kor lenge eg
　　　　　　　　　　　　　　　skal bli verande her. (NN)

*ya vayt ēēk-kuh vurr
leh-ng-uh ya skah blēē
vā-rruh-nuh hārr*　　　　　　　Jeg veit ikke hvor lenge jeg
　　　　　　　　　　　　　　　skal bli værende her. (BM)

Is there a lift?

*feens deh uhn **hays** hārr?*　　Finst det ein heis her? (NN)
*feens deh uhn **hays** hārr?*　　Fins det en heis her? (BM)

Where is the bathroom?

*kurr ārr **baa**-duh?*　　　　　　Kor er badet? (NN)
*vurr ārr **baa**-duh?*　　　　　　Hvor er badet? (BM)

Is there hot water all day?

*ā deh **vahrrmt** vahtn
der-ng-nuh **rrunt**?*　　　　Er det varmt vatn døgnet
　　　　　　　　　　　　　　　rundt? (NN)

*ā deh **vah-rnt** vahn
döy-nuh **rrünt**?*　　　　　　Er det varmt vann døgnet
　　　　　　　　　　　　　　　rundt? (BM)

Do you have a safe where I
can leave my valuables?

*haa rdü ehn **sayf** därr eh
kan **lehg**-guh va-**rdēē**-saa-
kuh-nuh **mēē**-nuh?*

*haa rdü ehn **sayf** därr ya
kan **lehg**-guh va-**rdēē**-saa-
kuh-nuh **mēē**-nuh?*

Har du ein safe der eg kan
leggje verdisakene mine?
(NN)

Har du en safe der jeg kan
legge verdisakene mine?
(BM)

Is there somewhere to wash
clothes?

*kahn eh vahs-kuh **klē**-ah
mēē-nuh **ehng**-kahn staan?*

*kahn ya vahs-kuh **klā**-rnuh
mēē-nuh noon-**stēts**?*

Kan eg vaske kleda mine
einkvan staden? (NN)

Kan jeg vaske klærne mine
noensteds? (BM)

Can I use the kitchen?

*ä rdeh **lor**-v o **brrüü**-kuh
cher-k-kuh-nuh?*

Er det lov å bruke
kjøkkenet?

Can I use the telephone?

*kahn eh for **lor**-nuh
tē-lē-**foon**-n?*

*kahn ya for **lor**-nuh
tē-lē-**foon**-n?*

Kan eg få låne telefonen?
(NN)

Kan jeg få låne telefonen?
(BM)

Requests & Complaints

Please wake me up at ...

*vä sho **sneel** o **vehch**-uh
meh ...*

*vä sho **sneel** o **vehk**-kuh
mä ...*

Ver så snill å vekkje meg ...
(NN)

Vær så snill å vekke meg ...
(BM)

The room needs to be cleaned.
*deht-tuh **rrum**-muh **bērr**-rr
yā-rrahst **rraynt***
*deht-tuh **rrum**-muh **bērr**-rr
yēr-rruhs **rraynt***

Dette rommet bør gjerast
reint. (NN)
Dette rommet bør gjøres
reint. (BM)

Please change the sheets.
*vā sho sneel o **sheeft**-uh
sehng-uh-töy*
*vā sho sneel o **sheeft**-uh
sehng-uh-töy*

Ver så snill å skifte
sengetøy. (NN)
Vær så snill å skifte
sengetøy. (BM)

I can't open/close the window.
*eh **grray**-uhrr eech-uh **or**-p-
nuh/luk-kuh **veen**-dü-uh*
*ya **grray**-uhrr eek-kuh **or**-p-
nuh/luk-kuh **veen**-dü-uh*

Eg greier ikkje opne/lukke
vindauget. (NN)
Jeg greier ikke åpne/lukke
vinduet. (BM)

I've locked myself out of my
room.
*eh haa **lor-st** meh **üü**-tuh
aa **rrum**-muh meet*
*ya haa **lor-st** mā **üü**-tuh aa
rrum-muh meet*

Eg har låst meg ute av
rommet mitt. (NN)
Jeg har låst meg ute av
rommet mitt. (BM)

The toilet won't flush.
*eh **for**-rr eech-uh spȳȳlt nē
po tua-**leht**-tuh*
*ya **for**-rr eek-kuh spȳȳlt nē
po tua-**leht**-tuh*

Eg får ikkje spylt ned på
toalettet. (NN)
Jeg får ikke spylt ned på
toalettet. (BM)

I don't like this room.
*eh **lēē**-kuhrr eechuh
deht-tuh **rrum**-uh*
*ya **lēē**-kuhrr eek-kuh
deht-tuh **rrum**-uh*

Eg liker ikkje dette rommet.
(NN)
Jeg liker ikke dette rommet.
(BM)

It's too small.	*deh ārr fo lee-tuh*	Det er for lite.
It's noisy.	*deh ārr fo-rr mӯӯ-yuh brror-k*	Det er for mye bråk.
It's too dark.	*deh ārr fo-rr mer-rrt*	Det er for mørkt.
It's expensive.	*deh ā rdӯӯ-rt*	Det er dyrt.

Some Useful Phrases

I am leaving now/tomorrow.

| *eh rray-suhrr nor/ee-mo-rro* | Eg reiser … nå/i morgon (NN) |
| *ya rray-suhrr nor/ee-mo-rro* | Jeg reiser … nå/i morgon (BM) |

I would like to pay the bill.

| *kahn eh for rrehk-neeng-ah tahk?* | Kan eg få rekninga, takk? (NN) |
| *kahn ya for rrehng-neeng-ah tahk?* | Kan jeg få rekninga, takk? (BM) |

name	*nahmn*	namn (NN)
	nahvn	navn (BM)
surname	*eht-tuh-nahmn*	etternamn (NN)
	eht-tuh-nahvn	etternavn (BM)
room number	*rrum-num-muhrr*	romnummer

Some Useful Words

address	*ah-drrehs-suh*	adresse
air-conditioning	*klēē-mah-ahn-lehg*	klimaanlegg
balcony	*bahl-kong*	balkong
bathroom	*baad*	bad
bed	*sehng*	seng
bill	*rrehk-neeng*	rekning (NN)
	rrehng-neeng/rray-neeng	rekning/regning (BM)
blanket	*tehp-puh*	teppe

candle	*steh-ah-**rrēēn**-lȳȳs*	stearinlys
chair	*stool*	stol
clean	*rrayn*	rein
cupboard	*skaap*	skap
dark	*mer-rrk*	mørk
dirty	***sheet**-n*	skitten
double bed	***dob**-buhlt-sehng*	dobbeltseng
electricity	*strrohw-m*	straum (NN)
	strrer-m	strøm (BM)
excluded	***ehks**-klü-sēēv*	eksklusiv
fan	***veef**-tuh*	vifte
included	*eeng-klü-**dē**-rt*	inkludert
key	***ner**-k-kuhl*	nøkkel
lift (elevator)	*hays*	heis
light bulb	*lȳȳs-pā-rruh*	lyspære
lock (n)	*lor-s*	lås
mattress	*mah-**drrahs***	madrass
mirror	*spē-guhl*	spegel (NN)
	spayl	speil (BM)
padlock	***hehng**-uh-lor-s*	hengelås
pillow	***püü**-tuh*	pute
quiet	***steel**-luh*	stille
room (in hotel)	*rrum*	rom
	*vā-**rruhl**-suh*	værelse (BM)
sheet	*laa-kuhn*	laken
shower	*düsh*	dusj
soap	*sor-puh*	såpe
suitcase	*kuf-fuh-rt*	koffert
swimming pool (indoor)	*sȳm-yuh-hahl*	symjehall (NN)
	sver-m-muh-hahl	svømmehall (BM)
table	*boo-rr*	bord

toilet	*toa-leht*	toalett
toilet paper	*doo-pah-pēē-rr*	dopapir
towel	*hahng-kluh*	handkle (NN)
	hong-kluh	håndkle (BM)
water	*vaht-n*	vatn
	vahn	vann (BM)
cold water	*kahlt vahtn*	kaldt vatn
	kahlt vahn	kaldt vann (BM)
hot water	*vah-rnt vahtn*	varmt vatn (NN)
	vah-rnt vahn	varmt vann (BM)
window	*veen-dohw-uh*	vindauge (NN)
	veen-dü	vindu (BM)

Around Town

I'm looking for ...
eh lay-tuhrr eht-tuhrr ...   Eg leiter etter ... (NN)
ya lay-tuhrr eht-tuhrr ...   Jeg leiter etter ... (BM)

the art gallery	*künst-gahl-luh-rrēē-uh*	kunstgalleriet
a bank	*bahng-kuhn*	banken
the church	*chȳrr-chah*	kyrkja (NN)
	cheerr-kah	kirka (BM)
the city centre	*sehn-trrüm*	sentrum
the ... embassy	*den ... ahm-bahs-saa-duh*	den ... ambassade
my hotel	*hutehl-luh meet*	hotellet mitt
the market	*to-rr-guh*	torget
the museum	*mü-sē-uh*	museet
the police	*pu-lee-tee-uh*	politiet
the post office	*post-kun-too-rruh*	postkontoret

a public toilet	*eht of-fuhntleh* *toa-leht*	eit offentleg toalett (NN)
	eht of-fuhntlee *toa-leht*	et offentlig toalett (BM)
the telephone centre	*tē-luh-varr-kuh*	televerket
the tourist information office	*tü-rreest-een-fo-rr-mah-shoon*	turistinformasjon

What time does it open?
  kaa tēē ārr ahn up-puh?   Kva tid er han oppe? (NN)
  no-rr ā rdehn up-puh?   Når er den oppe? (BM)
What time does it close?
  kaa tēē stehng-uhrr ahn?   Kva tid stenger han? (NN)
  no-rr stehng-uh rdehn?   Når stenger den? (BM)

What ... is this?
  kvaa fo-rr ... ā dē?   Kva for ... er det? (NN)
  veelkuhn ... ā rdē?   Hvilken ... er det? (BM)
street   *gaa-tuh*   gate
suburb   *fo-rr-staad*   forstad

For directions, see the Getting Around section, page 211.

At the Bank

I want to exchange some
money/traveller's cheques.

*eh veel **yā**-rnuh **vehks**-luh
pehng-ahrr/**hē**-vuh nok-
rruh **rra**-ysuh-shehk-kahrr*

Eg vil gjerne veksle pengar/
heve nokre reisesjekkar.
(NN)

*ya veel **yā**-rnuh **vehks**-luh
pehng-uhrr/**hē**-vuh noon
rray-suh-shehk-kuhrr*

Jeg vil gjerne veksle
penger/heve noen reisesjek-
ker. (BM)

What is the exchange rate?

*kvaa **ārr** vah-**lüü**-tah-kü-
shuhn?*

Kva er valutakursen? (NN)

*vaa **ārr** vah-**lüü**-tah-kü-
shuhn?*

Hva er valutakursen? (BM)

How many Norwegian kroner
per dollar?

*kurr **mahng**-uh **krroo**-
nuhrr fo-rr **ayn** dol-lahrr?*

Kor mange kroner for ein
dollar? (NN)

*vurr **mahng**-uh **krroo**-
nuhrr fo-rr **ēn** dol-lahrr?*

Hvor mange kroner for en
dollar? (BM)

Can I have money transferred
here from my bank?

*kahn eh for or-**vuhrr**-fēr-rt
pehng-ahrr **hēēt** frror
bahng-kuhn meen?*

Kan eg få overført pengar
hit frå banken min? (NN)

*kahn ya for or-**vuhrr**-fēr-rt
pehng-uhrr **hēēt** frraa
bahng-kuhn meen?*

Kan jeg få overført penger
hit fra banken min? (BM)

How long will it take to
arrive?

kurr lehng-yuh veel deh taa? — Kor lenge vil det ta? (NN)
vurr lehng-uh veel deh taa? — Hvor lenge vil det ta? (BM)

Has my money arrived yet?

haarr pehng-ah-nuh mēē-nu kor-muh noo? — Har pengane mine kome no? (NN)
haarr pehng-uh-nuh mēē-nuh kom-muht nor? — Har pengene mine kommet nå? (BM)

bank draft	*vehk-sl/rreh-mees-suh*	veksel/remisse
bank notes	*pehng-uh-seht-lahrr*	pengesetlar (NN)
	pehng-uh-sehd-luhrr	pengesedler (BM)
cashier	*kah-sē-rrahrr*	kasserar (NN)
	kah-sē-rruhrr	kasserer (BM)
coins	*mȳn-tahrr*	myntar (NN)
	mȳn-tuhrr	mynter (BM)
credit card	*krreh-deet-ko-rt*	kredittkort
exchange	*vehk-sleeng*	veksling
loose change	*vehk-sluh-pehng-ahrr*	vekslepengar (NN)
	vehk-sluh-pehng-uhrr	vekslepenger (BM)
signature	*ün-nuhrr-skrreeft*	underskrift

At the Post Office

I would like to send

eh veel sehn-duh ... — Eg vil sende ... (NN)
ya skah sehn-nuh ... — Jeg skal sende ... (BM)

a letter	*eht brrēv*	eit brev (NN)
	eht brrēv	et brev (BM)
a postcard	*eht post-ku-rt*	eit postkort (NN)
	eht post-ku-rt	et postkort (BM)

a parcel	*ay **pahk**-kuh*	ei pakke
a telegram	*eht tē-luh-**grrahm***	eit telegram (NN)
	*eht tē-luh-**grrahm***	et telegram (BM)

I would like some stamps.

| *eh veel yā-rnuh **haa** nok-rruh **frrēē**-marr-kuh* | Eg vil gjerne ha nokre frimerke. (NN) |
| *ya veel yā-rnuh **haa** noon **frrēē**-marr-kuh* | Jeg vil gjerne ha noen frimerker. (BM) |

How much does it to send this to …?

| *kurr **mȳch**-uh kos-tahrr deh o sehn-duh dēh-tuh til …?* | Kor mykje kostar det å sende dette til …? (NN) |
| *vurr **mȳȳ**-yuh kos-tuhrr deh o sehn-nuh dēh-tuh til …?* | Hvor mye koster det å sende dette til …? (BM) |

an aerogram	*eht aa-ē-rru-**grrahm***	eit aerogram (NN)
	*eht aa-ē-rru-**grrahm***	et aerogram (BM)
air mail	*lüft-post*	luftpost
envelope	*kon-vu-lüt*	konvolutt
mail box	***post**-kahs-suh*	postkasse
parcel	***pahk**-kuh*	pakke
registered mail	*rreh-kom-mahn-dē-rt post*	rekommandert post
surface mail	*or-vuhrr-flaa-tuh-post*	overflatepost

Telephone

I want to ring …

| *eh veel **rreeng**-yuh teel …* | Eg vil ringje til … (NN) |
| *ya veel **rreeng**-uh teel …* | Jeg vil ringe til … (BM) |

The number is …
   num-muh-rruh ārr …

Nummeret er …

I want to speak for three minutes.
   eh veel snahk-kuh ee trrē mee-nüt

Eg vil snakke i tre minutt. (NN)

   ya veel snahk-kuh ee trrē mee-nüt-tuhrr

Jeg vil snakke i tre minutter. (BM)

How much does a three-minute call cost?
   kurr mӯch-uh kos-tahrr ehn trrē mee-nüts sahm-taa-luh?

Kor mykje kostar ein tre minutts samtale? (NN)

   vurr mӯӯ-yuh kos-tuhrr ehn trē mee-nüt-tuhsh sahm-taaluh?

Hvor mye koster et tre minutters samtale? (BM)

How much does each extra minute cost?
   kurr mӯch-uh kos-tahrr kvah-rt ehks-trrah mee-nüt?

Kor mykje kostar kvart ekstra minutt? (NN)

   vurr mӯӯ-yuh kos-tuhrr va-rt ehks-trrah mee-nüt?

Hvor mye koster hvert ekstra minutt? (BM)

I would like to speak to Mr Sælen.
   eh skül-luh yā-rnuh for snahk-kuh mē harr sē-luhn

Eg skulle gjerne få snakke med herr Sælen. (NN)

   ya skül-luh yā-rnuh for snahk-kuh mē harr sē-luhn

Jeg skulle gjerne få snakke med herr Sælen. (BM)

I want to make a reverse-
charges phone call.

*eh veel **teeng**-uh ehn **sahm**-
taa-luh meh noo-**tē**-rreengs-
or-vuhrr-**fēr**-rreeng*

Eg vil tinge ein samtale
med noteringsoverføring.
(NN)

*ya veel buh-**steel**-luh ehn
sahm-taa-luh meh noo-**tē**-
rreengs-or-vuhrr-**fēr**-rreeng*

Jeg vil bestille en samtale
med noteringsoverøring.
(BM)

It's engaged.

*deh **ārr** **upp**-taht*

Det er opptatt.

I've been cut off.

*sahm-taa-luhn blay
brror-tuhn*

Samtalen blei broten. (NN)

*sahm-taa-luhn blay **brrüt***

Samtalen ble brutt. (BM)

Sightseeing

Do you have a guidebook/
local map?

*haa rdü ehn **gaid**/eht om-
rror-duh-kah-rt?*

Har du ein guide/eit
områdekart? (NN)

*haa rdü ehn **gaid**/eht om-
rror-duh-kah-rt?*

Har du en guide/et
områdekart? (BM)

What are the main attractions?

*kvaa ā rday **veek**-tee-ahs-
tuh aht-trrahk-shoo-nah-
nuh?*

Kva er dei viktigaste
attraksjonane? (NN)

*vaa ā rdee **veek**-tee-stuh sē-
varr-dee-hē-tuhr?*

Hva er de viktigste
severdigheter? (BM)

What is that?

*kvaa ā **rdē**?*

Kva er det? (NN)

*vaa ā **rdē**?*

Hva er det? (BM)

How old is it?
   *kurr **gahm**-mahlt ā rdeh?*   Kor gammalt er det? (NN)
   *vurr **gahm**-muhlt ā rdeh?*   Hvor gammelt er det? (BM)
Can I take photographs?
   *for-rr eh taa **bēē**-lētuh?*   Får eg ta bilete? (NN)
   *for-rr ya taa **beel**-duhrr?*   Får jeg ta bilder? (BM)
What time does it open/close?
   *kaa tēē **or-p**-nahrr deh?*   Kva tid opnar det? (NN)
   *no-rr **or-p**-nuhrr deh?*   Når åpner det? (BM)

ancient	***gahm**-mahl*	gammal
beach	***strrahn***	strand
castle	*shlot*	slott
cathedral	*kah-teh-**drraal***	katedral
church	*chȳrr-chuh*	kyrkje (NN)
	cheerr-kuh	kirke (BM)
concert hall	*kon-**sa-rt**-hüüs*	konserthus
library	*bee-blee-yu-**tēk***	bibliotek
main square	*(**stoo-rr**)-to-rrguh*	(stor)torget
market	*to-rr-guh*	torget
monastery	*klos-turr*	kloster
monument	*hees-too-rreesk **bȳg**-neeng*	historisk bygning
mosque	*mos-**kē***	moskē
old town	*gahm-mahl **bȳȳ***	gammal by
	*gahm-muhl **bȳȳ***	gammel by (BM)
the old city	***gahm**-luh-**bȳȳ**-yuhn*	gamlebyen
opera house	*oo-puh-**rrah**-hüüs*	operahus
palace	*shlot*	slott
ruins	*rrü-**ēē**-nahrr*	ruinar (NN)
	*rrü-**ēē**-nuhrr*	ruiner (BM)

stadium	**staa**-dee-on	stadion
statues	**bee**-lēt-ster-tuh	biletstøtte (NN)
	beel-luhd-ster-tuhrr	billedstøtter (BM)
synagogue	**sȳ**-nah-goo-guh	synagoge
temple	**hor**-v/**tehm**-puhl	hov/tempel
university	**ü**-nee-va-shee-tēt	universitet

Entertainment

What's there to do in the evenings?

kvaa kahn ayn yā-rruh um
kvehl-n?

Kva kan ein gjere om
kvelden? (NN)

vaa kahn mahn yēr-rruh
om kvehl-n?

Hva kan man gjøre om
kvelden? (BM)

Are there any discos?

ā rdeh nor-kon dees-ku-tēk?

Er det nokon diskotek? (NN)

ā rdeh noon dees-ku-tēk-
uhrr?

Er det noen diskoteker?
(BM)

Are there places where you
can hear local folk music?

ā rdeh nor-kon staarr dārr
ayn kahn höy-rruh po
noshk fol-kuh-mü-seek?

Er det nokon stader der ein
kan høyre på norsk
folkemusikk? (NN)

ā rdeh noo-uhn stē-duhrr
dārr ehn kahn her-rruh po
noshk fol-kuh-mü-seek?

Er det noen steder der en
kan høre på norsk
folkemusikk? (BM)

How much does it cost to get
in?

kurr mȳch-uh kostahrr deh
fo-rr o kor-muh een?

Kor mykje kostar det for å
kome inn? (NN)

vurr mȳȳ-yuh kostuhrr deh
fo-rr o ko-muh een?

Hvor mye koster det for å
komme inn? (BM)

cinema	*chēē-nu*	kino
concert	*kon-sa-rt*	konsert
discotheque	*dees-ku-tēk*	diskotck
theatre	*tē-aa-tuhrr*	teater

In the Country
Weather

What's the weather like?
kaa ärr värr-mehl-leeng-ah? — Kva er vermeldinga? (NN)
vaa ärr värr-mehl-leeng-ah? — Hva er værmeldinga? (BM)

The weather is today.
vä-rruh ärr ... ee-daag — Veret er ... i dag. (NN)
vä-rruh ärr ... ee-daag — Været er ... i dag. (BM)
Will it be ... tomorrow?
va-rt deh ... ee-mo-rr-go? — Vert det ... i morgon? (NN)
blēē rdeh ... ee-mo-rn? — Blir det ... i morgen? (BM)

cloudy	*or-vuh-shȳȳ-yah*	overkya
cold	*kahlt*	kaldt
foggy	*tor-kuh*	tåke
frosty	*frrost-vä-rr*	frostvêr (NN)
	frrost-vä-rr	frostvær (BM)
hot	*vah-rrmt*	varmt (NN)
	vah-rnt	varmt (BM)
raining	*rrehng-n*	regn
	rrayn	regn (BM)
snowing	*sn̄ør*	snø

sunny	*mӯ-chuh **sool***	mykje sol (NN)
	*mӯӯ-yuh **sool***	mye sol (BM)
windy	*mӯ-chuh **veen***	mykje vind (NN)
	*mӯӯ-yuh **veen***	mye vind (BM)

Camping

Am I allowed to camp here?
(tent)

| *for-rr eh **lorv** teel o **shlor** up tehl-tuh meet hãrr?* | Får eg lov til å slå opp teltet mitt her? (NN) |
| *for-rr ya **lorv** teel o **shlor** op tehl-tuh meet hãrr?* | Får jeg lov til å slå opp teltet mitt her? (BM) |

Is there a campsite nearby?

| *feenst deh ehn **kam**-peeng ee nãrr-lay-kuhn?* | Finst det ein camping i nærleiken? (NN) |
| *feens deh ehn **kam**-peeng ee nãrr-ē-tuhn?* | Finst det ein camping i nærheten? (BM) |

backpack	*rrӯg-sehk*	ryggsekk
can opener	*boks-or-pnahrr*	boksopnar (NN)
	boks-or-pnuhrr	boksåpner (BM)
compass	*kom-pahs*	kompass
crampons	*brrod-dahr*	broddar (NN)
	brrod-duhr	brodder (BM)
firewood	*vē*	ved
gas cartridge	*prru-**paan**-buh-hahl-dahrr*	propanbehaldar (NN)
	*prru-**paan**-buh-hol-luhrr*	propanbeholder (BM)
ice axe	*ēēs-er-ks*	isøks
mattress	*mah-drrahs*	madrass

penknife	*lum-muh-knēēv*	lommekniv
rope	*tohw*	tau
tent	*tehlt*	telt
tent pegs	*tehlt-plüg-gahrr*	teltpluggar (NN)
	tehlt-plüg-guhrr	teltplugger (BM)
torch (flashlight)	*lum-muh-lÿkt*	lommelykt
sleeping bag	*sor-vuh-poo-suh*	sovepose
stove	*koo-kuh-ahp-pah-rraat*	kokeapparat
water bottle	*vahss-flahs-kuh*	vassflaske (NN)
	vahn-flahs-kuh	vannflaske (BM)

Food

breakfast	*frrüü-kost*	frukost (NN)
	frroo-kost	frokost (BM)
lunch	*ler-nsh*	lunsj
dinner	*meed-daag*	middag

Table for ..., please.
  eht boo-rr teel ..., tahk Eit bord til ..., takk.
Can I see the menu please?
  kahn eh for meh-nÿÿ-yuhn, tahk Kan eg få menyen, takk. (NN)
  kahn ya for meh-nÿÿ-yuhn, tahk Kan jeg få menyen, takk. (BM)
I would like today's special, please.
  eh veel yá-rnuh haa daa-guhns rreht, takk Eg vil gjerne ha dagens rett, takk. (NN)
  ya veel yá-rnuh haa daa-guhns rreht, takk Jeg vil gjerne ha dagens rett, takk. (BM)

What does it include?
*kvaa um-**faht**-tah rdē?* Kva omfattar det? (NN)
*vaa om-**faht**-tuh rdē?* Hva omfatter det? (BM)
Is service included in the bill?
*árr buh-va-**rt**-neeng-ah* Er bevertninga medrekna?
*mē-**rrek**-nah?* (NN)
*árr buh-va-**rt**-neeng-ah* Er bevertninga iberegnet?
ēē-buh-rray-nuht? (BM)
Not too spicy please.
*eech-uh fo **shtarrt*** Ikkje for sterkt krydra, takk.
krrüd-drrah tahk (NN)
*eek-kuh fo **shtarrt*** Ikke for sterkt krydra, takk.
krrüd-drrah tahk (BM)

ashtray	*os-kuh-bē-guhrr*	oskebeger (NN)
	ahs-kuh-bē-guhrr	askebeger (BM)
the bill	*rrehk-neeng-ah*	rekninga (NN)
	rray-neeng-uhn	regningen (BM)
a cup	*ehn kop*	ein kopp (NN)
	uhn kop	en kopp (BM)
dessert	*deh-sárr*	dessert
a drink	*ehn drreengk*	ein drink (NN)
	uhn drreengk	en drink (BM)
a fork	*ehn gahf-fuhl*	ein gaffel (NN)
	uhn gahf-fuhl	en gaffel (BM)
fresh	*fashk*	fersk
a glass	*eht glaas*	eit glas (NN)
	uht glahs	et glass (BM)
a knife	*ehn knēēv*	ein kniv (NN)
	uhn knēēv	en kniv (BM)

NORWEGIAN

a plate	*ehn tahl-larrk*	ein tallerk (NN)
	uhn tahl-larr-kuhn	en tallerken (BM)
spicy	*starrkt (krrȳd-rrah)*	sterkt (krydra)
a spoon	*ay shay*	ei skei
	ay shē	ei skje (BM)
stale	*dor-vuhnt*	dovent
starter	*fo-rr-reht*	forrett
sweet	*sēr-t*	søt
teaspoon	*tē-shay*	teskei
	tē-shē	teskje (BM)
toothpick	*tahn-peerr-kahrr*	tannpirkar (NN)
	tahn-peerr-kuhrr	tannpirker (BM)

Vegetarian Meals

I am a vegetarian.

ēg árr veh-geh-tah-rree-aa-nahrr	Eg er vegetarianar. (NN)
ya árr veh-geh-tah-rree-aa-nuhrr	Jeg er vegetarianer. (BM)

I don't eat meat.

ēg ēt eech-uh cher-t	Eg et ikkje kjøtt. (NN)
ya spee-suhrr eek-uh cher-t	Jeg spiser ikke kjøtt. (BM)

I don't eat chicken, fish, or ham.

ēg ēt korr-chuh chȳl-leeng, ehl-luhrr feesk ,ehl-luh sheeng-kuh	Eg et korkje kylling, eller fisk, eller skinke. (NN)
ya spēē-suhrr varr-kuhn chül-leeng ehl-luhrr feesk ehl-luh sheeng-kuh	Jeg spiser verken kylling eller fisk eller skinke. (BM)

Breakfasts & Breads

koldtbord	buffet of cold dishes (fish, meat, cheese, salad and a sweet)
rømmegraut	boiled sour cream porridge with cinnamon and sugar
sildesalat	salad with slices of herring, cucumber, onions, etc
brød	bread, loaf
flatbørd	thin wafer of rye/barley
fleskepølse	pork sandwich spread
frokost, frukost	breakfast

biscuit	*kjeks*
brown bread	*grovbrød*
crisp-bread	*knekkebrød*
cured ham	*spekeskinke*
food on top of a sandwich, like cold cuts	*pålegg*
honey	*honning*
jam	*syltetøy*
oatmeal biscuits	*havrekjeks*
oatmeal porridge	*havregraut*
open sandwich	*smørbrød*
peanut butter	*peanøttsmør*
porridge, cereal	*graut, grøt*
roll	*rundstykke*
rusk	*kavring*
slice	*skive*
thin pancake	*lefse*
white bread	*loff*
wholemeal bread	*heilkornbrød*

NORWEGIAN

Potatoes & Staples

mashed potatoes	*potetmos*
potato chips	*pommes frites*
potato dumplings	*raspeballar, kumle*
potato pancake	*lompe, lumpe*
rice	*ris*

Dairy Products

gammalost	semi-hard brown cheese with strong flavour
geitost	sweet brown goat cheese
gudbrands dalsost	cheese similar to *geitost*
mysost	brown whey cheese
normannaost	Danish Blue
pultost	soft fermented cheese, often with caraway seeds
riddarost	Munster cheese
remuladesaus	cream mayonnaise with chopped gherkins and parsley

butter	*smør*
cheese	*ost*
cream	*fløyte, fløte*
cream cheese	*fløyteost*
sour cream	*rømme*
whipped cream	*krem, piska krem*

Eggs

fried egg (sunny side up)	*speilegg*
hard-boiled	*hardkokt*
scrambled eggs	*eggerøre forlorent*
soft-boiled	*blautkokt, bløtkokt*

NORWEGIAN

Soups & Mixed Dishes

dagens rett	today's special
fårikål	lamb in cabbage stew
gryte(rett)	casserole
italiensk salat	salad of diced cold meat, potatoes, apples and vegetables in mayonnaise
lapskaus	thick stew of diced meat, potatoes, onions and other vegetables
koldtbord	buffet of cold dishes (fish, meat, cheese, salad and a sweet)
pyttipanne	chunks of meat and potatoes, fried with onions, etc
suppe	soup
surkål	boiled cabbage flavoured with caraway seeds, sugar and vinegar

Meat

bankebiff	slices/chunks of beef simmered in gravy
beinlause fuglar, benløse fugler	rolled slices of veal stuffed with minced meat
blodpudding	black pudding
bris, brissel	sweetbread
dyresteik	roast venison
elgsteik	roast elk
fena(d)lår	cured leg of lamb
fleskepannekake	thick pancake with bacon, baked in the oven
fyll	stuffing, forcemeat
fårikål	lamb in cabbage stew
kålrulettar	minced meat in cabbage leaves
kalvetunge	calf's tongue

kjøttdeig	minced meat
kjøttkake	small hamburger steak
kjøttpålegg	cold cuts
kjøttpudding	meat loaf
lam(mebog)	(shoulder of) lamb
lever(postei)	liver (pâté)
lungemos	hash of pork lungs and onions
medaljong	small round fillet
medisterkake	pork hamburger steak
okserull	rolled stuffed beef, cold
pai	pie
pinnekjøtt	salted and fried lamb ribs
postei	meat pie
sauesteik	leg of lamb
skive	slice
smalehovud	roast head of lamb
spekemat, spike-mat	cured meat (lamb, beef, pork, reindeer, often served with scrambled eggs)
spekepølse	air-dried sausage
syltelabb	boiled, salt-cured pig's trotter

beef	*oksekjøtt*
fillet of beef	*oksefilet*
game	*vilt*
ham	*skinke*
kid	*geitekilling*
kidney	*nyre*
lamb/mutton	*sauekjøtt*
meat	*kjøtt*
meatball	*kjøttbolle*
pork	*svinekjøtt*

pork chop	*svinekotelett*
roast beef	*oksesteik*
roast pork	*svinesteik*
roast reindeer	*reinsdyrsteik*
rump steak	*mørbrad*
sausage	*pølse*
spare rib	*svineribbe*
veal	*kalvekjøtt*

Seafood

fiskebolle	fish ball
fiskegrateng	fish casserole
fiskekabaret	fish, shellfish and vegetables in aspic
fiskekake	fried fishball
gaffelbitar	salt- and sugar-cured sprat/herring fillets
gravlaks	salt- and sugar-cured salmon with dill and a creamy sauce
kaviar	smoked cod-roe spread
klippfisk	salted and dried cod
lutefisk	stockfish treated in lye solution, boiled
postei	fish pie
plukkfisk	poached fish in white sauce
rakefisk	cured and fermented fish (often trout)
sildesalat	salad with slices of herring, cucumber, onions, etc
spekesild	salted herring, often served with pickled beetroot, potatoes and cabbage
torsketunger	codtongues, often in sour cream sauce

anchovy	*ansjos*
catfish	*steinbit*
coalfish	*sei*
cod	*torsk*
crab	*krabbe*
crayfish	*kreps*
eel	*ål*
flounder	*flyndre*
frog fish/angler fish	*breiflabb*
haddock	*hyse, kolje*
halibut	*hellefisk, kveite*
herring	*sild*
lobster	*hummer*
mackerel	*makrell*
mussel	*blåskjel(l)*
plaice	*raudspette, rødspette*
rainbow trout	*regnbogeaure/regnbueørret*
roe	*rogn*
salmon	*laks*
sea trout	*sjøaure, sjøørret*
shellfish	*skaldyr, skalldyr*
shrimps	*reker*
small mackerel	*pir*
smoked salmon	*røykelaks*
sole	*sjøtunge*
soused herring	*kryddersild, sursild*
sprat/sardine	*brisling*
trout	*aure, ørret*
tuna	*tunfisk*
whale steak	*hvalbiff, kvalbiff*
young coalfish	*pale*

NORWEGIAN

Poultry & Wildfowl

black grouse	*årfugl, orrfugl*
chicken	*kylling*
chicken fricassee	*hønsefrikasse*
duck	*and*
fowl	*fugl*
goose (liver)	*gås(elever)*
partridge	*rapphøne*
ptarmigan	*rype*
quail	*vaktel*
turkey	*kalkun*

Vegetables

beans	*bønner*
beetroot	*raudbete, rødbete*
Brussels sprouts	*rosenkål*
butter beans	*voksbønner*
button mushroom	*sjampinjong*
cabbage	*kål*
carrots	*gulrøter*
cauliflower	*blomkål*
chives	*grasløk/gressløk*
cucumber	*agurk, slangeagurk*
French beans	*brekkbønner*
horseradish	*peparrot/pepperrot*
leek	*langeløk, purre*
lentils	*linser*
marrow/squash	*graskar/gresskar*
mushroom	*sopp*
onion	*løk/lauk*
peas	*erter*
pickled gherkin	*sylteagurk*

radish	*reddik*
red cabbage	*raudkål, rødkål*
sliced French beans	*snittebønner*
spinach	*spinat*
sugar peas	*sukkererter*
tomato	*tomat*
vegetables	*grøn(n)saker*

Spices, Herbs & Condiments

caraway seeds	*karve*
cardamom	*kardemomme*
chives	*grasløk/gressløk*
cinnamon	*kanel*
curry	*karri*
garlic	*hvitløk/kvitløk*
mustard	*sennep*
parsley	*persille*
pepper	*pepar, pepper*
spices, herbs	*krydder*
stuffing/forcemeat	*fyll*
sugar	*sukker*
tarragon	*estragon*
thyme	*timian*
vinegar	*eddik*

Methods of Cooking

baked	*bakt*
boiled/cooked	*kokt*
crumbed	*panert*
fried/roasted	*steikt, stekt*
grilled	*grilla, grillet*
grilled/toasted	*rista, ristet*

NORWEGIAN

home-made	*heimelaga, hjemmelaget*
rare	*råsteikt*
raw	*rå*
sautéed	*lettsteikt*
smoked	*røykt, røk(e)t*
stewed (fruit); creamed (vegetables)	*stua; stuet*

Fruit

apple	*eple*
apricot	*aprikos*
banana	*banan*
bilberries	*blåbær*
blackberries	*bjørnebær*
blackcurrants	*solbær*
cherry, morello	*kirsebær*
cranberries	*tyttebær*
currant	*korint*
fruit	*frukt*
fruit salad	*fruktsalat*
gooseberries	*stikkelsbær*
grapes	*druer*
lemon	*sitron*
orange	*appelsin*
peach	*fersken*
pear	*pære*
pineapple	*ananas*
plum	*plomme*
raisin	*rosin*
raspberries	*bringebær*
redcurrants	*rips*

NORWEGIAN

rhubarb	*rabarbra*
stewed plums	*plommegraut*
stewed prunes	*sviskegraut*
strawberries	*jordbær*

Desserts, Cakes & Cookies

arme riddarar, riddere	slices of bread dipped in batter, fried and served with jam
bløtkake	rich sponge layer cake with whipped cream
fløyteis, fløteis	ice-cream made of cream
fløytevaffel	cream-enriched waffle with jam
fromasj	mousse, blancmange
fruktis	sherbet, water ice
havrekjeks	oatmeal biscuit
hasselnøtt	hazelnut
julekake	rich fruit cake
kveitebolle	bun, sweet roll
kransekake	pile of almond-macaroon rings
kringle	ring-twisted bread with raisins
lefse	thin pancake (without eggs)
napoleonskake	custard slice
ris(gryns)graut	rice pudding with cinnamon and sugar, warm
riskrem	boiled rice with whipped cream, with raspberry jam
rislapp	small sweet rice cake
rødgrød	fruit pudding with vanilla cream
rømmegraut	boiled sour cream porridge with cinnamon and sugar
rørte tyttebær	mashed uncooked cranberries
sirupsnipp	ginger cookie

tilslørte bonde-piker	layers of apple sauce and breadcrumbs, topped with whipped cream
vannbakkels, vassbakkels	cream puff
vørterkake	spiced malt bread
wienerbrød	Danish pastry

almonds	*mandlar/mandler*
apple cake	*eplekake*
biscuit, cookie	*småkake*
bun, sweet roll	*hvetebolle*
cake	*kake*
chocolate	*sjokolade*
jam	*syltetøy*
ice cream	*is*
meringue	*marengs*
nut	*nøtt*
pancake	*pannekake*
sponge cake	*sukkerbrød*
tart	*terte*
wafer	*vaffel*
walnut	*valnøtt*

Drinks – Nonalcoholic

brus	fizzy fruit drink
kefir	fermented milk, kefir
kulturmjølk	cultured thick milk
vørterøl	nonalcoholic beer

apple juice	*eplemost*
cocoa	*kakao*
coffee	*kaffi/kaffe*

NORWEGIAN

fruit juice	*fruktsaft*
ice	*is*
milk	*mjølk/melk*
mineral water	*farris*
nonalcoholic	*alkoholfri*
orangeade	*appelsinbrus*
squash	*saft*
tea	*te*
water	*vatn, vann*

Drinks – Alcoholic

akevitt	kind of gin flavoured with spices
dram	drink/tot/shot
exportøl	strong, light-coloured beer
gløgg	kind of mulled wine, with brandy and spices
heimebrent	home-made brandy
lett-	with little/less alcohol or sugar
pils	lager
pjolter	long drink of whisky and soda water
toddi	mulled wine

beer	*øl*
bock	*bokkøl*
brandy	*brennevin*
cognac	*konjakk*
dark beer	*bayer*
double	*dobbel*
dry	*tørr*
light lager	*lager*
liqueur	*likør*

neat	*bar, berr*	
port	*portvin*	
red wine	*rødvin/raudvin*	
rum	*rom*	
sparkling	*musserande*	
white wine	*hvitvin/kvitvin*	
wine	*vin*	

Shopping

How much is it …?

korr mȳchuh kos-tarr deh …?	Kor mykje kostar det …? (NN)	
vorr mȳȳyuh kos-tuhrr deh …?	Hvor mye koster det …? (BM)	

bookshop	*book-hahn-dl*	bokhandel
camera shop	*foo-tu-fo-rreht-neeng*	fotoforretning
clothing store	*klēs-bü-teek*	klesbutikk
delicatessen	*deh-lee-kah-tehs-suh-fo-rreht-neeng*	delikatesseforretning
general store, shop	*daa-leh-vaa-rruh-fo-rreht-neeng*	daglegvareforretning (NN)
	daa-lee-vaa-rruh-fo-rreht-neeng	dagligvareforretning (BM)
laundry	*rrayn-suh-rrēē*	reinseri (NN)
	rrehnsuh-rrēē	renseri (BM)
market	*mahrrk-nah*	marknad (NN)
	mahrr-kuhd	marked (BM)
newsagency/ stationers	*chyosk*	kiosk

NORWEGIAN

pharmacy	*ah-pu-tēk*	apotek
shoeshop	*skoo-töy-fo-rreht-neeng*	skotøyforretning
souvenir shop	*süü-vuh-nēē-rr-shahp*	suvenirsjapp
supermarket	**snaarr**-*cherp(s-bü-teek)*	snarkjøp(sbutikk)
vegetable shop	*grer-n-saaks-hahn-dlahrr*	grønsakshandlar (NN)
	grer-n-saaks-hahn-dluhrr	grønnsakshandler (BM)

I would like to buy …
   eh kahn for …   Eg kan få … (NN)
   ya kahn for …   Jeg kan få … (BM)
Do you have others?
   *haa rdü **ahn**-drruh?*   Har du andre? (NN)
I don't like it.
   deh lēē-kuhrr ehg eech-uh   Det liker eg ikkje. (NN)
   deh lēē-kuhrr ya eek-kuh   Det liker jeg ikke. (BM)
Can I look at it?
   kahn eh for shor po dē?   Kan eg få sjå på det? (NN)
   kahn ya for sē po dē?   Kan jeg få se på det? (BM)
I'm just looking.
   eh ba-rruh sē-rr meh rrünt   Eg berre ser meg rundt. (NN)
   ya baa-rruh sē-rr ma rrünt   Jeg bare ser meg rundt. (BM)
Can you write down the price?
   kahn du skrrēē-vuh up   Kan du skrive opp prisen?
   prrēē-sn?

Do you accept credit cards?
taa rdü ee-moot krrē-deet-ko-rt?

Tar du imot kredittkort?

Could you lower the price?
kün-nuh dü seht-tuh ned prrēē-sn?

Kunne du sette ned prisen?

I don't have much money.
eh haarr eech-uh mȳch-uh pehng-ahrr ēg

Eg har ikkje mykje pengar, eg. (NN)

ya haarr eek-kuh mȳȳ-yuh pehng-uhrr yay

Jeg har ikke mye penger, jeg. (BM)

Can I help you?
kahn eh yehl-puh dēg?

Kan eg hjelpe deg? (NN)

kahn ya yehl-puh day?

Kan jeg hjelpe deg? (BM)

Will that be all?
vaa rdeh sor nor-ko ahn-nah?

Var det så noko anna? (NN)

vaa rdeh sor noo aant?

Var det så noe annet? (BM)

Would you like it wrapped?
skahl eh pahk-kuh deh een fo rdēg?

Skal eg pakke det inn for deg? (NN)

skahl ya pahk-kuh deh een fo rday?

Skal eg pakke det inn for deg? (BM)

Sorry, this is the only one.
eh ā rlay fo rdē mehn deht-tuh ā rduhn ay-nahs-tuh

Eg er lei for det, men dette er den einaste. (NN)

buh-klaa-guhrr deht-tuh ā rduhn ē-nuhs-tuh

Beklager, dette er den eneste. (BM)

How much/many do you
want?

kurr **mȳch**-*uh*/**mahng**-*uh* *veel dü haa?*	Kor mykje/mange veel du ha? (NN)
vurr **mȳȳ**-*yuh*/**mahng**-*uh* *veel dü haa?*	Hvor mye/mange veel du ha? (BM)

Souvenirs

earrings	*öy-rruh-dob-bahrr*	øyredobbar (NN)
	ēr-rruh-dob-buhrr	øredobber (BM)
glasswork	*glahs-töy*	glastøy, glasstøy
handicraft	*künst-hahn-varrk*	kunsthandverk
necklace	*hahls-chē-duh*	halskjede
Norwegian vest	*kuf-tuh*	kufte, kofte
pottery	*stayn-töy*	steintøy
ring	*rreeng*	ring
rug	*rrȳȳ-yuh*	rye

Clothing

clothing	*klē-yuh*	klede (NN)
	klärr	klær (BM)
coat	*frrahk*	frakk
dress	*choo-luh*	kjole
jacket	*yahk-kuh*	jakke
jumper (sweater, jersey)	*gehn-suhrr*	genser
shirt	*shu-rtuh*	skjorte
shoes	*skoo*	sko
skirt	*sher-rt*	skjørt
trousers	*buk-suhrr*	bukser

It doesn't fit.
	*deh **pahs**-sahrr eech-uh*	Det passar ikkje. (NN)
	*deh **pahs**-suhrr eek-kuh*	Det passer ikke. (BM)

It is …
	deh ärr …	Det er …
too big	*fo **shtoo**-rt*	for stort
too small	*fo **lēē**-tuh*	for lite
too short	*fo-rr **ko**-rt*	for kort
too long	*fo-rr **lahngt***	for langt
too tight	*fo **teht**-seet-tahn-nuh*	for tettsittande
too loose	*fo **lohw**-st*	for laust

Materials

cotton	***bum**-ül*	bomull
handmade	***hahn-laa**-gah*	handlaga (NN)
	***hon-laa**-guht*	håndlaget (BM)
leather	*lärr*	lêr (NN)
	lärr	lær (BM)
of brass	***mehs**-seeng*	messing-
of gold	*gül*	gull-
of silver	*ser-lv*	sølv-
silk	*seelk*	silk
wool	*ül*	ull

Toiletries

comb	*kahm*	kam
condoms	***kun-doom***	kondom
deodorant	*dē-yu-du-**rrahnt***	deodorant
hairbrush	***hor**-rr-ber-shte*	hårbørste
moisturising cream	***fuk**-tee-hēts-krrēm*	fuktighetskrem

razor	*bahrr-bē-rr-hør-vuhl*	barberhøvel
sanitary napkins	**daa**-muh-been	damebind
shampoo	**shahm**-poo	sjampo
shaving cream	*bahrr-bē-rr-krrēm*	barberkrem
soap	*sor-puh*	såpe
sunblock cream	**ser**-n-blok-ul-yuh	sunblock-olje
tampons	*tahm-pong-ahrr*	tampongar (NN)
	tahm-pong-uhrr	tamponger (BM)
tissues	*pah-pēē-rr-lum-muh-ter-rr-kluh*	papirlommetørkle
toilet paper	**doo**-pah-pēē-rr	dopapir
toothbrush	**tahn**-ber-shtuh	tannbørste
toothpaste	**tahn**-krrēm	tannkrem

Stationery & Publications

map	*kah-rt*	kart
newspaper	*ah-vēēs*	avis
newspaper in English	**ehng**-uhlsk-sprror-kleh ah-vēēs	engelskspråkleg avis (NN)
	ehng-uhlsk-sprror-klee ah-vēēs	engelskspråklig avis (BM)
novels in English	**ehng**-uhl-skuh rru-**maa**-nahrr	engelske romanar (NN)
	ehng-uhl-skuh rru-**maa**-nuhrr	engelske romaner (BM)
paper	*pah-pēē-rr*	papir
pen (ballpoint)	*pehn (küü-luh-pehn)*	penn (kulepenn)
scissors	*sahks*	saks

Photography

How much is it to process this film?

> *kurr mӯch-uh kos-tahrr deh o frrahm-kahl-luh dehn-nuh feel-muhn?*

Kor mykje kostar det å framkalle denne filmen? (NN)

> *vurr mӯӯ-yuh kos-tuhrr deh o frrahm-kahl-luh dehn-nuh feel-muhn?*

Hvor mye koster det å framkalle denne filmen? (BM)

When will it be ready?

> *no-rr ā rduhn fa-rdee?*

Når er den ferdig?

I'd like a film for this camera.

> *eh veel yā-rnuh haa ehn feelm teel dehn-nuh kaa-muh-rrahn*

Eg vil gjerne ha ein film til denne kameraen. (NN)

> *ya veel yā-rnuh haa uhn feelm teel dehn-nuh kaa-muh-rrahn*

Jeg vil gjerne ha en film til denne kameraen. (BM)

B&W (film)	*svahrrt-kveet*	svart-kvitt (NN)
	svah-rt-veet	svart-hvitt (BM)
camera	*kaa-muh-rrah*	kamera
colour (film)	*fahrr-guh(-feelm)*	farge(film)
film	*feelm*	film
flash	*bleets*	blitz
lens	*leen-suh*	linse
light meter	*lӯӯs-mor-lahrr*	lysmålar (NN)
	lӯӯs-mor-luhrr	lysmåler (BM)

Smoking

A packet of cigarettes, please.

*ay pahk-kuh see-gah-**rreht-** tahrr, tahk*	Ei pakke sigarettar, takk. (NN)
*ay pahk-kuh see-gah-**rreht-** tuhrr, tahk*	Ei pakke sigaretter, takk. (BM)

Are these cigarettes strong/ mild?

*ã rdehs-suh see-gah-**rreht-** tah-ne **krrahf**-tee-yuh/**meel-** luh?*	Er desse sigarettane kraftige/milde? (NN)
*ã rdees-suh see-gah-**rreht-** tuh-ne **krrahf**-tee-yuh/**meel-** luh?*	Er disse sigarettene kraftige/milde? (BM)

Do you have a light?

haa rdü fÿÿrr?	Har du fyr?

cigarette papers	***rrül**-luh-pah-pēē-rr*	rullepapir
cigarettes	*see-gah-**rreht**-tahrr*	sigarettar (NN)
	*see-gah-**rreht**-tuhrr*	sigaretter (BM)
filtered	***feel**-tuhrr*	filter
lighter	***lai**-tuhrr*	lighter
matches	*fÿÿ-**shteek**-kuhrr*	fyrstikker
menthol	***mehn**-tol*	mentol
pipe	***pēē**-puh*	pipe
tobacco (pipe)	*(**pēē**-puh)-tu-**bahk***	(pipe)tobakk

Colours

black	*svah-rt*	svart
blue	*blor*	blå
brown	*brrüün*	brun

green	*grrēr-n*	grøn (NN)
	grrer-n	grønn (BM)
pink	*rroo-sah*	rosa
red	*rohw*	raud (NN)
	rør	rød (BM)
white	*kvēēt*	kvit (NN)
	vēēt	hvit (BM)
yellow	*güül*	gul

Sizes & Comparisons

small	*lēē-tn*	liten
big	*stoo-rr*	stor
heavy	*tung*	tung
light	*leht*	lett
more	*mayrr*	meir (NN)
	mehrr	mer (BM)
less	*meen-drruh*	mindre
too much/many	*fo-rr mÿch-uh/*	for mykje/mange
	mahng-uh	(NN)
	fo-rr mÿÿ-yuh/	for mye/mange
	mahng-uh	(BM)
many	*mahng-uh*	mange
enough	*nok*	nok
also	*ok-so*	også (NN)
	os-so	også
a little bit	*leet*	litt

NORWEGIAN

Health

Where is …?
kurr/kvaarr ārr …?		Kor/kvar er …? (NN)
vurr ārr …?		Hvor er …? (BM)
the doctor	***lē-guhn***	legen
the hospital	***shüü-kuh-hüü-suh***	sjukehuset
the chemist	***ah-pu-tē-kuh***	apoteket
the dentist	***tahn-lē-guhn***	tannlegen

I am sick.
ehg ā shüük	Eg er sjuk. (NN)
ya ā shüük	Jeg er syk. (BM)

My friend is sick.
vehn-n meen ā shüük	Vennen min er sjuk.

Could I see a female doctor?
kahn eh for snahk-kuh mēn	Kan eg få snakke med ein
kveen-nuh-leh lē-guh?	kvinneleg lege? (NN)
kahn ya for snahk-kuh mēn	Kan jeg få snakke med en
kveen-nuh-lee lē-guh?	kvinnelig lege? (BM)

What's the matter?
kvaa ārr ee vē-guhn?	Kva er i vegen? (NN)
vaa ārr ee vay-uhn?	Hva er i vegen? (BM)

Where does it hurt?
kurr yā rdeh vunt?	Kor gjer det vondt? (NN)
vurr yōr rdeh vunt?	Hvor gør det vondt? (BM)

It hurts here.
deh yārr vunt hārr	Det gjer vondt her. (NN)
deh yōr-rr vunt hārr	Dette gjør vondt. (BM)

My … hurts.
deh yārr vunt ee …	Det gjer vondt i … (NN)
deh yōr-rr vunt ee …	Det gjør vondt i … (BM)

Parts of the Body
(my/your)

ankle	*uk-lah*	okla (NN)
	ahng-kuh-luhn	ankelen (BM)
arm	*ahrr-muhn*	armen
back	*rrȳg-guhn*	ryggen
chest	*brrȳst-kahs-sah*	brystkassa
ear	*öy-rruh*	øyret (NN)
	ēr-rruh	øret
eye	*ohw-guh*	auget (NN)
	öy-uh	øyet (BM)
finger	*feeng-uh-rruhn*	fingeren
foot	*foo-tn*	foten
hand	*hahn-nah*	handa (NN)
	hon-nah	hånda (BM)
head	*hor-wuh*	hovudet (NN)
	hoo-duh	hodet (BM)
heart	*yahrr-tuh*	hjartet (NN)
	ya-rtuh	hjertet (BM)
leg	*bay-nuh*	beinet
mouth	*mün-n*	munnen
nose	*naa-suhn*	nasen (NN)
	nē-sah	nesa (BM)
skin	*hüü-dah*	huda (NN)
	hüü-dn	huden (BM)
teeth	*tehn-n-nuh*	tennene
throat	*strrüü-puhn*	strupen

NORWEGIAN

Ailments

I have ...

eh haarr ...	Eg har ... (NN)	
ya haarr ...	Jeg har ... (BM)	
an allergy	*ehn ahl-lehrr-gēē*	ein allergi (NN)
	uhn ahl-lehrr-gēē	en allergi (BM)
anaemia	*bloo-mahng-uhl*	blodmangel
a burn	*eht brrehn-sor-rr*	eit brennsår (NN)
	uht brrehn-sor-rr	et brennsår (BM)
a cold	*snüü-uh*	snue
constipation	*fo-shtop-peeng*	forstopping (NN)
	fo-shtop-puhlsuh	forstoppelse (BM)
a cough	*hus-tuh*	hoste
diarrhoea	*maa-guh-shohw*	magesjau
fever	*fē-buhrr*	feber
a headache	*vunt ee hor-wuh*	vondt i hovudet (NN)
	vunt ee hoo-duh	vondt i hodet (BM)
hepatitis	*güül-sot*	gulsòtt
indigestion	*dor-rleh fo-rdöy-e eng*	dårlég fordøying (NN)
	dor-rlee fo-rdöy-uhl-suh	dårlig fordøyelse (BM)
an infection	*ehn buh-tehn-uhl-suh*	ein (BM en) betennelse
influenza	*een-flü-ehn-sah*	influensa
low/high blood pressure	*lor-kt/her-kt bloo-trrȳk*	lågt/høgt blodtrykk (NN)
	laaft/höyt bloo-trrȳk	lavt/høyt blodtrykk (BM)
a pain	*sma-rtuh*	smerte
sore throat	*vunt ee hahl-sn*	vondt i halsen

sprain	*ay foshtüü-eeng*	ei forstuing
sunburn	*sool-brrehnt-hayt*	solbrentheit (NN)
	sool-brrehnt-hēt	solbrenthet (BM)
a venereal	*ehn cher-n-*	ein (BM en)
disease	*shüükdom*	kjønnssjukdom
worms	*een-vor-ls-mahk*	innvolsmakk (NN)
	een-vols-mahrrk	innvollsmark (BM)

Some Useful Words & Phrases
I'm ...
eh haarr ...   Eg har ... (NN)
ya haarr ...   Jeg har ... (BM)

diabetic	*suk-kuh-shüü-kuh*	sukkersjuke
epileptic	*fahl-luh-shüü-kuh*	fallesjuke
asthmatic	*ahst-mah*	astma

I'm allergic to ...
ēg ārr ah-lehrr-geesk moot ... Eg er allergisk mot ... (NN)
ya ārr ah-lehrr-geesk moot ... Jeg er allergisk mot ... (BM)

| antibiotics | *ahn-tee-bee-yoo-tee-kah* | antibiotika |
| penicillin | *pehn-nee-see-lēēn* | penicillin |

I'm pregnant.
ēg ārr grrah-vēēd   Eg er gravid. (NN)
ya ārr grrah-vēēd   Jeg er gravid. (BM)

I'm on the pill.
eh tēk pē-peel-lah   Eg tek P-pilla. (NN)
ya taarr pē-peel-luhn   Jeg tar P-pillen. (BM)

NORWEGIAN

I haven't had my period for
... months.

    *eh haarr **eech**-uh haht vē-*   Eg har ikkje hatt veka på ...
    *kah por ... **mornaarr***   måneder. (NN)

    *ya haarr **eek**-kuh haht vē-*   Jeg har ikke hatt veka på ...
    *kah por ... **mor-ntuhrr***   måneder. (BM)

I have been vaccinated.

    *ēg ärr vahk-see-**nē-rt***   Eg er vaksinert. (NN)

    *ya ärr vahk-see-**nē-rt***   Jeg er vaksinert. (BM)

I have my own syringe.

    *eh haarr meen **ay**-guhn*   Eg har min eigen
    ***sprröy**-tuh-spees*   sprøytespiss. (NN)

    *ya haarr meen **ē**-guhn*   Jeg har min egen
    ***sprröy**-tuh-spees*   sprøytespiss. (BM)

I feel better/worse.

    *eh **chehn**-nuhrr meh bē-*   Eg kjenner meg betre/verre.
    *rruh/**varr**-uh*   (NN)

    *ya **fēr**-luhrr meh bē-*   Jeg føler meg bedre/verre.
    *drruh/**varr**-uh*   (BM)

accident	*üü-lÿk-kuh*	ulykke
addiction	*aav-**hehng**-ee-hayt*	avhengigheit (NN)
	*aav-**hehng**-ee-hēt*	avhengighet (BM)
aspirin	*dees-**prreel***	dispril
bandage	*bahn-**daa**-shuh*	bandasje
blood test	*bloo-**prrør**-vuh*	blodprøve
contraceptive	*prrē-vehn-**shoons**-meedl*	prevensjonsmiddel
injection	***sprröy**-tuh*	sprøyte
menstruation	*mehns-trrü-ah-**shoon***	menstruasjon

At the Chemist
I need medication for ...
*eh trrehng eht **meedl** moot ...* Eg treng eit middel mot ... (NN)
*ya trrehng-uhrr eht **meedl** moot ...* Jeg trenger et middel mot ... (BM)
I have a prescription.
*eh haarr ehn rruh-**sehpt*** Eg har ein resept. (NN)
*ya haarr uhn rruh-**sehpt*** Jeg har en resept. (BM)

Time & Dates
What time is it?
*kvaa ärr **klok-kah?*** Kva er klokka? (NN)
*vaa ärr **klok-kah?*** Hva er klokka? (BM)

It is ... (am/pm)
klok-kah ärr ... Klokka er ...
in the morning *um **fo-rr**-meed-daa-guhn* om formiddagen
in the afternoon *um **eht-tuhrr**-meed-daa-guhn* om ettermiddagen
in the evening *um **kvehl**-n* om kvelden

What date is it today?
*kvaa **daa**-tu ärr deh ee-**daag?*** Kva dato er det i dag? (NN)
*vaa **daatu** ärr deh ee-**daag?*** Hva dato er det i dag? (BM)

Days of the Week
Monday *mon-daa(g)* måndag (NN)
  mahn-daa(g) mandag (BM)
Tuesday *tÿÿs-daa(g)* tysdag (BM)
  tēēsh-daa(g) tirsdag (BM)
Wednesday *uns-daa(g)* onsdag

NORWEGIAN

Thursday	*toosh-daa(g)*	torsdag
Friday	*frrē-daa(g)*	fredag
Saturday	*lohw-rdaa(g)*	laurdag (NN)
	ler-rdaa(g)	lørdag (BM)
Sunday	*ser-n-daa(g)*	søndag
	sun-daa(g)	sundag (NN)

Months

January	*yah-nü-waarr*	januar
February	*feh-brrü-waarr*	februar
March	*maash*	mars
April	*ah-prreel*	april
May	*maa-ee*	mai
June	*yüü-nee*	juni
July	*yüü-lee*	juli
August	*ohw-güst*	august
September	*sehp-tehm-buhrr*	september
October	*uk-too-buhrr*	oktober
November	*no-vehm-buhrr*	november
December	*dē-sehm-buhrr*	desember

Seasons

summer	*soo-mahrr*	sommar (NN)
	som-muhrr	sommer (BM)
autumn	*hohw-st*	haust (NN)
	her-st	høst (BM)
winter	*veen-tuhrr*	vinter
spring	*vor-rr*	vår

Present

today	*ee-daag*	i dag
this morning	*ee-daag mo-rr-gon*	i dag morgon (NN)
	ee-mo-rr-uhs	i morges (BM)

tonight (evening)	*ee-kvehl*	i kveld
this week	*dehn-nuh vē-kah*	denne veka (NN)
	dehn-nuh üü-kah	denne uka (BM)
this year	*ee-yor-rr*	i år
now	*nor*	nå
	noo	no (NN)

Past

yesterday	*ee-gor-rr*	i går
day before yesterday	*ee fēr-rr-dahks*	i førdags (NN)
	ee fo-rr-gor-sh	i forgårs (BM)
yesterday morning	*ee-gor-rr fo-rr-meed-daag*	i går formiddag
last night	*ee-naht*	i natt
last week/month	*sees-tuh vē-kuh/ mor-nah*	siste veke/månad (NN)
	sees-tuh üü-kuh/ mor-nt	siste uke/måned (BM)
last year	*ee-fyoo-rr*	i fjor

Future

tomorrow	*ee-mo-rr-gon*	i morgon (NN)
	ee-mor-rn	i morgen (BM)
day after tomorrow	ee-or-vuhrr-mo-rr-gon	i overmorgon (NN)
	ee-or-vuhrr-mor-rn	i overmorgen (BM)
tomorrow morning	ee-mo-rr-gon fo-rr-meed-daag	i morgon formiddag (NN)
next week	**nehs-tuh vē-kah**	neste veka (NN)
	nehs-tuh üü-kuh	neste uke (BM)
next year	**nehs-tuh or-rr**	neste år

During the Day

afternoon	*eht-tuhrr-meed-daag*	ettermiddag
dawn, very early morning	*daa-grrȳȳ*	daggry
day	*daag*	dag
early	*tēē-lehg*	tidleg (NN)
	tēē-lee	tidlig (BM)
midnight	*meet-naht*	midtnatt
morning	*fo-rr-meed-daag*	formiddag
night	*naht*	natt
noon	*klok-kah tol*	klokka tolv
sundown	*sool-nē-gahng*	solnedgang
sunrise	*sool-up-gahng*	soloppgang

Numbers & Amounts

0	*nül*	null
1	*ayn*	ein (NN)
	ēn	en (BM)
2	*too*	to
3	*trrē*	tre
4	*fēē-rruh*	fire
5	*fehm*	fem
6	*sehks*	seks
7	*shüü*	sju
	sȳȳv	syv (BM)
8	*ot-tuh*	åtte
9	*nēē*	ni
10	*tēē*	ti
11	*el-vuh*	elleve
12	*tol*	tolv
20	*chü-uh*	tjue
	tȳȳ-vuh	tyve (BM)

30	*trreht-tee*	tretti
	trrehd-vuh	tredve
40	*fer-rtee*	førti
50	*fem-tee*	femti
60	*sehks-tee*	seksti
70	*sȳt-tee*	sytti (NN)
	ser-tee	sytti (BM)
80	*ot-tee*	åtti
90	*neet-tee*	nitti
100	*hün-drruh*	hundre (BM)
1000	*tüüs-uhn*	tusen
one million	*ayn mee-lee-yoon*	ein million (NN)
	ēn mee-lee-yoon	en million (BM)
¼	*ehn kvah-rt*	ein (BM en) kvart
⅓	*ehn trrē-dēl*	ein (BM en) tredel
½	*ehn hahl*	ein (BM en) halv
¾	*trrē-kvah-rt*	trekvart
1st	*fer-sh-tuh*	første
2nd	*aa-uhn*	annen, (NN) annan
	ahn-drruh	andre
3rd	*trreh-dyuh*	tredje

Some Useful Words

a little (amount)	*leet*	litt
double	*dob-buhlt*	dobbelt
a dozen	*tol*	tolv
Enough!	*nok!*	nok!
few	*for*	få

less	*meen-drruh*	mindre
many	*mahng-uh*	mange
more	*mayrr/**flay**-rruh*	meir/fleire (NN)
	*mē-rr/**flē**-rruh*	mer/flere (BM)
once	*ayn gong*	ein gong (NN)
	ēn gahng	en gang (BM)
a pair	*eht paarr*	eit par (NN)
	eht pahrr	et par (BM)
percent	*prru-**sehnt***	prosent
some	*noo-n*	noen
	nok-rruh	nokre (NN)
too much	*fo-rr **mȳȳ**-yuh*	for mye
	*fo-rr **mȳch**-uh*	for mykje (NN)
twice	*too gong-uhrr*	to gonger
	too gahng-uhrr	to ganger (BM)

Abbreviations

AS	company
EF	EC
e.Kr./f.Kr.	AD/BC
FN	UN
f.o.m.	from (eg. today)
gt./vn.	St/Rd
hovudpostkontor	GPO
Herr/Fru	Mr/Mrs/MS
m.o.h.	meter above sealevel
NAF	AA (Automobile Association)
nord/sør	Nth/Sth
NSB	Norwegian Railway Company
postnummer	ZIP-code
Storbritannia	UK

NORWEGIAN

Swedish

Swedish

Introduction

Swedish is a Germanic language, belonging to the Nordic branch, and spoken by the Swedes, who number about 8.5 million, and some small numbers of Finns and Estonians. Swedes, Danes and Norwegians can, however, make themselves understood as the languages are similar. Since Swedish is spoken by so few, most Swedes speak English as a second language.

Since they share common roots in Old Norse, you will find many similarities between English and Swedish. However, the pronunciations alter, and there are sounds in Swedish which are not found in English. There are, for instance, three more letters in the Swedish alphabet: **å**, **ä** and **ö**. Swedish grammar follows the Nordic Germanic languages. Verbs are the same regardless of person: 'I am, you are, etc' is, in Swedish, *Jag är, du är,* and so on. Definite articles in Swedish ('the' in English) are determined by the ending of a noun: *-en* and *-et* for singular nouns and *-na* or *-n* for plural. To determine if it is *-en* or *-et* as an ending can be difficult and has to be learnt word by word.

One last suggestion is to try to learn the common phrases for politeness, as your attempts will be greatly appreciated by the Swedes, who are not used to foreigners speaking Swedish.

Pronunciation

Sweden is a large country but with a relatively small population. Since people in the past lived scattered and isolated, there is a great variety of dialects. There are sounds in Swedish which do not exist in English, so we have tried to give as close approximations as possible.

Vowels

The vowels are pronounced as short sounds if there is a double consonant afterwards, otherwise they are long sounds. Sometimes the **o** in Swedish sounds like the **å**, and **e** as the **ä**. There are, however, not as many exceptions to the rules as there are in English, and you'll find the best way to learn these sounds is to listen to speakers during your travels.

Swedish	Long	Short
a	as the 'a' in 'father'	as in 'cut', or the French *ami*
o	as in 'zoo'	as in 'pot'
u	sounds like 'ooo!' when you don't like something	as in 'pull'
i	as in 'see'	as in 'in'
e	as in 'fear'	as in 'bet'
å	as in 'poor' (rendered in the pronunciation guide as *oo-a*)	almost like the 'o' in 'pot'
ä	as in 'act'	as in the French *et*
ö	similar to the 'er' in 'fern', closer to the *ö* in the German *schön*	as in the French *deux*
y	as in German *über*	as in the French *tu*

Consonants

The consonants are pronounced almost the same as in English, although the following variations and combinations are specific to Swedish:

c	like the 's' in 'sit'; sometimes as 'k'
ck	like a double 'k', which gives the vowel before a short sound
tj, rs	a 'sh' sound, as in 'ship'
sj, ch	a thin gutteral 'ch' sound, similar to the Scottish *loch*, or the German *ich*
g, lj	a 'y' sound, as in 'onion'. Sometimes the **g** is pronounced as the 'g' in 'good'

Greetings & Civilities
Top Useful Phrases

Hello.
hay　　　　　　　　　　　　　Hej.
Goodbye.
ah-yer/hay da!　　　　　　　　Adjö/Hej då!
Yes./No.
yaa/nay　　　　　　　　　　　Ja./Nej.
Excuse me.
ur-zhak-taa may　　　　　　　Ursäkta mig.
May I? Do you mind?
foo-ar yaagh? yer deat　　　　Får jag? Gör det något?
noo-agh-ot?
Sorry. (excuse me, forgive me)
fer-laht (ur-shak-ta may,　　　Förlåt. (ursäkta mig, förlåt
fer-loo-at may)　　　　　　　　mig)
Please.
snal-ah, van-ligh-ehn　　　　　Snälla, vänligen.
Thank you.
tahk　　　　　　　　　　　　　Tack.
Many thanks.
stoort tahk　　　　　　　　　　Stort tack.

That's fine. You're welcome.
| *deat ar braa* | Det är bra. |
| *vaar-soo-a-good* | Varsågod. |

Greetings
Good morning.
| *good-mor-ghon* | Godmorgon. |

Good afternoon.
| *good-ehft-ear-mi-daagh* | Godeftermiddag. |

Good evening/night.
| *good-kval/naht* | Godkväll/natt. |

How are you?
| *hur moo-ar du?* | Hur mår du? |

Well, thanks.
| *braa, tahk* | Bra, tack. |

Forms of Address
Madam/Mrs	*daam/fru*	Dam/Fru
Sir/Mr	*hehrn/hehr*	Herrn/Herr
Miss	*frer-kehn*	Fröken
companion, friend	*kahm-raat, van*	kamrat, vän

Small Talk
Meeting People
What is your name?
| *vaad heat-ehr du?* | Vad heter du? |

My name is ...
| *yaagh heat-ehr ...* | Jag heter ... |

I'd like to introduce you to ...
| *foo-ar yaagh preh-sehn-tear-ah day ferr ...* | Får jag presentera dig för ... |

I'm pleased to meet you.
ahn-yeh-namt aht traf-ah day   Angenämt att träffa dig.

Nationalities

Where are you from?
vaar ar du ee-froo-an?   Var är du ifrån?

I am from ...
yaagh ar froo-an ...   Jag är från ...

Australia	*ah-u-straa-lee-ehn*	Australien
Canada	*kah-nah-dah*	Kanada
England	*ehng-lahnd*	England
Ireland	*ir-lahnd*	Irland
New Zealand	*nü-ah sea-lahnd*	Nya Zealand
Scotland	*skot-lahnd*	Skottland
the USA	*u-s-aa*	USA
Wales	*vayls*	Wales

Age

How old are you?
hur gahm-ahl ar du?   Hur gammal är du?

I am ... years old.
yaagh ar ... oo-ar gahm-ahl   Jag är ... år gammal.

Occupations

What (work) do you do?
vilk-eht ar dit ür-keh   Vilket är ditt yrke?

I am (a/an) ...
yaagh ar ...   Jag är ...

artist	*ahr-tist*	artist
business person	*ah-fars-mahn*	affärsman
doctor	*dok-toor*	doktor

English	Pronunciation	Swedish
engineer	*ing-khehn-yerr*	ingengör
farmer	*boon-deh*	bonde
journalist	*khoor-nah-list*	journalist
lawyer	*ahd-voo-kaat*	advokat
manual worker	*hahnt-vehrk-ahr-eh*	hantverkare
mechanic	*meh-kaan-i-kehr*	mekaniker
nurse	*khert-ehr-zhkah*	sköterska
office worker	*kon-toor-ist*	kontorist
scientist	*veat-ehn-skaaps-mahn*	vetenskapsman
student	*stu-dehnt*	student
teacher	*lar-ahr-eh*	lärare
waiter	*sehr-vee-trees*	servitris (f)
	sehr-vee-terr	servitör (m)
writer	*ferr-faht-ahr-eh*	fårfattare

Religion

What is your religion?
  vil-kehn ar din rehl-ee-oon?   Vilken är din religon?
I am not religious.
  yaagh ar int-eh rehl-ee-khers   Jag är inte religös.

I am ...
  yaagh ar ...   Jag är ...

English	Pronunciation	Swedish
Buddhist	*bud-ist*	Buddist
Catholic	*kat-oo-leek*	Katolik
Christian	*krist-ehn*	Kristen
Hindu	*hin-du*	Hindu
Jewish	*yu-deh*	Jude
Muslim	*mu-sleem*	Muslim

Family

Are you married?
  ar du yift?   Är du gift?

I am single.
  yaagh ar oo-yift   Jag är ogift.

I am married.
  yaagh ar yift   Jag är gift.

How many children do you
have?
  hur moo-ang-ah baarn   Hur många barn har du?
  haar du?

I don't have any children.
  yaagh haar ing-ah baarn   Jag har inga barn.

I have a daughter/a son.
  yaagh har ehn dot-ehr/   Jag har en dotter/son.
  soo-an

How many brothers/sisters do
you have?
  hur moo-ang-ah brer-dehr/ Hur många bröder/systrar
  süs-trahr haar du?   har du?

Is your husband/wife here?
  ar din mahn/fru har?   Är din man/fru här?

Do you have a boyfriend/
girlfriend?
  har du ehn poyk-van/   Har du en pojkvän/flickvän?
  flik-van?

brother	*broor*	bror
children	*baarn*	barn
daughter	*dot-ehr*	dotter
family	*fah-mily*	familj

father	*faar*	far
husband	*mahn*	man
mother	*moor*	mor
sister	*süs-tehr*	syster
son	*soo-an*	son
wife	*fru*	fru

Feelings

I like ...
   yaagh tük-ehr om ...   Jag tycker om ...
I don't like ...
   yaagh tük-ehr int-eh om ...   Jag tycker inte om ...
I am in a hurry.
   yaagh haar broo-at-om   Jag har bråttom.
I am right.
   yaagh haar rat   Jag har rätt.
I am sorry. (condolence)
   yaagh bea-klaagh-ahr   Jag beklagar.
I am grateful.
   yaagh ar tahk-sahm   Jag är tacksam.

I am ...
   yaagh ar ...   Jag är ...

cold/hot	*kahl/vahrm*	kall/varm
hungry/thirsty	*hung-righ/terrs-tigh*	hungrig/törstig
sleepy	*trert*	trött
angry	*ahry*	arg
happy/sad	*ghlaad/lehs-ehn*	glad/ledsen
tired	*trert*	trött
well	*frisk*	frisk
worried	*oo-roo-ligh*	orolig

Language Difficulties

Do you speak English?
taal-ahr du ehng-ehl-skah?   Talar du engelska?

Does anyone speak English?
taal-ahr noo-ag-on   Talar någon engelska?
ehng-ehl-skah?

I speak a little ...
yaagh taal-ahr lee-teh ...   Jag talar lite ...

I don't speak ...
yaagh taal-ahr int-eh ...   Jag talar inte ...

I (don't) understand.
yaagh ferr-stoo-ar (int-eh)   Jag förstår (inte).

Could you speak more slowly
please?
kahn du van-lig-ehn taal-ah   Kan du vänligen tala lite
lee-teh loo-ang-sahm-ahr-   långsammare?
eh?

Could you repeat that?
kahn du up-reap-ah deat?   Kan du upprepa det?

How do you say ...?
hur sayer mahn ...?   Hur säger man ...?

What does ... mean?
vaad beh-tüd-ehr ...?   Vad betyder ...?

I speak ...
yaagh taal-ahr ...   Jag talar ...

English	Pronunciation	Swedish
Danish	*dahn-skah*	Danska
Dutch	*hol-land-skah*	Holländska
English	*ehng-ehl-skah*	Engelska
Finnish	*fin-skah*	Finska
French	*frahn-skah*	Franska

| German | *tü-skah* | Tyska |
| Italian | *ital-yen-skah* | Italienska |

Some Useful Phrases

Sure.
  yaa-vist   Javisst.
Just a minute.
  drery ehn mi-nut   Dröj en minut.
It's (not) important.
  deat ar (int-eh) vikt-ight   Det är (inte) viktigt.
It's (not) possible.
  deat ar (int-eh) mery-light   Det är (inte) möjligt.
Good luck!
  lüka til!   Lycka till!

Signs

BAGGAGE COUNTER	BAGAGE INLÄMNING
CHECK-IN COUNTER	INCHECKNING
CUSTOMS	TULL
EMERGENCY EXIT	NÖDUTGÅNG
ENTRANCE	INGÅNG
EXIT	UTGÅNG
FREE ADMISSION	GRATIS INTRÄDE
HOT/COLD	VARM/KALL
INFORMATION	INFORMATION
NO ENTRY	INGEN INGÅNG
NO SMOKING	RÖKFÖRBUD
OPEN/CLOSED	ÖPPEN/STÄNGD
PROHIBITED	FÖRBJUDET
RESERVED	RESERVERAD
TELEPHONE	TELEFON
TOILETS	TOALETTER

SWEDISH

Emergencies

POLICE POLICE STATION	POLIS POLISSTATION

Help!
yalp! — Hjälp!

It's an emergency!
deat ar ehn nerd-sit-u-ah-khoon! — Det är en nödsituation!

There's been an accident!
deat haar hant ehn oo-lük-ah! — Det har hänt en olycka!

Call a doctor!
ring ehf-tehr ehn dok-toor! — Ring efter en doktor!

Call an ambulance!
ring ehf-tehr ehn ahm-bu-lahns! — Ring efter en ambulans!

I've been raped.
yaagh haar bleev-it voo-ald-taagh-ehn — Jag har blivit våldtagen.

I've been robbed!
yaagh haar bleev-it roo-an-ahd! — Jag har blivit rånad!

Call the police!
ring poo-lees-ehn! — Ring polisen!

Where is the police station?
vaar ar poo-lees-stah-khoon-ehn? — Var är polisstationen?

Go away!
ferr-svin! — Försvinn!

I'll call the police!
yaagh ring-ehr poo-lees-ehn!
Jag ringer polisen!

Thief!
zhuv!
Tjuv!

I am/My friend is ill.
yaagh ar/min van ar khuk
Jag är/Min vän är sjuk.

I am lost.
yaagh ar vils-eh
Jag är vilse.

Where are the toilets?
vaar ar too-ah-leht-ehr-nah?
Var är toaletterna?

Could you help me please?
kahn du van-lig-ehn yalp-ah may?
Kan du vänligen hjälpa mig?

Could I please use the telephone?
kahn yaagh van-lig-ehn foo-a ahn-van-dah tehl-eh-foo-an-ehn?
Kan jag vänligen få använda telefonen?

I'm sorry. I apologise.
yaagh ar leh-sehn. yaagh bear om ur-sakt
Jag är ledsen. Jag ber om ursäkt.

I didn't realise I was doing anything wrong.
yaagh fer-stood int-eh aht yaagh yoor-deh noo-ag-ot feal
Jag förstod inte att jag gjorde något fel.

I didn't do it.
yaagh yoor-deh deat int-eh
Jag gjorde det inte.

292 Swedish

I wish to contact my embassy/
consulate.
> *yaagh ern-skahr kon-tahk-*
> *tah min ahm-bah-saad/mit*
> *kon-su-laat*

Jag önskar kontakta min
ambassad/mitt konsulat.

I speak English.
> *yaagh taal-ahr ehng-ehl-*
> *skah*

Jag talar engelska.

I have medical insurance.
> *yaagh haar khuk-fer-sak-*
> *ring*

Jag har sjukförsäkring.

My possessions are insured.
> *minag agh-o-deal-ahr ar*
> *fer-sak-rad-eh*

Mina ägodelar är försäkrade.

My ... was stolen.
> *min ... bleav stul-ehn*

Min ... blev stulen.

I've lost ...
> *yaagh haar fer-loor-aht ...*

Jag har förlorat ...

my bags	*min-ah vask-oor*	mina väskor
my handbag	*min hahnd-vask-ah*	min handväska
my money	*mina pehng-ahr*	mina pengar
my travellers' cheques	*min-ah reas-eh-shehk-ahr*	mina resecheckar
my passport	*mit pahs*	mitt pass

Paperwork

name	*nahmn*	namn
address	*ah-drehs*	adress
date of birth	*fer-dehl-seh-daat-um*	födelsedatum

place of birth	*fer-dehl-seh-ort*	födelseort
age	*oo-ald-ehr*	ålder
sex	*shern*	kön
nationality	*naht-khoo-nahl-i-teat*	nationalitet
religion	*rehl-i-yoon*	religon
reason for travel	*reas-ahns and-ah-moo-al*	resans ändamål
profession	*ürk-eh*	yrke
marital status	*yift/oo-yift*	gift/ogift
passport	*pahs*	pass
passport number	*pahs-num-ehr*	passnummer
visa	*vee-sum*	visum
tourist card	*tur-ist-kort*	turistkort
identification	*lehg-i-ti-mah-khoon*	legitimation
birth certificate	*ferd-ehl-seh-beh-vees*	födelsebevis
driver's licence	*ker-kort*	körkort
customs	*tul*	tull
immigration	*i-meh-grah-khoon*	imegration
border	*ghrans*	gräns

Getting Around

ARRIVALS	INKOMMANDE
BUS STOP	BUSSHÅLLPLATS
DEPARTURES	AVGÅENDE
STATION	STATION
SUBWAY	TUNNELBANA
TICKET OFFICE	BILJETTKONTOR
TIMETABLE	TIDTABELL
TRAIN STATION	TÅGSTATION

What time does the ... leave/
arrive?

nar ahv-goo-ar/kom-ehr ...?   När avgår/kommer ...?

(air)plane	*flüg-plaan-eht*	flygplanet
boat	*boo-at-ehn*	båten
bus (city)	*stahds-bus-ehn*	stadsbussen
bus (intercity)	*lahnds-orts-bus-ehn*	landsortsbussen
train	*too-ag-eht*	tåget
tram	*spoo-ar-vahngn-ehn*	spårvagnen

Directions

Where is ...?
vaar ar ...?   Var är ...?

How do I get to ...?
hur kom-ehr yaagh til ...?   Hur kommer jag till ...?

Is it near here?
ar deat loo-angt har-i-froo-an?   Är det långt härifrån?

Can I walk there?
kahn yaagh goo-a deet?   Kan jag gå dit?

Can you show me (on the map)?
kahn du vees-ah may (poo-a kaart-ahn)?   Kan du visa mig (på kartan)?

Are there other means of getting there?
kahn yaagh kom-ah deet poo-a ahn-drah sat?   Kan jag komma dit på andra sätt?

I want to go to ...
yaagh vil goo-a til ...   Jag vill gå till ...

SWEDISH

Go straight ahead.
  goo-a raakt frahm   Gå rakt fram.
It's two blocks down.
  deat ar tvoo-a kvahr-tear   Det är två kvarter neråt.
  near-oo-at
Turn left ...
  svang vans-tehr ...   Sväng vänster ...
Turn right ...
  svang herg-ehr ...   Sväng höger...

at the next corner	*veed nast-ah hern*	vid nästa hörn
at the traffic lights	*veed trah-feek-yus-eht*	vid trafikljuset
behind	*bak-om*	bakom
in front of	*frahm-ferr*	framför
far	*loo-angt*	långt
far	*nar-ah*	nära
opposite	*moot-saht*	motsatt

Booking Tickets

Excuse me, where is the ticket office?
  ur-sakt-ah may, vaar ar bil-yet-kon-toor-eht?   Ursäkta mig, var är biljettkontoret?
Where can I buy a ticket?
  vaar kahn yaagh kerpa ehn bil-yet?   Var kan jag köpa en biljett?
I want to go to ...
  yaagh vil oo-ak-ah til ...   Jag vill åka till ...
Do I need to book?
  moo-as-teh yaagh book-ah?   Måste jag boka?

You need to book.
  du moo-as-teh book-ah   Du måste boka.
I would like to book a seat
to ...
  yaagh skul-eh vil-yah book-   Jag skulle vilja boka en
  ah ehn plahts til ...   plats till ...

I would like ...
  yaagh skul-eh vil-yah   Jag skulle vilja ha ...
  haa ...

a one-way ticket	*ehn ehnk-ehl-bil-yeht*	en enkelbiljett
a return ticket	*ehn reh-tur-bil-yeht*	en returbiljett
two tickets	*tvoo-a bil-yeht-ehr*	två biljetter
tickets for all of us	*bil-yeht-ehr fer os ahlah*	biljetter för oss alla
a student's fare	*stud-ehnt-bil-yht*	studentbiljett
a child's/pensioner's fare	*baarn-bil-yeht/pehn-kho-nars-bil-yeht*	barnbiljett/pensionärsbiljett
1st class	*fers-tah klahs*	första klass
2nd class	*ahnd-rah klahs*	andra klass

It is full.
  deat ar fult   Det är fullt.
Is it completely full?
  ar deat healt fult?   Är det helt fullt?
Can I get a stand-by ticket?
  fins deat ehn vant-eh-lis-   Finns det en väntelista?
  tah?

Air

CHECKING IN	INCHECKNING
LUGGAGE PICKUP	BAGAGEHÄMTNING
REGISTRATION	INSKRIVNING

Is there a flight to ...?
fins deat eht flügh til ...? Finns det ett flyg till ...?

When is the next flight to ...?
nar goo-ar nast-ah flügh til ...? När går nästa flyg till ...?

How long does the flight take?
hur loo-ang teed taar flügh-tur-ehn? Hur lång tid tar flygturen?

What is the flight number?
vaad ar flügh-num-reht? Vad är flygnummret?

You must check in at ...
du moo-ast-eh shek-ah in veed ... Du måste checka in vid ...

airport tax	*flügh-plahts-skaht*	flygplatsskatt
boarding pass	*ehm-bahr-kear-ings-kort*	embarkeringskort
customs	*tul*	tull

Bus

| BUS/TRAM STOP | BUSS-/SPÅRVAGNS-HÅLLPLATS |

Where is the bus/tram stop?
vaar ar bus/spoo-ar-vahngns-hoo-al-plahts-ehn?

Var är buss/spårvagnshållplatsen?

Which bus goes to ...?
vil-kehn bus goo-ar til ...?

Vilken buss går till ...?

Does this bus go to ...?
goo-ar dehn-ah bus til ...?

Går denna buss till ...?

How often do buses pass by?
hur of-tah goo-ar bus-ahr-nah?

Hur ofta går bussarna?

Could you let me know when we get to ...?
kahn du mea-deal-ah nar vee kom-ehr til ...?

Kan du meddela när vi kommer till ...?

I want to get off!
yaagh vil goo-a aav!

Jag vill gå av!

What time is the ... bus?
nar goo-ar ... bus?

När går ... buss?

next	*nas-tah*	nästa
first	*fers-tah*	första
last	*sis-tah*	sista

Metro

METRO/UNDERGROUND	TUNNELBANA
CHANGE (for coins)	VÄXEL
THIS WAY TO	DENNA VÄG TILL
WAY OUT	UTGÅNG

Which line takes me to ...?
vil-kehn leen-yeh goo-ar til ...?
Vilken linje går till ...?

What is the next station?
vil-kehn ar nast-ah stah-khoon?
Vilken är nästa station?

Train

DINING CAR	RESTURANGVAGN
EXPRESS	EXPRESS
PLATFORM NO	PERRONG NR
SLEEPING CAR	SOVVAGN

Is this the right platform for ...?
ar deht-ah rat pear-ong fer ...?
Är detta rätt perrong för ...?

Passengers must change trains/platforms.
pas-ah-khear-ahr-eh moo-as-teh büt-ah too-agh/pear-ong
Passagerare måste byta tåg/perrong.

The train leaves from platform ...
too-ag-eht aav-goo-ar froo-an pear-ong ...
Tåget avgår från perrong ...

| dining car | *rehs-tu-rahng-vahngn* | resturangvagn |
| express | *ehx-prehs* | express |

| local | *loo-kaal* | lokal |
| sleeping car | *soov-vahngn* | sovvagn |

Taxi

Can you take me to ...?
  kahn du ker-ah may til ...? Kan du köra mig till ...?
Please take me to ...
  van-ligh-ehn ker til ... Vänligen kör till ...
How much does it cost to go
to ...?
  vaad kost-ahr deat til ...? Vad kostar det till ...?

Instructions

Here is fine, thank you.
  har bleer braa, tahk Här blir bra, tack.
The next corner, please.
  nast-ah hern, tahk Nästa hörn, tack.
Continue!
  foort-sat! Fortsätt!
The next street to the left/right.
  nast-ah gaat-ah til Nästa gata till vänster/höger.
  vans-tehr/herg-ehr
Stop here!
  stahn-ah har! Stanna här!
Please slow down.
  van-lig-ehn sahk-tah near Vänligen sakta ner.
Please wait here.
  van-lig-ehn van-tah har Vänligen vänta här.

Some Useful Phrases

The train is delayed/cancelled.
*too-ag-eht ar fer-sean-aht/
in-stalt* Tåget är försenat/inställt.

How long will it be delayed?
*hur mük-eht ar deat
ferr-sean-aht?* Hur mycket är det försenat?

There is a delay of ... hours.
*deat ar ferr-sean-aht ... tim-
ahr* Det är försenat ... timmar.

Can I reserve a place?
*kahn yaagh reas-ehr-vear-
ah ehn plahts?* Kan jag reservera en plats?

How long does the trip take?
*hur loo-ang teed taar
reas-ahn?* Hur lång tid tar resan?

Is it a direct route?
*ar deat ehn dir-ehkt-ferr-
bind-ehl-seh?* Är det en direktförbindelse?

Is that seat taken?
ar sat-eht up-taag-eht? Är sätet upptaget?

I want to get off at ...
yaagh vil goo-a aav veed ... Jag vill gå av vid ...

Excuse me.
ur-sakt-ah may Ursäkta mig.

Where can I hire a bicycle?
*vaar kahn yaagh hür-ah
ehn sük-ehl?* Var kan jag hyra en cykel?

SWEDISH

Car

FREEWAY	MOTORVÄG
GARAGE	GARAGE
GIVE WAY	VÄJA
MECHANIC	VERKSTAD
NO ENTRY	INGEN PÅFART
NO PARKING	PARKERINGSFÖRBUD
ONE WAY	ENKELRIKTAT
REPAIRS	REPARATION
SELF SERVICE	SJÄLVBETJÄNING
STOP	STOPP
SUPER	SUPER
UNLEADED	BLYFRI

Where can I rent a car?
vaar kahn yaagh hür-ah ehn beel?
Var kan jag hyra en bil?

How much is it daily/weekly?
hur mük-eht kos-tahr deat daagh-lig-ehn/vehk-oo-vees?
Hur mycket kostar det dagligen/veckovis?

Does that include insurance/mileage?
in-klu-dear-ahr deat fer-säk-ring/free-ah meel?
Inkluderar det försäkring/fria mil?

Where's the next petrol station?
vaar ar nast-ah behn-seen-stah-khoon?
Var är nästa bensinstation?

Please fill the tank.
van-lig-ehn fül tahnk-ehn
Vänligen fyll tanken.

I want ... litres of petrol (gas).
yaagh vil haa ... leet-ehr begn-seen
Jag vill ha ... liter bensin.

Please check the oil and water.
van-lig-ehn kol-ah ol-ya ok vaht-ehn
Vänligen kolla olja och vatten.

How long can I park here?
hur lang-eh kahn yaagh pahr-kear-ah har?
Hur länge kan jag parkera här?

Does this road lead to?
lead-ehr dehn-ah vag til?
Leder denna väg till?

air (for tyres)	*luft*	luft
battery	*baht-ehr-ee*	batteri
brakes	*broms-ahr*	bromsar
clutch	*kop-ling*	koppling
driver's licence	*kerr-kort*	körkort
engine	*moo-toor*	motor
lights	*lil-eh*	lyse
oil	*ol-ya*	olja
puncture	*punk-tear-ing*	punktering
radiator	*kül-ahr-eh*	kylare
road map	*vagh-kahr-tah*	vägkarta
tyres	*dak*	däck
windscreen	*vind-rut-ah*	vindruta

Car Problems

I need a mechanic.
yaagh beher-vehr ehn meh-kaan-ik-ehr
Jag behöver en mekaniker.

What make is it?
vil-keht mark-eh ar deat?
Vilket märke är det?

The battery is flat.
baht-eh-ri-eht ar slut Batteriet är slut.

The radiator is leaking.
kül-ahr-ehn lak-ehr Kylaren läcker.

I have a flat tyre.
yaagh haar punk-tear-ing Jag har punktering.

It's overheating.
dehn kok-ahr Den kokar.

It's not working.
dehn ar traas-igh Den är trasig.

Accommodation

CAMPING GROUND	CAMPINGPLATS
FULL/NO VACANCIES	FULLT/INGA LEDIGA RUM
GUESTHOUSE	GÄSTHUS
HOTEL	HOTELL
MOTEL	MOTELL
ROOMS AVAILABLE	LEDIGA RUM
YOUTH HOSTEL	VANDRARHEM

I am looking for ...
yaagh leat-ahr ehf-tehr Jag letar efter ...

Where is a ...?
vaar finns ...? Var fins ...?

cheap hotel	*bil-igh-ah hot-ehl*	billiga hotell
good hotel	*braa hot-ehl*	bra hotell
nearby hotel	*nar-lig-ahn-deh hot-ehl*	närliggande hotell

What is the address?
   vilk-ehn ah-drehs?   Vilken adress?
Could you write the address,
please?
   kaan du van-lig-ehn
   skreev-ah ah-drehs-ehn?   Kan du vänligen skriva
                            adressen?

At the Hotel

Do you have any rooms
available?
   fins deat noo-agr-ah   Finns det några lediga rum?
   lead-igh-ah rum?

I would like ...
   yaagh skul-eh vil-ya haa ...   Jag skulle vilja ha ...

a single room	*eht ehn-kehl-rum*	ett enkelrum
a double room	*eht dub-ehl-rum*	ett dubbelrum
a room with a	*eht rum mead*	ett rum med
bathroom	*baad-rum*	badrum
to share a dorm	*deal-ah soov-saal*	dela sovsal
a bed	*ehn sang*	en säng

I want a room with a ...
   yaagh vil haa eht rum   Jag vill ha ett rum med ...
   mead ...

bathroom	*baad-rum*	badrum
shower	*duzh*	dusch
television	*tehl-eh-vi-khoon*	television
window	*fern-stehr*	fönster

I'm going to stay for ...
yaagh stahn-ahr ...   Jag stannar ...

one day	*ehn daagh*	en dag
two days	*tvoo-a daagh-ehr*	två dagar
one week	*ehn vehk-ah*	en vecka

Do you have identification?
haar du lehgh-i-ti-mah-khoon?   Har du legitimation?

Your membership card, please.
dit mead-lehms-kort, tahk   Ditt medlemskort, tack.

Sorry, we're full.
tü-var, deat ar fult   Tyvärr, det är fullt.

How long will you be staying?
hur lang-eh kom-ehr nee stahn-ah?   Hur länge kommer ni stanna?

How many nights?
hur moo-ang-ah nat-ehr?   Hur många nätter?

It's ... per day/per person.
... par daag/par par-soon   ... per dag/per person.

How much is it per night/per person?
hur mük-eht kost-ahr deat par naht/par par-soon?   Hur mycket kostar det per natt/per person?

Can I see it?
foo-ar yaagh sea deat?   Får jag se det?

Are there any others?
fins deat noo-agh-ot ahn-aht?   Finns det något annat?

Are there any cheaper rooms?
fins deat bil-igh-ahr-eh rum?

Finns det billigare rum?

Can I see the bathroom?
foo-ar yaagh sea baad-rum-eht?

Får jag se badrummet?

Is there a reduction for students/children?
fins deat stu-dehnt-rah-baht/baarn-rah-baht?

Finns det studentrabatt/barnrabatt?

Does it include breakfast?
in-klu-dear-ahs fru-kost?

Inkluderas frukost?

It's fine, I'll take it.
deat bleer braa, yaagh taar deat

Det blir bra, jag tar det.

I'm not sure how long I'm staying.
yaagh veat int-eh hur lang-eh yaagh stahn-ahr

Jag vet inte hur länge jag stannar.

Is there a lift?
fins deat his?

Finns det hiss?

Where is the bathroom?
vaar ar baad-rum-eht?

Var är badrummet?

Is there hot water all day?
fins deat vaarm-vaht-ehn heal-ah daagh-ehn?

Finns det varmvatten hela dagen?

Do you have a safe where I can leave my valuables?
fins deat ferr-vaar-ings-box vaar yaagh kahn lamn-ah var-deh-saak-ehr?

Finns det förvaringsbox var jag kan lämna värdesaker?

Is there somewhere to wash
clothes?
*kahn yaagh tvat-ah klad-
ehr noo-ag-ahn-stahns?*

Kan jag tvätta kläder
någonstans?

Can I use the kitchen?
*kahn yaagh ahn-van-dah
kerk-eht?*

Kan jag använda köket?

May I use the telephone?
*foo-ar yaagh ahn-van-dah
tehl-eh-foon-ehn?*

Får jag anväda telefonen?

Requests & Complaints

Please wake me up at ...
van-lig-ehn vak may veed ...

Vänligen väck mig vid ...

The room needs to be cleaned.
*rum-eht bea-herv-ehr
stad-ahs*

Rummet behöver städas.

Please change the sheets.
van-lig-ehn büt laak-ahn

Vänligen byt lakan.

I can't open/close the window.
*yaagh kahn int-eh erp-nah/
stang-ah fernst-reht*

Jag kan inte öppna/stänga
fönstret.

I've locked myself out of my
room.
*yaagh haar loo-ast may
ut-eh*

Jag har låst mig ute.

The toilet won't flush.
*too-ah-leht-ehn spool-ahr
int-eh*

Toaletten spolar inte.

I don't like this room.
*yaagh yil-ahr int-eh
deht-ah rum*

Jag gillar inte detta rum.

It's too ...
deat ar ...   Det är ...

small	*err leet-eht*	för litet
noisy	*bul-right*	bullrigt
dark	*ferr merkt*	för mörkt
expensive	*ferr dürt*	för dyrt

Some Useful Phrases

I am/We are leaving now.
   yaagh/vee lamn-ahr nu   Jag/Vi lämnar nu.

I would like to pay the bill.
   yaagh skul-eh vil-ya   Jag skulle vilja betala
   beh-taal-ah rak-ning-ehn   räkningen.

name	*nahmn*	namn
surname	*ehft-ehr-nahmn*	efternamn
room number	*rums-num-ehr*	rumsnummer

Some Useful Words

address	*ah-drehs*	adress
air-conditioned	*luft-kon-di-khoo-near-aht*	luftkonditionerat
balcony	*bahl-kong*	balkong
bathroom	*baad-rum*	badrum
bed	*sang*	säng
bill	*rak-ning*	räkning
blanket	*filt*	filt
candle	*yus*	ljus
chair	*stool*	stol
clean	*sta-dah*	städa
cupboard	*skoo-ap*	skåp
dark	*merrkt*	mörkt

dirty	*smut-sight*	smutsigt
double bed	*dub-ehl-sang*	dubbelsäng
electricity	*ehl-ehk-tri-si-teat*	elektrisitet
excluded	*ut-eh-slut-eht*	uteslutet
fan	*flakt*	fläkt
included	*in-bea-rak-naht*	inberäknat
key	*nük-ehl*	nyckel
lift (elevator)	*hiss*	hiss
light bulb	*lahm-pah*	lampa
lock (n)	*loo-as*	lås
mattress	*mah-drahs*	madrass
mirror	*seagh-ehl*	spegel
padlock	*ligh-mah-drahs*	liggmadrass
pillow	*kud-eh*	kudde
quiet	*tüst*	tyst
room (in hotel)	*rum*	rum
sauna	*bahs-tu*	bastu
sheet	*laak-ahn*	lakan
shower	*duzh*	dusch
soap	*tvoo-al*	tvål
suitcase	*reas-vas-kah*	resväska
swimming pool	*sim-bah-sang*	simbassäng
table	*boord*	bord
toilet	*too-ah-leht*	toalett
toilet paper	*too-ah-leht-pahp-ehr*	toalettpapper
towel	*hahnd-duk*	handduk
water	*vaht-ehn*	vatten
cold water	*kahl-vaht-ehn*	kallvatten
hot water	*vahrm-vaht-ehn*	varmvatten
window	*ferns-tehr*	fönster

Around Town

I'm looking for ...
yaag leat-ahr ehft-ehr ...   Jag letar efter ...

the art gallery	*konst-gahl-eh-ree-eht*	konstgalleriet
a bank	*ehn bahnk*	en bank
the church	*shürk-ahn*	kyrkan
the city centre	*stahds-sehnt-rum*	stadscentrum
the ... embassy	*... ahm-bah-saad-ehn*	... ambassaden
my hotel	*mit ho-tehl*	mitt hotell
the market	*mahrk-nahd-ehn*	marknaden
the museum	*mu-sea-eht*	museet
the police	*poo-lees-ehn*	polisen
the post office	*post-kon-toor-eht*	postkontoret
a public toilet	*ehn ahl-man-too-ah-leht*	en offentlig toalett
the telephone centre	*teal-eh-foon-cehnt-reht*	telefoncentret
the tourist information office	*tur-ist-in-form-ah-khoon*	turistinformation

What time does it open?
nar erpn-ahr dea?   När öppnar de?

What time does it close?
nar stang-ehr dea?   När stänger de?

What ... is this?
vilk-ehn ... ar deht-ah?   Vilken ... är detta?

street	*gaat-ah*	gata
suburb	*ferr-ort*	förort

For directions, see the Getting Around section, 294.

At the Post Office

I would like to send ...
yaagh skul-eh vil-ya khik-ah ...   Jag skulle vilja skicka ...

a letter	*eht breav*	ett brev
a postcard	*eht vü-kort*	ett vykort
a parcel	*eht pah-keat*	ett paket
a telegram	*eht tehl-eh-grahm*	ett telegram

I would like some stamps.
yaagh skul-eh vil-ya haa noo-agr-ah free-mark-ehn   Jag skulle vilja ha några frimärken.

How much is the postage?
hur mük-eht ar port-ot?   Hur mycket är portot?

How much does it cost to send this to ...?
hur mük-eht kost-ahr deat aht khik-ah deht-ah til ...?   Hur mycket kostar det att skicka detta till ...?

an aerogram	*eht ah-ear-o-grahm*	ett aerogram
air mail	*flüg-post*	flygpost
envelope	*ku-var*	kuvert
mail box	*breav-loo-ad-ah*	brevlåda
parcel	*pah-keat*	paket
registered mail	*reh-kom-ehn-dear-ahd post*	rekommenderad post
surface mail	*üt-post*	ytpost

Telephone

I want to ring ...
> *yaagh vil ring-ah ...*

Jag vill ringa ...

The number is ...
> *num-reht ar ...*

Nummret är ...

I want to speak for three minutes.
> *yaagh vil taal-ah ee trea mi-nut-ehr*

Jag vill tala i tre minuter.

How much does a three-minute call cost?
> *hur mük-eht kost-ahr eht trea mi-nut-ehrs sahm-taal?*

Hur mycket kostar ett tre minuters samtal?

How much does each extra minute cost?
> *hur mük-eht kost-ahr vahr-yeh ehx-trah mi-nut?*

Hur mycket kostar varje extra minut?

I would like to speak to Mr Perez.
> *yaagh skul-eh vil-ya taal-ah mead hehr perez*

Jag skulle vilja tala med herr Perez.

I want to make a reverse-charges phone call.
> *yaagh vil gerr-ah eht b-aa-sahm-taal*

Jag vill göra ett ba-samtal.

It's engaged.
> *deat ar up-taagh-eht*

Det är upptaget.

I've been cut off.
> *sahm-taal-eht brert*

Samtalet bröt.

At the Bank

I want to exchange some
money/traveller's cheques.
  yaagh vil vax-lah pehng-ahr/reas-eh-shek-ahr
Jag vill växla pengar/resecheckar.

What is the exchange rate?
  vaad ar vax-ehl-kurs-ehn?
Vad är växelkursen?

How many kronor per dollar?
  hur moo-ang-ah kroon-oor par dol-ahr?
Hur många kronor per dollar?

Can I have money transferred
here from my bank?
  kaan yaagh flüt-ah erv-ehr pehng-ahr heet froo-an min bahnk?
Kan jag flytta över pengar hit från min bank?

How long will it take to
arrive?
  hur loo-ang teed taar deat aht kom-ah fraam?
Hur lång tid tar det att komma fram?

Has my money arrived yet?
  haar meen-ah pehng-ahr kom-it an?
Har mina pengar kommit än?

bank draft	*kvit-o*	kvitto
bank notes	*sead-lahr*	sedlar
cashier	*ehx-peh-deet*	expedit
coins	*münt*	mynt
credit card	*krea-deet-kort*	kreditkort
exchange	*vax-lah*	växla
loose change	*lers vax-ehl*	lös växel
signature	*und-ehr-skrift*	underskrift

SWEDISH

Sightseeing

Do you have a guidebook/
local map?

*haar du ehn reas-eh-hahnd-
book/loo-kaal kaart-ah?*

Har du en resehandbok/
lokal karta?

What are the main attractions?

*vilk-ah ar huv-ud-aht-rahk-
khoon-ehr-nah?*

Vilka är
huvudattraktionerna?

What is that?

vaad ar deat?

Vad är det?

How old is it?

hur gahm-ahl ar dehn?

Hur gammal är den?

May I take photographs?

*foo-ar yaagh foo-too-grah-
fear-ah?*

Får jag fotografera?

What time does it open/close?

*vilk-ehn teed erp-nahr/
stang-ehr det?*

Vilken tid öppnar/stänger
det?

ancient	*foorn-teed-ah*	forntida
archaeological	*ahrk-eh-ol-o-gee*	arkeologi
beach	*strahnd*	strand
bridge	*broo*	bro
building	*büg-nahd*	byggnad
castle	*slot*	slott
cathedral	*dom-shür-kah*	domkyrka
church	*shür-kah*	kyrka
concert hall	*kon-sar-saal*	konsertsal
island	*er*	ö
lake	*kher*	sjö
library	*bib-lee-o-teak*	bibliotek

main square	*stoor-tory-eht*	stortorget
market	*tory (hahn-deal)*	torg (handel)
monastery	*klost-ehr*	kloster
monument	*min-ehs-mark-eh*	minnesmärke
mosque	*mosk-ea*	moské
old city	*gahm-lah staan*	gamla stan
palace	*pah-lahts*	palats
opera house	*oop-ear-ah-hus-eht*	operahuset
ruins	*ru-een-ehr*	ruiner
sea	*haav*	hav
square	*tory*	torg
stadium	*ee-drots-ah-rean-ah*	idrottsarena
statues	*stah-tü-ehr*	statyer
synagogue	*sün-ah-ghoogh-ah*	synagoga
temple	*tehmp-ehl*	tempel
university	*un-ee-vehr-see-teat*	universitet

Activities

trekking (backpacking)	*vahn-drah*	vandra
canoeing	*pah-dlah kah-noot*	paddla kanot
downhill skiing	*slaa-lom*	slalom
fishing	*fisk-ah*	fiska
running	*spring-ah*	springa
sailing	*seag-lah*	segla
skating	*oo-ak-ah skree-skoor*	åka skridskor
skiing	*oo-ak-ah shee-dor*	åka skidor
swimming	*baa-dah*	bada

Entertainment

What's there to do in the evenings?
vaad fins aht ger-ah poo-a kval-ahr-nah?

Vad finns att göra på kvällarna?

Are there any discos?
fins deat noo-aghr-ah disk-oo-teak?

Finns det några diskotek?

Are there places where you can hear local folk music?
fins deat noo-agh-on-stahns vaar mahn kahn her-ah loo-kaal folk-mu-seek?

Finns den någonstans var man kan höra lokal folkmusik?

How much does it cost to get in?
hur mük-eht kost-ahr deat aht kom-ah in?

Hur mycket kostar det att komma in?

cinema	*bee-oo*	bio
concert	*kon-sar*	konsert
discotheque	*disk-oo-teak*	diskotek
theatre	*tea-aa-tehr*	teater

In the Country
Weather

What's the weather like?
hur ar vad-reht?

Hur är vädret?

The weather is ... today.
vad-reht ar ... i-daag

Vädret är ... idag.

cloudy	*moo-aln-ight*	molnigt
cold	*kahlt*	kallt
foggy	*dim-ight*	dimmigt
frosty	*frost*	frost
hot	*vahrmt*	varmt
raining	*rehng-night*	regnigt
snowing	*sner-ahr*	snöar
sunny	*sool-ight*	soligt
windy	*bloo-as-ight*	blåsigt

Camping

Am I allowed to camp here?
   foo-ar yaagh kahm-pah   Får jag kampa här?
   har?

Is there a campsite nearby?
   fins deat ehn kahmp-ing-   Finns det en kampingplats
   plahts ee nar-heat-ehn?   i närheten?

backpack	*rüg-sak*	ryggsäck
can opener	*kon-sehrv-erp-nahr-eh*	konservöppnare
compass	*kom-pahs*	kompass
crampons	*ees-brod*	isbrodd
firewood	*vead*	ved
gas cartridge	*gaas-pah-troon*	gaspatron
hammock	*hang-maht-ah*	hängmatta
ice axe	*hah-hah*	hacha
mattress	*mah-drahs*	madrass
penknife	*fik-kneev*	fickkniv
rope	*reap*	rep
tent	*talt*	tält
tent pegs	*talt-pin-ahr*	tältpinnar

torch (flashlight)	*fik-lahmp-ah*	ficklampa
sleeping bag	*soov-sak*	sovsäck
stove	*spees*	spis
water bottle	*vaht-ehn-flahsk-ah*	vattenflaska

Food

Swedish dishes vary greatly. Probably the most famous Swedish food is the smorgasbord, *smörgårdbord*, which is a variety of many dishes.

Spring

Spring starts with the *semla*, a bun associated with Lent. And after that comes Easter which has its tradition of Easter eggs. The eggs are painted by children, and eaten with fish dishes like smoked salmon, *gravad lax* (salmon marinated in salt only).

Summer

During the summer, Swedes enjoy the warm weather and long daylight. The food is therefore very light – fish is a main dish, and a lot of fruit and berries are eaten. During the midsummer celebrations, pickled herring is a must, with Swedish *snaps*, a spirit similar to vodka. And remember the Swedes often sing and say *skål* before they drink *snaps*, so don't get worried when singing starts. *Strömming* and *gravad lax* are other fish dishes eaten during the summer. In the summer everybody tries to be outdoors as much as possible, so there are plenty of BBQ's.

Autumn

The major celebration of this period, towards the end of the summer, is the crayfish season. In many cases crayfish is the only thing served, together with bread (usually crispbread, *knäckebröd*), and of course *snaps* and singing. During this time, berries like *hjortron* and *lingon* are enjoyed, as are mushrooms picked in the forests.

Winter
The cold winter requires hot food, and a tradition is to have pea soup on Thursdays. At Christmas time there are a lot of dishes served, and the tradition probably varies a little among the households. Some major dishes are ham, herring, *lutfisk* (dried ling soaked in lye), smoked salmon and the smorgasbord dishes. Also gingerbread biscuits, *pepparkakor*, and the alcoholic beverage, *glögg* are associated with Christmas.

At the Restaurant
There are plenty of restaurants serving the Swedish *husmanskost* (Swedish classic cooking on the old country side) and the Swedish specialities, but there are a lot of foreign restaurants as well. There is one drawback with Swedish restaurants – they can be a bit expensive.

breakfast	*fru-kost*	frukost
lunch	*lunzh*	lunch
dinner	*mid-daagh*	middag
bakery	*baagh-eh-ree*	bageri
grocery	*spes-eh-ree-ehr*	specerier
delicatessen	*dehl-i-kah-tehs-ehr*	delikatesser
restaurant	*rehs-tu-rahng*	resturang

Table for ..., please.
   boord ferr ..., tahk   Bord för ..., tack.

Can I see the menu please?
    foo-ar yaagh sea meh-nün,
    tahk
                               Får jag se menyn, tack.

I would like the set lunch,
please.
    yaagh skul-eh vil-ya haa   Jag skulle vilja ha
    lunzh-meh-nün, tahk   lunchmenyn, tack.

What does it include?
    vaad in-eh-faht-ahr deat? Vad innefattar det?

Is service included in the bill?
    ar sehr-vear-ings-aav-yift Är serveringsavgift inräknat
    in-rak-naht ee noot-ahn? i notan?

Not too spicy please.
    int-eh fer krüd-stahrkt, tahk Inte för kryddstarkt, tack.

ashtray	*ahsk-faat*	askfat
the bill	*noot-ahn*	notan
a cup	*ehn kop*	en kopp
dessert	*ehft-ehr-rat*	efterrätt
a drink	*ehn drink*	en drink
a fork	*ehn gahf-ehl*	en gaffel
fresh	*frazh*	fräsch
a glass	*eht glaas*	ett glas
a knife	*ehn kneev*	en kniv
a plate	*ehn tahl-rik*	en tallrik
spicy	*krüd-aht*	kryddat
a spoon	*ehn khead*	en sked
stale	*unk-ehn*	unken
sweet	*sert*	söt
teaspoon	*tea-khead*	tesked
toothpick	*tahnd-peat-ahr-eh*	tandpetare

Vegetarian Meals

I am a vegetarian.
   yaagh ar veh-gheh-tahr-ee-aan   Jag är vegetarian.

I don't eat meat.
   yaagh at-ehr int-eh kert   Jag äter inte kött.

I don't eat chicken, or fish, or ham.
   yaagh at-ehr int-eh shük-ling, ehl-ehr fisk, ehl-ehr khink-ah   Jag äter inte kyckling, eller fisk, eller skinka.

Breakfast   Frukost

There is a special breakfast dish often eaten by Swedes which consists of fermented milk together with cereal. Sometimes one will find a smorgasbord for breakfast, which tends to be more of a brunch.

butter	*smör*
boiled egg	*kokt ägg*
cereal and milk	*flingor & mjölk*
fried egg	*stekt ägg*
milk	*mjölk*
oatmeal	*havregrynsgröt*
pancakes	*pankakor*
toast	*rostat bröd*

Sandwiches   Smörgåsar

There is a special Swedish bread called *knäckebröd*, a crisp bread that is eaten with, among other things, *leverpastej*, paté, and *sill*, herring. Sometimes small sandwiches are eaten as starters. The Swedish word *pålägg* is a common word for the things one can put on a sandwich.

SWEDISH

Räksmörgås
  Shrimp sandwich usually with egg and mayonnaise.
Landgång
  A large gourmet sandwich with a variety of pålägg.
Sillsmörgås
  Sandwich with sill and boiled potato slices.

bread	*bröd*
butter	*smör*
chicken	*kyckling*
ham	*skinka*
turkey	*kalkon*

Soup   Soppa

Ärtsoppa
  Yellow pea soup, traditionally eaten on Thursdays.
Nässelsoppa
  Nettle soup served with half a hardboiled egg.

chicken soup	*kyckling soppa*
fish soup	*fisksoppa*
vegetable soup	*grönsakssoppa*

Meat   Kött

Pytt i panna
  Potato, meat and onion, cut into small cubes. Served with egg
  and beet.

Sjömansbiff (Sailor's beef)
  Sliced beef (rump), potatoes and vegetables, with spices, in a casserole. Served as winter meal.

Viltgryta
  Game casserole, usually elk or reindeer.

Kalops
  A Swedish type of beef stew with onions and herbs.

Leverpastej
  A liver paté served at smörgasbords, and for breakfast on crispbread.

chicken	*kyckling*
lamb chops	*lammkotletter*
minced meat	*köttfärs*
roast beef	*oxstek*
roast lamb	*lammstek*
sausage	*korv*
steak	*biff*
turkey	*kalkon*

Seafood

There is a great variety of fish dishes in Sweden, and you shouldn't leave the country without trying some.

Gravad lax
  Salmon marinated in salt, pepper and dill – a summer dish.

Sill
  Sweet pickled herring, usually served with many different herbs. Also a summer dish associated with midsummer and *snaps*.

Stromming
  A herring type of fish.

Strömmingsflundror
　　Fried stromming.
Sotare
　　Grilled stromming, which are slightly salted, over a fire.
Böckling
　　Smoked herring.
Lutfisk
　　Dried codfish soaked in lye. A fish dish which is associated
　　with Christmas.
Janssons frestelse (Jansson's Temptation)
　　Anchovy and potato dish made in the oven. Often served at
　　a smorgasbord.

cod	*torsk*
crab	*krabba*
crayfish	*kräftor*
halibut	*helgeflundra*
herring	*sill*
oyster	*ostron*
perch	*abborre*
pike	*gädda*
plaice	*rödspätta*
salmon	*lax*
shrimp	*räkor*
sole	*sjötunga*
trout	*forell*

Vegetables	**Grönsaker**
cabbage	*kål*
capsicum	*paprika*
carrot	*morot*
cauliflower	*blomkål*

cucumber	*gurka*
lettuce	*sallad*
mushroom	*champinjon*
onions	*lök*
peas	*ärter*
potato	*potatis*
tomato	*tomater*

Desserts — Efterrätt

apple pie	*äppelkaka*
cake	*tårta*
cheese cake	*ostkaka*
ginger snaps	*pepparkakor*
ice cream	*glass*
oatmeal wafers	*havreflarn*

Drinks – Nonalcoholic — Dricka

coffee	*kaffe*
milk	*mjölk*
orange juice	*apelsin juice*
soft drink	*läsk*
tea	*te*
water	*vatten*

Drinks – Alcoholic — Alkoholhaltiga Drycker

glögg
  A Christmas Spirit.

snaps
  A similar spirit to vodka. It may be flavoured with different kind of herbs, or just plain.

punsch
  A Swedish liqueur flavored with arrack (a coarse spirit). It has a distinct taste and is traditionally served with pea soup.

beer	*öl*
wine	*vin*
liqueur	*likör*

Shopping

How much is it?
hur mük-eht kost-ahr dehn?   Hur mycket kostar den?

bookshop	*book-hahn-dehl*	bokhandel
camera shop	*kaam-ehr-ah-ah-far*	kameraaffär
clothing store	*klad-ah-far*	klädaffär
delicatessen	*deh-lee-kah-tehs-ah-far*	delikatessaffär
general store, shop	*div-ehrs-eh-hahnd-ehl*	diversehandel
laundry	*tvat-ehr-ee*	tvätteri
market	*mahrk-nahd*	marknad
newsagency/ stationers	*nü-heats-bür-oo-a/ pahp-ehrs-hahnd-ehl*	nyhetsbyrå/pappers handel
pharmacy	*ahp-oo-teak*	apotek
shoeshop	*skoo-ah-far*	skoaffär
souvenir shop	*soov-eh-neer-ah-far*	souveniraffär
supermarket	*snahb-sherp*	snabbköp
vegetable shop	*grern-saaks-ah-far*	grönsaksaffär

I would like to buy ...
yaagh skul-eh vil-ya kerp-ah ...   Jag skulle vilja köpa ...
Do you have others?
haar du ahn-drah?   Har du andra?
I don't like it.
yaagh yil-ahr dehn int-eh   Jag giller den inte.

May I look at it?
   foo-ar yaagh tit-ah poo-a dehn?   Får jag titta på den?

I'm just looking.
   yaagh tit-ahr baar-ah   Jag tittar bara.

Can you write down the price?
   kahn du skreev-ah near prees-eht?   Kan du skriva ner priset?

Do you accept credit cards?
   taar du eh-moot kreh-deet-kort?   Tar du emot kreditkort?

Could you lower the price?
   kahn du goo-a near ee prees?   Kan du gå ner i pris?

I don't have much money.
   yaagh haar int-eh soo-a mük-eht pehng-ahr   Jag har inte så mycket pengar.

Can I help you?
   kahn yaagh yalp-ah day?   Kan jag hjälpa dig?

Will that be all?
   vaar deat ahlt?   Var det allt?

Would you like it wrapped?
   vil du haa deat in-slaagh-eht?   Vill du ha det inslaget?

Sorry, this is the only one.
   tüv-ar, deht-ah ar deat ehnd-ah ehx-ehm-plaar-eht   Tyvärr, detta är det enda exemplaret

How much/many do you want?
   hur mük-eht/moo-ang-ah vil du haa?   Hur mycket/många vill du ha?

Souvenirs

earrings	*err-hang-ehn*	örhängen
handicraft	*hahnt-vark*	hantverk
necklace	*hahls-bahnd*	halsband
pottery	*poor-sleen*	porslin
ring	*ring*	ring

Clothing

clothing	*klad-ehr*	kläder
coat	*rok*	rock
dress	*drakt*	dräkt
jacket	*yak-ah*	jacka
jumper (sweater)	*trery-ah*	tröja
shirt	*khoort-ah*	skjorta
shoes	*skoor*	skor
skirt	*shool*	kjol
trousers	*büx-oor*	byxor

It doesn't fit.
dehn pahs-ahr int-eh   Den passar inte.

It is too ...
dehn ar ferr ...   Den är för ...

big	*stoor*	stor
small	*leet-ehn*	liten
short	*kort*	kort
long	*loo-ang*	lång
tight	*smaal*	smal
loose	*lers*	lös

Materials

cotton	*boo-mul*	bomull
handmade	*hahnd-yoord*	handgjord
leather	*lad-ehr*	läder
of brass	*aav mas-ing*	av mässing
of gold	*aav guld*	av guld
of silver	*aav silv-ehr*	av silver
silk	*silk-eh*	silke
wool	*ül-eh*	ylle

Toiletries

comb	*kahm*	kam
condoms	*koon-doom-ehr*	kondomer
deodorant	*dea-oo-doo-rahnt*	deodorant
hairbrush	*hoo-ar-borst-eh*	hårborste
moisturising cream	*fukt-kram*	fuktkräm
razor	*raak-hüv-ehl*	rakhyvel
sanitary napkins	*daam-bind-ah*	dambinda
shampoo	*khahmp-oo*	schampo
shaving cream	*raak-lerd-ehr*	raklödder
soap	*tvoo-al*	tvål
sunblock cream	*sool-kram*	solkräm
tampons	*tahm-pong-ehr*	tamponger
tissues	*nas-duk-ahr*	näsdukar
toilet paper	*too-ah-leht-pahp-ehr*	toalettpapper
toothbrush	*tahnd-borst-eh*	tandborste
toothpaste	*tahnd-kram*	tandkräm

Stationery & Publications

map	*kaart-ah*	karta
newspaper	*teed-ning*	tidning

newspaper in English	*ehng-ehlsk teed-ning*	engelsk tidning
novels in English	*ehng-ehlsk-ah roo-maan-ehr*	engelska romaner
paper	*pahp-ehr*	papper
pen (ballpoint)	*pehn-ah*	penna
scissors	*sahx*	sax

Photography

How much is it to process this film?
hur mük-eht kost-ahr frahm-kahl-ning aav dehn-ah film? — Hur mycket kostar framkallning av denna film?

When will it be ready?
nar ar dehn klaar? — När är den klar?

I'd like a film for this camera.
yaagh skul-eh vil-yah haa ehn film ferr dehn-ah kaam-ehr-ah — Jag skulle vilja ha en film för denna kamera.

B&W (film)	*svahrt-veet film*	svart-vit film
camera	*kaam-ehr-ah*	kamera
colour (film)	*fary-film*	färgfilm
film	*film*	film
flash	*blixt*	blixt
lens	*ob-yehk-teev*	objektiv
light meter	*yus-mat-ahr-eh*	ljusmätare

Smoking

A packet of cigarettes, please.
eht pah-keat sigh-ahr-eht-ehr, tahk — Ett paket cigaretter, tack.

Are these cigarettes strong/
mild?

ar dehs-ah sigh-ahr-eht-ehr
stahrk-ah/svaagh-ah?

Är dessa cigaretter starka/
svaga?

Do you have a light?

haar du ehld?

Har du eld?

cigarette papers	*sigh-ahr-eht-pahp-ehr*	cigarettpapper
cigarettes	*sigh-ahr-eht-ehr*	cigaretter
filtered	*filt-ehr*	filter
lighter	*tand-ahr-eh*	tändare
matches	*tand-stik-oor*	tändstickor
menthol	*mehn-too-al*	mentol
pipe	*pee-pah*	pipa
tobacco (pipe)	*peep-too-bahk*	piptobak

Colours

black	*svahrt*	svart
blue	*bloo-a*	blå
brown	*brun*	brun
green	*grern*	grön
orange	*oo-rahnkh*	orange
pink	*roo-as-ah*	rosa
purple	*lee-lah*	lila
red	*rerd*	röd
white	*veet*	vit
yellow	*gul*	gul

Sizes & Comparisons

small	*lee-tehn*	lite
big	*stoor*	stor
heavy	*tung*	tung
light	*yus*	ljus
more	*mear*	mer
less	*mind-reh*	mindre
too much/many	*fer mük-eht/moo-ang-ah*	för mycket/många
many	*moo-ang-ah*	många
enough	*til-rak-light*	tillräckligt
also	*ok-soo-a*	också
a little bit	*ehn leet-ehn beet*	en liten bit

Health

Where is ...?
  var ar ...? — Var är ...?

the doctor	*dok-toorn*	doktorn
the hospital	*khuk-hus-eht*	sjukhuset
the chemist	*ah-poo-teak-eht*	apoteket
the dentist	*tahnd-lak-aar-ehn*	tandläkaren

I am sick.
  yaagh ar khuk — Jag är sjuk.
My friend is sick.
  min van ar khuk — Min vän är sjuk.
Could I see a female doctor?
  kahn yaagh foo-a traf-ah ehn kvin-ligh lak-ah-reh? — Kan jag få träffa en kvinnlig läkare?
What's the matter?
  vaad ar deat ferr feal? — Vad är det för fel?

Where does it hurt?
vaar ger deat oont? Var gör det ont?
I have ...
yaagh haar ... Jag har ...
It hurts here.
deat ger oont har Det gör ont här.
My ... hurts.
min ... ger ont Min ... gör ont.

Parts of the Body

ankle	*vrist*	vrist
arm	*ahrm*	arm
back	*rüg*	rygg
chest	*brerst-kory*	bröstkorg
ear	*er-ah*	öra
eye	*erg-ah*	öga
finger	*fing-ehr*	finger
foot	*foot*	fot
hand	*hahnd*	hand
head	*huv-ud*	huvud
heart	*yart-ah*	hjärta
leg	*bean*	ben
mouth	*mun*	mun
nose	*nas-ah*	näsa
ribs	*reav-bean*	revben
skin	*hud*	hud
spine	*rüg-raad*	ryggrad
stomach	*maagh-eh*	mage
teeth	*tand-ehr*	tänder
throat	*hahls*	hals

SWEDISH

Ailments

English	Pronunciation	Swedish
an allergy	*ahl-ehr-ghee*	allergi
anaemia	*ah-neh-mee*	anemi
a blister	*ehn bloo-as-ah*	en blåsa
a burn	*eht bran-soo-ar*	ett brännsår
a cold	*ehn ferr-shül-ning*	en förkylning
constipation	*ferr-stop-ning*	förstoppning
a cough	*hos-tah*	hosta
diarrhoea	*dee-ah-rea*	diarré
fever	*feab-ehr*	feber
glandular fever	*kert-ehl-feab-ehr*	körtelfeber
a headache	*huv-ud-vark*	huvudvärk
hepatitis	*heh-pah-teet*	hepatit
indigestion	*maag-beh-svar*	magbesvär
an infection	*ehn in-fehk-khoon*	en infektion
influenza	*in-flu-ehns-ah*	influensa
lice	*lers*	löss
low/high blood pressure	*loo-aght/herght blood-trük*	lågt/högt blodtryck
a pain	*smart-oor*	smärtor
sore throat	*hahls-oont*	halsont
sprain	*stuk-ah*	stuka
a stomachache	*maag-oont*	magont
sunburn	*sool-bran-ah*	solbränna
a venereal disease	*ehn kerns-khuk-doom*	en könssjukdom
worms	*mahsk-ahr*	maskar

Some Useful Words & Phrases

I'm ...

yaagh ar ...   Jag är ...

diabetic	*dee-ah-beat-ik-ehr*	diabetiker
epileptic	*ehp-ee-lehpt-ik-ehr*	epileptiker
asthmatic	*ahst-maat-ik-ehr*	astmatiker

I'm allergic to antibiotics/
penicillin
   yaagh ar ahl-ehrgh-isk   Jag är allergisk mot anti-
   moot ahnt-i-bi-oot-ik-ah/   biotika/penicillin
   pehn-i-si-leen

I'm pregnant.
   yaagh ar grah-veed   Jag är gravid.

I'm on the pill.
   yaagh at-ehr p-pil-ehr   Jag äter p-piller.

I haven't had my period for ...
months.
   yaagh haar int-eh hahft   Jag har inte haft mens sen ...
   mehns sehn ... moo-an-ahd-   månader.
   ehr

I have been vaccinated.
   yaagh ar vahk-see-near-ahd   Jag är vaccinerad.

I have my own syringe.
   yaagh haar min eagh-ehn   Jag har min egen spruta.
   sprut-ah

I feel better/worse.
   yaagh moo-ar bat-reh/   Jag mår bättre/sämre.
   sam-reh

accident	*oo-lük-ah*	olycka
addiction	*mis-bruk*	missbruk

antibiotics	*ahnt-ee-bee-oo-tik-ah*	antibiotika
antiseptic	*ahnt-ee-sehpt-isk*	antiseptisk
aspirin	*ahsp-i-reen*	aspirin
bandage	*fer-bahnd*	förband
bite	*beht*	bett
blood pressure	*blood-trük*	blodtryck
blood test	*blood-proov*	blodprov
contraceptive	*preh-vehn-teev-meahd-ehl*	preventivmedel
injection	*sprut-ah*	spruta
injury	*skaad-ah*	skada
itch	*kloo-ad-ah*	klåda
medicine	*mehd-i-seen*	medicin
menstruation	*mehn-stru-ah-khoon*	menstruation
nausea	*il-ah-moo-end-eh*	illamående
oxygen	*sür-eh*	syre
vitamins	*veet-ah-meen-ehr*	vitaminer
wound	*soo-ar*	sår

At the Chemist

I need medication for ...
yaagh bea-herv-ehr mehd-i-seen ferr ...
Jag behöver medicin för ...

I have a prescription.
yaagh haar eht rea-sehpt
Jag har ett recept.

At the Dentist

I have a toothache.
yaagh haar tahnd-vark
Jag har tandvärk.

I've lost a filling.
yaagh haar tahp-aht ehn plomb
Jag har tappat en plomb.

SWEDISH

I've broken a tooth.
min tahnd haar spruk-it   Min tand har spruckit.
My gums hurt.
mit tahnd-kert vark-ehr   Mitt tandkött värker.
I don't want it extracted.
yaagh vil int-eh haa dehn   Jag vill inte ha den
bort-taagh-ehn   borttagen.
Please give me an anaesthetic.
van-lig-ehn ye may   Vänligen ge mig
bea-derv-nings-mead-ehl   bedövningsmedel.

Time & Dates

Swedes use the twenty-four-hour system for telling the time.

What time is it?
vaad ar klok-ahn?   Vad är klockan?
It is ...
dehn ar ...   Den är ...
What date is it today?
vilk-eht daat-um ar deht   Vilket datum är det idag?
i-daag?

in the morning	*poo-a morgh-on-ehn*	på morgonen
in the afternoon	*poo-a ehft-ehr-mi-*	på eftermiddagen
	daagh-ehn	
in the evening	*poo-a kval-ehn*	på kvällen

Days of the Week

Monday	*moo-an-daagh*	måndag
Tuesday	*tees-daagh*	tisdag
Wednesday	*oons-daagh*	onsdag

Thursday	*toors-daagh*	torsdag
Friday	*frea-daagh*	fredag
Saturday	*lerr-daagh*	lördag
Sunday	*sern-daagh*	söndag

Months

January	*jahn-u-aar-i*	januari
February	*fehb-ru-aar-i*	februari
March	*mahrs*	mars
April	*ahp-ril*	april
May	*mahy*	maj
June	*ju-ni*	juni
July	*ju-li*	juli
August	*ah-u-ghust-i*	augusti
September	*sehp-tehmb-ehr*	september
October	*ok-toob-ehr*	oktober
November	*noo-vehmb-ehr*	november
December	*deh-sehmb-ehr*	december

Seasons

summer	*som-ahr*	sommar
autumn	*herst*	höst
winter	*vint-ehr*	vinter
spring	*voo-ar*	vår

Present

today	*i-daagh*	idag
this morning	*i-mors-eh*	imorse
tonight	*i-kval*	ikväll
this week	*dehn-ah vehk-ah*	denna vecka
this year	*deht-ah oo-ar*	detta år
now	*nu*	nu

Past

yesterday	*i-goo-ar*	igår
day before yesterday	*i-fer-goo-ar*	iförrgår
yesterday morning	*i-goo-ar mors-eh*	igår morse
last night	*i-goo-ar kval*	igår kväll
last week	*fer-ah vehk-ahn*	förra veckan
last year	*fer-ah oo-ar-eht*	förra året

Future

tomorrow	*i-morgh-on*	imorgon
day after tomorrow	*ee-erv-ehr-morgh-on*	iövermorgon
tomorrow morning	*ee-morgh-on-bit-i*	imorgonbitti
tomorrow afternoon/evening	*i-morgh-on ehft-ehr-mi-daagh/kval*	imorgon eftermiddag/kväll
next week	*nast-ah vehk-ah*	nästa vecka
next year	*nast-ah oo-ar*	nästa år

During the Day

afternoon	*ehft-ehr-mi-daagh*	eftermiddag
dawn, very early morning	*grün-ing, teed-igh*	gryning, tidig morgon
day	*daagh*	dag
early	*teed-ight*	tidigt
midnight	*meed-naht*	midnatt
morning	*morgh-on*	morgon
night	*naht*	natt
noon	*mi-daagh*	middag
sundown	*sool-nead-goo-ahng*	solnedgång
sunrise	*sool-up-goo-ahng*	soluppgång

Numbers & Amounts

0	*nol*	noll
1	*eht*	ett
2	*tvoo-a*	två
3	*trea*	tre
4	*für-ah*	fyra
5	*fehm*	fem
6	*sehx*	sex
7	*khu*	sju
8	*oo-at-ah*	åtta
9	*nee-oo*	nio
10	*tee-oo*	tio
11	*ehlv-ah*	elva
12	*tolv*	tolv
13	*treh-ton*	tretton
14	*fyoor-ton*	fjorton
15	*fehm-ton*	femton
16	*sehx-ton*	sexton
17	*khu-ton*	sjutton
18	*aar-ton*	arton
19	*ni-ton*	nitton
20	*shu-go*	tjugo
30	*treh-tee-oo*	trettio
40	*fur-tee-oo*	fyrtio
50	*fehm-tee-oo*	femtio
60	*sehx-tee-oo*	sextio
70	*khu-tee-oo*	sjuttio
80	*o-tee-oo*	åttio
90	*ni-tee-oo*	nittio
100	*eht hund-rah*	ett hundra
1000	*eht tu-sehn*	ett tusen

one million	*ehn mil-yoon*	en miljon
1st	*ferrst-ah*	första
2nd	*ahndr-ah*	andra
3rd	*tread-yeh*	tredje
¼	*ehn fyar-deh-deal*	en fjärdedel
⅓	*ehn trea-dyeh-deal*	en tredjedel
½	*ehn hahlv*	en halv
¾	*trea fyar-deh-deal-ahr*	tre tjärdedelar

Some Useful Words

a little (amount)	*leet-eh-grahn*	litegrand
double	*dub-ehl*	dubbel
a dozen	*eht dus-in*	ett dussin
Enough!	*til-rak-light*	tillräckligt!
few	*noo-aghr-ah*	några
less	*mind-reh*	mindre
many	*moo-ang-ah*	många
more	*mear*	mer
once	*ehn goo-ang*	en gång
a pair	*eht paar*	ett par
percent	*proo-sehnt*	procent
some	*noo-aghr-ah*	några
too much	*fer moo-ang-ah*	för många
twice	*tvoo-a goo-ang-ehr*	två gånger

Abbreviations

eKr/fKr	AD/BC
fm/em	am/pm
AB	Corporation
avd/HK	Dept/HQ
EG	EC
Hr/Fr/Frk	Mr/Mrs/Ms
v	week
SB	UK
FN	UN

Index

Finnish 72

Icelandic 141

Swedish 280

Guides to Europe

Eastern Europe on a shoestring
This guide has opened up a whole new world for travellers - Albania, Bulgaria, Czechoslovakia, eastern Germany, Hungary, Poland, Romania and Yugoslavia.
'...a thorough, well-researched book. Only a fool would go East without it.' - *Great Expeditions*

Finland - travel survival kit
Finland is an intriguing blend of Swedish and Russian influences. With its medieval stone castles, picturesque wooden houses, vast forest and lake district, and interesting wildlife, it is a wonderland to delight any traveller.

Iceland, Greenland & the Faroe Islands - travel survival kit
Iceland, Greenland & the Faroe Islands contain some of the most beautiful wilderness areas in the world. This practical guidebook will help travellers discover the dramatic beauty of this region, no matter what their budget.

Mediterranean Europe on a shoestring
Details on hundreds of galleries, museums and architectural masterpieces and information on outdoor activities including hiking, sailing and skiing. Information on travelling in Albania, Andorra, Cyprus, France, Greece, Italy, Malta, Morocco, Portugal, Spain, Tunisia, Turkey and former Socialist Federal Republics of Yugoslavia.

Poland - travel survival kit
Poland's beautiful beaches, tranquil lakes, rugged mountains and areas of unspoilt primeval forest are a delight for trekkers and nature lovers. This practical guide has all the details on rural Poland and lively cities such as Warsaw, Kraków and Gdansk.

Scandinavian & Baltic Europe on a shoestring
A comprehensive guide to travelling in this region. Countries featured include Denmark, Estonia, the Faroe Islands, Finland, Iceland, Latvia, Lithuania, Norway, Sweden.

Trekking in Spain
Aimed at both overnight trekkers and day hikers, this guidebook includes useful maps and full details on hikes in some of Spain's most beautiful wilderness areas.

USSR - travel survival kit
Invaluable advice on getting around and beating red tape for individual and group travellers alike. This comprehensive guide includes an unsanitised historical background and complete information on art and culture. Over 130 reliable maps, and all place names are given in Cyrillic script. (includes the independent states).

Western Europe on a shoestring
This long-awaited guide covers all of Western Europe's well-loved sights and provides routes for cycling and driving tours, plus details on hiking, climbing and skiing. All the travel facts on Andorra, Austria, Belgium, Britain, France, Germany, Ireland, Italy, Liechtenstein, Luxembourg, Netherlands, Portugal, Spain and Switzerland.

Also available:

Eastern Europe phrasebook
Bulgarian, Czech, Hungarian, Polish, Romanian, Slovak

Mediterranean Europe phrasebook
Albanian, Greek, Italian, Macedonian, Maltese, Serbian & Croatian, Slovenian

Western Europe phrasebook
Basque, Catalan, Dutch, French, German, Irish, Portuguese, Spanish (Castilian)

Phrasebooks

Brazilian
Burmese
Eastern Europe
Egyptian Arabic
Hindi/Urdu
Indonesian
Japanese
Korean
Latin American Spanish
Mandarin Chinese
Mediterranean Europe
Moroccan Arabic
Nepali

Papua New Guinea
Pilipino
Quechua
Russian
Scandinavian Europe
Sri Lanka
Swahili
Thai
Thai Hill Tribes
Tibet
Turkish
Western Europe

Where Can You Find Out.........

HOW to get a Laotian visa in Bangkok?
WHERE to go birdwatching in PNG?
WHAT to expect from the police if you're robbed in Peru?
WHEN you can go to see cow races in Australia?

In the Lonely Planet Newsletter!

Every issue includes:

- *a letter from Lonely Planet founders Tony and Maureen Wheeler*
- *a letter from an author 'on the road'*
- *the most entertaining or informative reader's letter we've received*
- *the latest news on new and forthcoming releases from Lonely Planet*
- *and all the latest travel news from all over the world*